The Generals of SHILOH

Character in Leadership, April 6–7, 1862

Larry Tagg

SB

Savas Beatie
California

Library of Congress Cataloging-in-Publication Data

Names: Tagg, Larry, author.
Title: The Generals of Shiloh: Character in Leadership, April 6-7, 1862 / by Larry Tagg.
Description: First edition. | El Dorado Hills, California: Savas Beatie LLC, 2017. | Includes bibliographical references and index.
Identifiers: LCCN 2017031695| ISBN 9781611213690 (alk. paper) | ISBN 9781611213706 (ebk.)
Subjects: LCSH: Shiloh, Battle of, Tenn., 1862. | United States—History—Civil War, 1861-1865—Biography. | Generals—United States—Biography. | Generals—Confederate States of America—Biography. | Command of troops—History—19th century.
Classification: LCC E473.54 .T34 2017 | DDC 973.7/31—dc23
LC record available at https://lccn.loc.gov/2017031695

First Edition, First Printing

SB

Savas Beatie LLC
989 Governor Drive, Suite 102
El Dorado Hills, CA 95762
Phone: 916-941-6896
(web) www.savasbeatie.com
(E-mail) sales@savasbeatie.com

Our titles are available at special discounts for bulk purchases. For more details, contact us at sales@savasbeatie.com.

Unless otherwise noted, all photos courtesy of the *Library of Congress*, *National Archives*, or *Generals in Blue* and *Generals in Gray*.

Proudly printed in the United States of America.

Table of Contents

Table of Contents (continued)

Table of Contents (continued)

List of Maps

The Convergence of the Armies on Shiloh

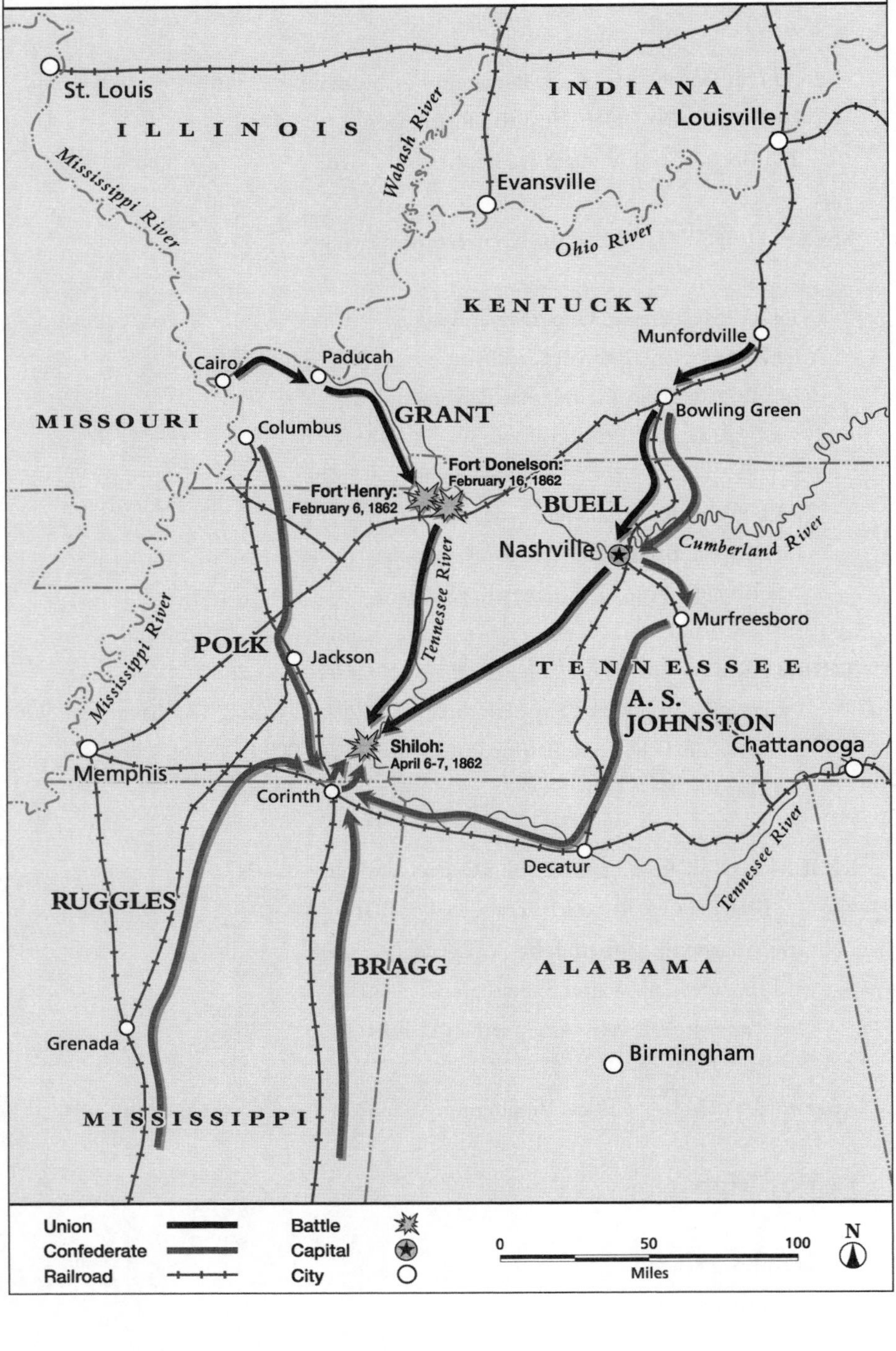
St. Louis
ILLINOIS
INDIANA
Louisville
Wabash River
Mississippi River
Evansville
Ohio River
KENTUCKY
Munfordville
Cairo
Paducah
MISSOURI
Columbus
GRANT
Bowling Green
Fort Donelson:
February 16, 1862
Fort Henry:
February 6, 1862
BUELL
Nashville
Cumberland River
Tennessee River
Murfreesboro
Mississippi River
POLK
Jackson
TENNESSEE
A. S.
JOHNSTON
Chattanooga
Memphis
Shiloh:
April 6-7, 1862
Corinth
Decatur
Tennessee River
RUGGLES
BRAGG
ALABAMA
Grenada
Birmingham
MISSISSIPPI
Union
Confederate
Railroad
Battle
Capital
City
0
50
100
Miles
N

Introduction

Character is both the archer and the bow that gives flight to the arrow whose arc describes a human life. Storytellers instinctively know the importance of character. Character is the engine of every great story.

Military history is too often limited to strategy, tactics, weaponry, and supplies. Battles, particularly, present a chaos so intense that merely describing events and sorting out causes and effects is an immense task. Historians must devote so much effort to faithfully reconstructing a battle's events that men's characters are often too little mentioned. However, if we look at the history of a battle as might a weaver plying his trade, events are only the warp threads—the threads running lengthwise through the narrative. In order to make a whole cloth, the soldiers' character must provide the woof threads—the threads drawn through, inserted over and under the events—that complete the fabric of the battle narrative. The stories of the men in this book—the leaders of brigades, divisions, corps, and armies that came together on April 6 and 7, 1862, near Pittsburg Landing, Tennessee—are meant to provide the threads necessary to create the whole fabric of the story of the Battle of Shiloh at the climax of the first year of the Civil War in the West.

The biographical approach to Shiloh is also valuable as a snapshot of American culture, fourscore and six years after the country's birth. The color and diversity of the battle's generals provide a kaleidoscopic view of the society of the period. The United States in 1860 was an young nation with a small standing army. When war broke out in Charleston Harbor in April 1861, hundreds of new generals had to be minted to command hundreds of thousands of new soldiers. These new chieftains were not professionals, but were elevated very quickly from a hodge-podge of street-level occupations. Of the 66 brigade-and-up leaders at Shiloh presented in this study, only 14 were serving as career soldiers one year before the battle when Fort Sumter fell. Thirteen more were lawyers, prominent in their communities and well- connected. Thirteen were politicians, including the previous vice president of the United States who now served in the Confederate Army. There were five businessmen (including an Iowa hatter), four plantation owners, two professors, a millwright, a sheriff, a blacksmith, a riverboatman, a geologist, a horse breeder, a bishop, a newspaper editor, a farmer, a cotton broker, a stagecoach operator, a bridge engineer, a Navy ordnance officer, and an architect. The most famous of them all, Ulysses S. Grant, was clerking at his father's dry goods store in Illinois.

A study of the generals of Shiloh also helps illuminate the entire history of the Western Theater in the first year of the war. This obscure woodland in western Tennessee was the improbable rendezvous of more 100,000 Americans. They were men who had fought in and brought experience from every engagement in the Western Theater over the previous twelve months, at a moment when the momentum of Union victory seemed irreversible. Grant would later write:

> Up to the battle of Shiloh I, as well as thousands of other citizens, believed that the rebellion against the Government would collapse suddenly and soon, if a decisive victory could be gained over any of its armies. Donelson and Henry were such victories. An army of more than 21,000 men was captured or destroyed. Bowling Green, Columbus and Hickman, Kentucky, fell in consequence, and Clarksville and Nashville, Tennessee, the last two with an immense amount of stores, also fell into our hands. The Tennessee and Cumberland rivers, from their mouths to the head of navigation, were secured.

The stories of the generals of Shiloh must necessarily include these previous episodes.

Overwhelmingly, however, Shiloh was a meeting of masses of young men, many of whom had never fired a gun in anger. Some of the new recruits had just received the first muskets they had ever held. That they fought so hard and so well for two long days in dense, ravine-crossed woods, under mostly amateur officers, is a mark of the intensity of their will to fight. That neither side could force a crushing victory is a mark of the balance of their abilities. Of the character of the men in the two opposing armies, Grant wrote his opinion that "It is possible that the Southern man started in with a little more dash than his Northern brother; but he was correspondingly less enduring."

The battle of Shiloh draws its interest in part because it is the story of the bloody meeting of not two armies, but three. It was the violent rite of passage of all the major armies of the Western Theater of the Civil War, and each—the Army of the Tennessee, the Army of the Ohio, and the Army of the Mississippi—had passed through its birth and early growth in its own peculiar way. Each was an accretion of regiments and batteries that had been added sometimes singly, and sometimes, as in the few weeks immediately leading up to the battle, in great numbers. More, each regiment of those armies that threaded its way through the first year of the war toward the rendezvous on the Shiloh plateau arrived with its own story. Even in this earliest of the major battles of the Civil War in the West—and the battle of Shiloh marks, within one week, the end of the first year of the war—the officers who commanded their brought with them their own unique background of experiences. None had yet fought a battle on the epic scale of Shiloh, but each man and command had traveled their own winding road to get there.

The use of character-as-history also invites the reader to find new stories that haven't yet been explored in Civil War literature. Sometimes a collection of stories, even short ones such as those found here, suggests its own themes. Sometimes it sparks new insights. In every case, it will be the characters, as well as the events, that enchant the reader.

Larry Tagg
Sacramento, California

Author's Note

Because *The Generals of Shiloh* is not intended as a new definitive battle or campaign history, I decided (together with my publisher) to forego the use of footnotes and instead include a Critical Bibliography, which readers will find at the end of this book.

The Shiloh Battlefield

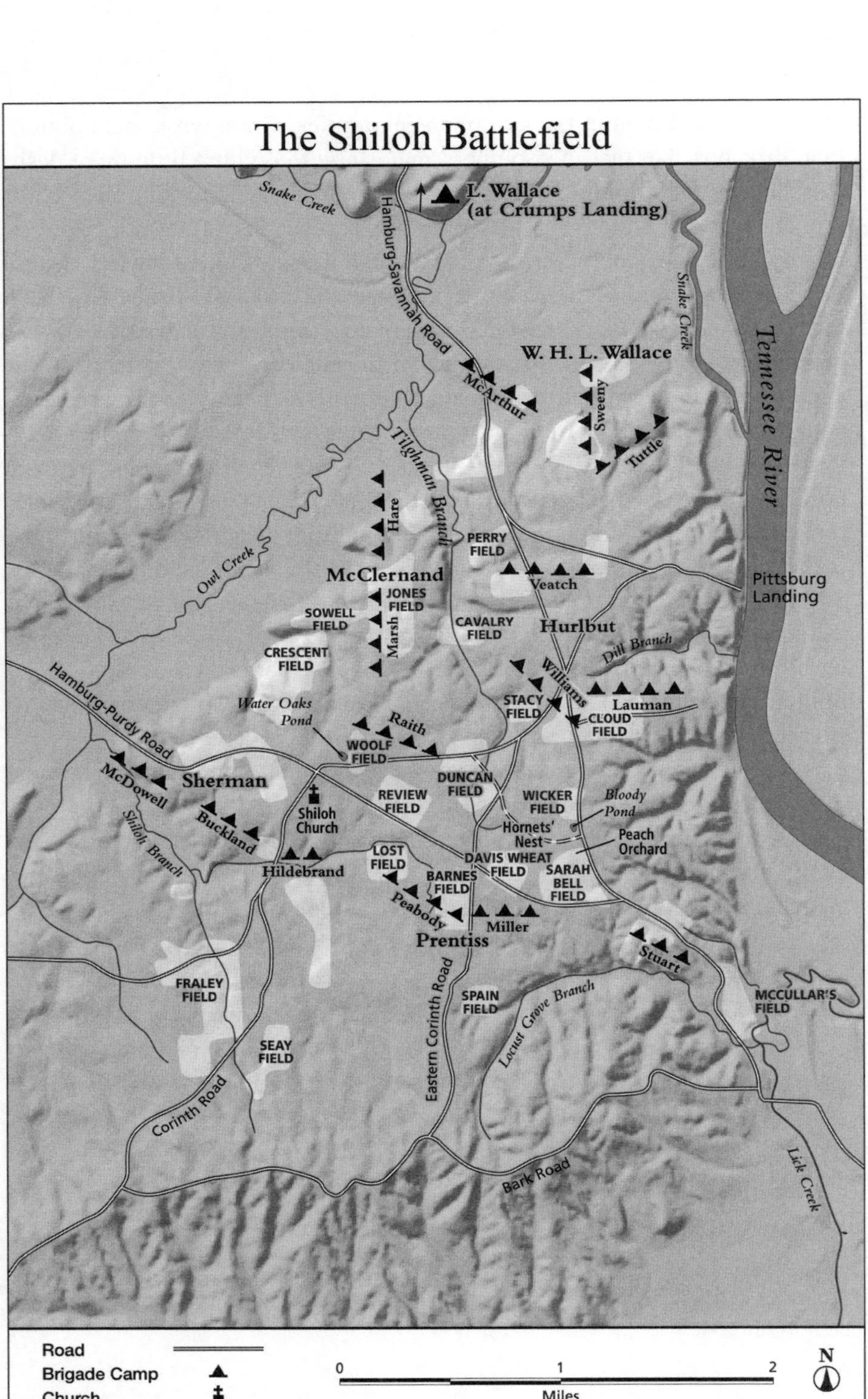

L. Wallace
(at Crumps Landing)
Snake Creek
Hamburg-Savannah Road
Snake Creek
Tennessee River
W. H. L. Wallace
McArthur
Sweeny
Tuttle
Tilghman Branch
Hare
Owl Creek
PERRY FIELD
McClernand
Veatch
Pittsburg Landing
JONES FIELD
SOWELL FIELD
Marsh
CAVALRY FIELD
Hurlbut
Dill Branch
CRESCENT FIELD
Williams
Hamburg-Purdy Road
Water Oaks Pond
STACY FIELD
Lauman
CLOUD FIELD
Raith
WOOLF FIELD
McDowell
Sherman
DUNCAN FIELD
Shiloh Church
REVIEW FIELD
WICKER FIELD
Bloody Pond
Buckland
Shiloh Branch
Hornets' Nest
Peach Orchard
LOST FIELD
DAVIS WHEAT FIELD
Hildebrand
BARNES FIELD
SARAH BELL FIELD
Peabody
Miller
Prentiss
Stuart
Eastern Corinth Road
SPAIN FIELD
Locust Grove Branch
MCCULLAR'S FIELD
FRALEY FIELD
SEAY FIELD
Corinth Road
Bark Road
Lick Creek
Road
Brigade Camp
Church
0
1
2
Miles
N

Army of the Tennessee

Major General Ulysses Simpson Grant

On the day Fort Sumter fell, Ulysses "Sam" Grant was working as a clerk at his family's leather goods store in his hometown of Galena, in the remote northwest corner of Illinois. Grant had lived in the town for less than a year and few people knew him. But because of his West Point education and 15-year career in the Army, a few townsmen persuaded him to preside over a Union rally two days later.

At the rally, Congressman Elihu Washburne and attorney John Rawlins gave stirring speeches and inspired enough enlistments to fill a full 100-man company from Galena. Afterward, the congressman made a point of seeking out Grant, intrigued that in his hometown there lived a West Pointer and Mexican War officer whom he did not know. Washburne was immediately impressed with Grant, whose ideas on politics and the organizing and equipping of the new Union regiments were already well developed.

Grant never returned to the family store. He spent the next two weeks drilling and uniforming Galena's new infantry company, although he declined to be its captain in order to remain available for a higher post. When the company went to Springfield for mustering-in, he went with it. After the Galena men boarded a train for Cairo, Illinois, with the 11th Illinois Infantry regiment on April 30, Grant was invited by Governor Richard Yates (who had heard about Grant from Washburne) to remain in the state capital, without rank but with the duty of organizing and mustering in new Illinois regiments.

Grant drew notice by doing his job ably and without fanfare, and Governor Yates (again, after conferring with Washburne) named Grant as colonel of the new 21st Illinois Infantry on June 15, 1861. Grant's regiment was assigned to guard a railway line in northern Missouri. Grant marched his regiment toward Missouri on July 3, and for the next six weeks, he earned valuable experience as the colonel of a regiment in the volunteer army. Perhaps his greatest epiphany came on July 14, after he had received orders to seek out and destroy a Confederate regiment under Col. Thomas Harris. As he approached the Rebel camp, Grant remembered later, "My heart kept getting higher and higher until it felt to me as though it was in my throat. I would have given anything then to have been back in Illinois, but I had not the moral courage to halt and consider what to do." When he found the enemy camp abandoned, Grant wrote:

> My heart resumed its place. It occurred to me at once that Harris had been as much afraid of me as I had been of him. This was a view of the question I had never taken before; but it was one I never forgot afterwards. From that event to the close of the war, I never experienced trepidation upon confronting an enemy, though I always felt more or less anxiety. I never forgot that he had as much reason to fear my forces as I had his.

During Grant's tenure at the head of the 21st Illinois in northern Missouri, on July 25 Abraham Lincoln appointed John C. Fremont to command the Western Department. A week or so later came news that Lincoln had created 34 new brigadiers to lead the new brigades of the Union army. For political reasons, he had parceled generalships out to states in the same manner as postmasterships and other Federal appointments. Illinois was entitled to four generals, to be chosen by the Illinois congressmen. The first one was given to Grant, at the request of Lincoln's and Grant's mutual friend, Elihu Washburne. (The other three were Stephen A. Hurlbut, Benjamin M. Prentiss, and John A. McClernand—all of whom would be division commanders under Grant nine months later at the battle of Shiloh.)

Fremont ordered Grant to assume command of the District of Southeast Missouri, with its tiny force of three regiments, headquartered at Cairo, Illinois. Although Fremont would say later that he recognized Grant's "dogged persistence" and "iron will," he almost certainly did not realize the significance of his choice. On September 1, 1861, Grant took the reins of what would soon prove to be the most important district in the West, and began to organize what would be the future Army of the Tennessee.

Aside from the capital at Washington, there was no strategic point valued so highly as Cairo, where the nation's mightiest rivers, the Mississippi and the Ohio, met, and which pointed downward like a dagger into the junction between two slave states, Kentucky and Missouri. Southern Illinois itself, settled largely by Virginians and Kentuckians, was strongly sympathetic to the Confederate cause.

The government's first act in the West, in the first week after the fall of Fort Sumter, had been to hurry 595 men onto trains in Chicago and speed them to Cairo. One town native wrote, "The importance of taking possession of this point was felt by all, and that, too, without waiting the arrival and organization of a brigade."

Once there, Grant was immediately and relentlessly aggressive. Col. Theodore Lyman, who worked with him later in the war, wrote, "He habitually wore an expression as if he had determined to drive his head through a brick wall and was about to do it." From his first days at Cairo, Grant was constantly scheming how to get at the stronger Confederate army camped at Columbus, Kentucky, a day's march away.

At the same time, Grant was fastidious in his attention to administrative detail, the same trait Congressman Washburne had discovered the previous spring in Galena. From his first days at his new headquarters at Cairo, he was unrelentingly thorough. When Major General Henry Halleck replaced Fremont as head of the Department of the Missouri on November 9, 1861, Halleck, whose strengths were organization and management, was impressed with the tidiness of Grant's command, and was persuaded to keep Grant on at his post in Cairo.

Grant was one of few Civil War generals who saw value in keeping his men active and giving them their head. He exercised his green recruits by sending them on constant patrols in the swampy lowlands of nearby Missouri and Kentucky. In those restless, watchful fall weeks, his little army operated entirely in this tiny but important tract of land, a semicircle extending south from Cairo with a radius of fifteen miles, with Columbus, Kentucky and Belmont, Missouri—the two Rebel strongpoints straddling the Mississippi River—at its southernmost edge. Grant's stance was always aggressive, always tugging at the leash, an attitude which he imparted to the men under his command. Here was the major difference between himself and his opposite at Columbus, Confederate General Leonidas Polk, who was content to play a defensive role and "let sleeping dogs lie." This difference would manifest itself in the fighting mettle of the armies at the great tests of Fort Donelson and Shiloh in the coming winter and spring.

After two months of probes and patrols, the men were spoiling for a fight. To oblige their lust for battle, Grant on November 6, 1861 put 3,500 men in five regiments, plus artillery and cavalry, onto transports, floated them down the Mississippi, landed them on the Missouri shore above Belmont and rode at their head toward the Rebel camp.

After the battle of Belmont that followed, both sides claimed victory, but Grant ever afterward maintained that, by fighting their way through the Rebel line not just once, into the enemy camp, but again, on the way back to their transports, his men gained confidence in their fighting ability, and that their baptism of fire at Belmont steeled them for what lay ahead.

Too, the battle of Belmont showed Grant as a battlefield leader, one his men trusted and loved as a soldier. Part of this derived from his unmatched ability as a horseman—his men loved seeing his grace on a mount—and part from his physical courage. He shared his men's danger when bullets started to fly, and had a horse shot from under him during the fighting. The men also saw for the first time the indomitability that he showed in battle. He would never incite the wild cheering and hat-waving that George McClellan did back East. Rather, he inspired a quiet loyalty.

Another talent crucial to Grant's success as a leader of men was his ability, rare among generals, to write clear orders—he spent hours in the evening personally writing out his instructions for the next day's maneuvers. When he was done with one order, he would push it from the table onto the floor and start on the next. When he went to bed, an orderly would gather up the paper slips and take them to the chief of staff, who would distribute them to his subordinates.

In December 1861, Grant's tiny District of Southeast Missouri was merged into the District of Cairo, Department of the Missouri. By this time Grant's command had grown to 16 regiments in four brigades, all clustered in riverfront posts near the junction of the Mississippi and the Ohio.

Early 1862 was a time of frustrating inactivity, east and west. In the nation's capital, George McClellan was in bed with typhoid fever, and Lincoln did not know what the general's plans were. Desperate at the impasse, President Lincoln moaned to his quartermaster general, "The bottom is out of the tub! What should I do?" General Halleck in St. Louis responded by ordering a "demonstration" into western Kentucky by Grant's force at Cairo, in concert with the new "turtles"—175-foot-long armored gunboats with 13 guns each, machines that would revolutionize warfare along the inland rivers. Halleck's order to move south, even though it was designed only as a feint, was one which the restless Grant eagerly accepted. The expedition went forward on January 14, and, although it accomplished little, it yielded one important result: when the gunboats neared Fort Henry in their ascent of the Tennessee River, they saw that it was weak and poorly sited.

The most promising avenue of advance into the Confederate interior was up the Tennessee and Cumberland rivers. Grant had for weeks been persistently requesting permission to attack Fort Henry, the gateway to the upper Tennessee Valley. In that desolate winter, at the nadir of Union fortunes, Halleck, on January 28, 1862, granted Grant's request.

On February 1, in preparation for an assault on Fort Henry, Grant transported his newly assembled army of about 15,000 men up the Ohio and Tennessee rivers and had it ashore near Fort Henry by February 5. Leading the column of steam transports up the river were four of the new ironclad gunboats, with three timberclad gunboats for added firepower. As it turned out, the capture of Fort Henry was accomplished the next day entirely by the gunboats while most of the garrison fled. As a result, the Tennessee River was opened to the Union army as far south as Muscle Shoals in northern Alabama.

Grant had already determined to "keep the ball moving" (his words) by advancing on the nearby Fort Donelson, ten miles to the east on the Cumberland River. He held a council of war with his subordinates (the only time in the war he would ever do so), and they voiced unanimous approval of the advance. On February 12, Grant plunged onto the muddy trails to Fort Donelson, the nearby gateway to the Cumberland and thus Nashville and central Tennessee.

There the combined Confederate garrisons of Forts Henry and Donelson, with reinforcements from nearby Tennessee and Kentucky brigades, waited behind their earthworks. In the crucible of the subsequent fighting at Ft. Donelson, Grant showed a willingness to improvise the command structure of his army according to the demands of the battle, improvising a new 3rd Division from regiments that arrived by steamboat during the combat.

Fort Donelson surrendered on February 16, 1862, and Grant was promoted to major general, effective the same day. As the news spread, gloom in the North over the war became euphoria. Grant's victory had deprived the South of an army of 13,000 Rebel soldiers captured there. Too, it completely collapsed the Confederate front. One week later, Gen. Albert Sidney Johnston, at the head of the main Confederate army in Bowling Green, Kentucky, retreated through Nashville, Tennessee, heading south. A week after that, Polk's army evacuated the "Gibraltar of the West" at Columbus on the Mississippi.

Halleck, from his office in St. Louis, created a new district, the District of West Tennessee, and made Grant the commander while Grant's headquarters were still at Fort Donelson. Grant's new district was unique in that it had no geographical limits, but consisted only in Grant's forces that were to operate with him on the Tennessee River.

On February 21, Grant reorganized the Army of the District of West Tennessee, now grown to 27,000 men, into four divisions. The 1st, 2nd and 3rd Divisions remained essentially the same as they were at Fort Donelson, and a 4th Division, under Brig. Gen. Stephen Hurlbut, was cobbled together from regiments more recently arrived by steamboat, mostly from Illinois.

Halleck simultaneously decided to create a fifth division for Grant. On February 14, immediately after the capture of Fort Henry, Halleck had given his friend, Brig. Gen. William T. Sherman—who was attempting to rebuild his reputation after being dismissed for "insanity" the previous November—command of a new division based at Paducah, consisting of regiments Halleck was forwarding from all over his department. On March 1, Halleck added it to Grant's command.

With the latest additions, Grant reported his army's strength as just under 40,000 men.

On the same day he added Sherman's division to Grant's army, Halleck ordered Grant to move his army up the Tennessee River on a raid with the purpose of destroying railroad bridges and telegraph lines vital to Confederate communications in western Tennessee. On March 4, Grant starting marching his forces at Fort Donelson, which then consisted of the 1st, 3rd, and 4th Divisions, back to Fort Henry to embark for the advance up the Tennessee River.

It was not clear that it was any longer Grant's army to command, however. After the victory at Fort Donelson, he had rushed C. F. Smith's 2nd Division up the Cumberland River to Clarksville, Tennessee—a leap toward the prize of Nashville. This placed Smith's division in Don Carlos Buell's neighboring Department of the Cumberland, and Halleck, always sensitive on the subject of department lines, hit the roof. Repeated misunderstandings in communications between Grant in Tennessee and Halleck at his headquarters in St. Louis—inevitable in the far-flung Western Theater—inflamed Halleck's petty jealousies now that Grant, the muddy-booted hero of Fort Donelson, was suddenly the nation's darling. So on March 4, Halleck wired Grant ordering him to hand control of the upcoming Tennessee River operation to Brig. Gen. Charles F. Smith. Halleck told Grant himself to wait behind at Fort Henry.

Smith, now leading the expedition, floated his 2nd Division back down the Cumberland and Ohio rivers, then up the Tennessee to Savannah, Tennessee, the river town closest to the Union army's next strategic objective: the crucial railroad hub at Corinth, Mississippi, only 34 miles to the southwest. Smith's flotilla arrived at Savannah in the second week of March, the same week the steamboat fleets bearing Brig. Gen. Lew Wallace's 3rd Division and Sherman's 5th Division labored upriver.

It took 24 hours for Sherman's 5th Division, on 17 steamboat transports, to cover the 100 miles from Paducah to Savannah, where it arrived on March 11.

Wallace's 3rd Division disembarked on March 12 at Crump's Landing, on the west bank of the Tennessee a mile or so upriver from Savannah. Wallace occupied the landing with his infantry, then sent his cavalry straight west on an expedition that destroyed the north-south Mobile & Ohio Railroad trestle north of Corinth at Beach Creek. (Within 36 hours, however, the Confederates had repaired the bridge.)

That same week, Halleck's relentless lobbying of Lincoln for unrivaled authority in the west was rewarded: Lincoln's "War Order #3" merged the three departments west of the Appalachians into a new Department of the Mississippi under Halleck, and made Brig. Gen. Buell's Army of the Ohio part of Halleck's command.

In another development important to the campaign, on March 12 General Smith fell while boarding a skiff at Savannah and cut his shin badly. Brig. Gen. W.H.L. "Will" Wallace replaced him as commander of the 2nd Division, while Grant was reinstated in control of the expedition. In the coming weeks, the seemingly minor injury would fester and kill Smith.

On March 14, Sherman steamed further upriver to accomplish the other bridge-burning mission. He moved his division to the mouth of Yellow Creek, from which he marched south and attempted to torch the Bear Creek bridge on the east-west Memphis & Charleston Railroad. Forced to abandon the movement because of rain and high water, Sherman put his men back on their transports and floated them back downstream to Pittsburg Landing—the only landing in the area, in that rain-soaked season, that was still above water—where, on March 16, he disembarked, along with Hurlbut's 4th Division, which had now arrived and was waiting in transports anchored at the landing. On orders from General Smith, both divisions went inland far enough to allow the whole army to camp in the space between them and the river. The 8,500 men of Sherman's division marched two miles southwest to Shiloh Church and encamped, and Hurlbut's division, 7,800 strong, camped to Sherman's left as they faced in the direction of the enemy, two days' march distant at Corinth.

The Shiloh plateau on which Sherman and Hurlbut camped was the only high, firm ground in an otherwise low, swampy region. It was well suited for defense, bounded by creeks running north and south—Lick Creek on the east and Owl and Snake Creeks on the west. Tributaries of these formed steep ravines carved into the plateau. Any attack on the plateau would have to be a straight-ahead frontal assault from the south, the only approach to Pittsburg Landing.

On March 13 Halleck, bowing to public pressure as well as the injury to C.F. Smith, telegraphed Grant at Fort Henry: "Instead of relieving you, I wish you as soon as your new army is in the field to assume the immediate command and lead it on to new victories." Grant, with his 10-day dressing-down now ended, arrived at Savannah on March 17. He was surprised to find his two newest divisions under Sherman and Hurlbut, entirely made of raw recruits, camped on the west bank of the Tennessee at Pittsburg Landing, nearest the Confederate army known to be concentrating at Corinth. His three veteran divisions meantime were scattered—the 7,500 men of Lew Wallace's 3rd Division four miles downriver from Pittsburg Landing at Crump's Landing; McClernand's 8,000 1st Division veterans camped around Savannah; and Smith's 2nd Division, 8,400 strong, still languishing on their transports at Savannah moorings. In choosing a place to concentrate, the Savannah location had the merit of having the Tennessee River to protect Grant's gathering army from any Confederate attack while Buell's Army of the Ohio moved to join them. However, caution was not in Grant's nature, and besides, Smith had already ordered a concentration of the army at Pittsburg Landing. Grant went ahead with a build-up at the Landing, characteristically planning for a strike on Corinth before the Rebels there could concentrate further. Halleck's Tennessee River raid on Confederate communications had by this time clearly become an invasion. That is, Grant meant to stay.

In the three weeks before the great battle, troop transports were docked at Pittsburg Landing five deep, busy unloading a growing army whose camps spread two miles inland. On March 19, the 2nd Division, now under Will Wallace, arrived at Pittsburg Landing and moved inland a short distance. On March 20, McClernand arrived with his division and camped behind Sherman's division.

On March 26, 1862, Brig. Gen. Benjamin Prentiss reported for duty and was assigned command of the unattached troops at Pittsburg Landing. As new regiments arrived, they were formed into two brigades commanded by the senior colonels, with supporting cavalry and artillery. There being no vacancy near Pittsburg Landing for the 7,500 men in the regiments and batteries of Prentiss's new 6th Division, their camps were laid out on the outer rim of the army, nearest the Confederate army.

Grant's army had been born one year earlier with 595 Chicago men heading south on a train to defend the levees of Cairo. By the time Grant took over in September, the army at Cairo had been reinforced to around 12,000 men. Through the fall of 1861, that figure held steady—around 12,000 District of Cairo soldiers took part in the maneuvers that accompanied the battle of Belmont on November 7, and about 15,000 started toward Fort Henry in the first week of February. From there, however, the number of men in Grant's army soared, as Halleck in St. Louis reinforced success. By mid-February, after the capture of Fort Donelson, Grant's army counted 24,000 men. Six weeks later, on the eve of the battle of Shiloh, after the army had steamed 100 miles into Confederate territory and threatened to deliver a crushing blow to the Confederate war effort in the west, the army Grant now called "The Army of Tennessee" numbered over 45,000 men.

In the field, Grant was bold to the point of recklessness. At the close of a victory in battle, he immediately looked ahead to the next battle, determined to keep the momentum. This dynamism, his greatest asset, almost led to the loss of his entire command in his first three battles—at Belmont, Fort Donelson, and Shiloh. But those near-disasters revealed another aspect of his character, which was the ability, even in the face of appalling casualties, to sense opportunity rather than defeat. This was a quality unique among Northern generals in the first year of the war. After the calamity of the first day at Shiloh, when a defeated General Sherman found Grant smoking a cigar under a tree and sighed, "Well, Grant, we've had the devil's own day, haven't we?" Grant famously shot back, "Yes. Lick 'em tomorrow, though." He traveled along the lines of his men, exhorting them quietly, telling them, "Boys, remember the watchword is 'Donelson'."

The numbers on the field of battle at Shiloh were the largest that Grant, or anyone in the United States at that time, had ever seen. He responded by declining to give orders from the rear, but instead choosing to see, and be seen by, his men. According to one of his escorts, Grant "continuously rode along the line of battle, through the hottest of their fire, for the whole distance of about five miles." During this day-long tour, a scout riding next to him had his head taken off by a cannonball, and Grant himself was narrowly saved from a serious wound by a canister shot when it hit and bent the scabbard of his sword. He took only a small part in the direction of the battle, moving reinforcements forward and directing the beginning of the final line.

Grant's habit of visiting all parts of the field impaired his control of his army, contributing to the skulkers estimated variously from 6,000 to 15,000, huddled at Pittsburg Landing at day's end. (He changed this habit: later in the war at the Wilderness, he would sit in one spot in the rear, whittling while he waited for reports.) The number of men listed as missing was enormous: 26% of his casualties. Buell, perhaps jealous of Grant's greater part in this mightiest conflict in the nation's history, wrote ungenerously of Grant's leadership that there was "want of cohesion and concert in the Union ranks," and that his men suffered from "the absence of a common head." It is true that the combat in the ravine-etched, wooded terrain devolved into a soldier's battle. One of Grant's own men called it "little more than a fearful melee at best." But Grant's peregrinations gave him a canny feel for the battle. Sherman remembered that, about 4:00 p.m., Grant told him "that at a certain period of the [Fort Donelson] battle he saw that either side was ready to give way if the other showed a bold front, and he was determined to do that very thing."

Ulysses S. Grant went on to be the most successful general of the Civil War. Afterward, at the rank of full General, he oversaw the military aspects of Reconstruction. In 1868, he was elected 18th President of the United States at the age of 46, the youngest elected president in the nation's history at that time, and served two terms, though both were blighted by financial scandals caused by Grant's inability to judge the character of his associates.

The same inability bedeviled Grant's post-presidential career, as when his business partner embezzled their financial firm, leaving Grant bankrupt in 1884. At the end of his life, while dying of throat cancer, he applied the same writing talent to composing his memoirs that had had so much to do with his success a general, and he hired his friend Mark Twain to publish them. Grant's Memoirs proved a classic work of American literature and provided a financial legacy for his family.

The Army of the Tennessee at Shiloh

At Shiloh, Grant's army had a slight advantage in numbers over the Confederate Army of Mississippi—about 45,000 to 40,000—which was balanced by the Confederate advantage of surprise. Grant's army enjoyed a superiority in the number and quality of its artillery: Grant fielded 127 guns in 26 batteries, while the Confederates had only 115 guns in 23 batteries. Nearly half of Grant's guns were rifled—against just 13 rifled guns in the Confederate army—and the rifled cannon had a longer range than smoothbores. The dense woods, however, nullified this advantage.

Grant's army had problems beside those posed by the wooded terrain. Three of his six divisions were composed almost entirely of green troops, many of whom had been rushed forward from their training camps before they had completed their instruction. Additionally, the too-rapid enlargement of Grant's army had caused widespread disruption among its officers and their commands. Colonels, many of whom had never seen a battle, found themselves suddenly at the heads of brigades hastily thrown together, and each of these colonels' regiments was forced to elevate an untested officer to its head in his place. The regiments were too big, averaging close to 600 men each, too large for their inexperienced colonels to lead effectively, especially in the confusion of woods, fighting much of the time without recognizable front lines.

Too, there were problems with munitions. There were too many ammunition types needed to supply the artillery batteries, which had ten different gun types. The infantry regiments, too, carried many different caliber weapons. Fortunately for the Union men, these same problems beset the Confederate army.

It is interesting that Grant decided to personally direct all six of his divisions himself, rather than dividing them into corps. This made command less efficient in his Army of the Tennessee than in Johnston and Beauregard's Army of the Mississippi, and demanded that he personally cover more ground in extremely difficult terrain. And if Grant were incapacitated, army command would have taken valuable time to sort out, since the army's other active major generals, John McClernand and Lew Wallace, had both been promoted on the same date, and neither outranked the other.

About half of the 62 regiments in Grant's army at Pittsburg Landing had combat experience, a bigger share than in the Confederate army. About half of Grant's batteries were also combat veterans, while the majority of his cavalry had been under fire at Fort Donelson or in skirmishes throughout the department in the past year.

On April 2, Grant refined the organization of his army and shuffled the assignments for all his artillery and cavalry units. It created confusion in the short run, since units that had previously been attached to a brigade in one division were often transferred to new, unfamiliar divisions. The confusion was still being sorted out when the Confederates attacked on April 6. Thus, at the battle of Shiloh, Grant's army was bewildered by the problem of managing cavalry and artillery that had recently lost their old attachments and had not yet been consolidated in their divisions.

On Sunday, April 6, the Army of the Tennessee was encamped on the west bank of the Tennessee River; the 1st, 2nd, 4th, 5th, and 6th divisions at Pittsburg Landing, with 39,830 officers and men present for duty, and the 3rd Division at Crump's Landing, with 7,250 more. General Grant's headquarters was downriver at Savannah, Tennessee, where he was awaiting the arrival of General Buell. While at breakfast early Sunday morning, Grant heard heavy firing at Pittsburg Landing, and, leaving instructions for the lead division of Buell's approaching Army of the Ohio to move up the east bank of the river to a point opposite Pittsburg Landing, Grant and his staff took a steamboat to the battlefield, where they arrived at about 8:00 a.m. Grant visited each of his divisions at the front, and, judging that he was attacked by the main force of the enemy and not a diversion, he sent an order for Lew Wallace's 3rd Division at Crump's Landing to march to the field and join him. He also sent a request to General Buell for reinforcements.

On the first day of the battle, the Army of the Tennessee was gradually driven back by the Confederate surprise attack, but maintained its cohesion and successfully resisted being pried away from its lifeline on the river at Pittsburg Landing. A. S. Johnston's forces made steady progress until about 11:00, when Union resistance stiffened. On the main Union defensive line, Benjamin M. Prentiss's 6th Division and W. H. L. Wallace's 2nd Division established a position nicknamed the "Hornets' Nest," along the road that came to be called the "Sunken Road," fronting a field. The Confederates assaulted this position for several hours, in perhaps a dozen separate charges. The men of Stephen A. Hurlbut's 4th Division protected this central position on its left, and those of John A. McClernand's 1st Division, after falling back from their early-morning positions, protected the right. At around 5:00 p.m., however, the troops to the left and right gave way, and the Hornets' Nest position collapsed, leading to the capture of more than 2,000 of its survivors. Their hours-long defense, however, bought time for Grant to establish a final defensive line near Pittsburg Landing, which allowed Buell's Army of the Ohio to start crossing the river during the night. These fresh troops, numbering about 17,000 men, took positions on the Union left, nearest the river. Across the Owl Creek bridge on the opposite flank came Lew Wallace's fresh 3rd Division, whose 7,000 men took positions on the Union right.

At the opening of the battle on the second day, led by Sherman, McClernand, and Hurlbut, the men of Grant's army, still suffering the effects of the beating they had taken the day before, did not move forward quickly, but still kept pace with the fresh troops on either side. By 8:00 a.m. they were moving forward warily, but were stopped again by a stream called Tilghman's Branch, which they did not cross until about 10:00 a.m. For the next four hours, they saw fighting just as hard as on the first day, but the outnumbered, fatigued Confederate army made an orderly retreat at about 2:30 on the afternoon of the second day.

At Shiloh, Grant's Army of the Tennessee lost 1,513 killed, 6,601 wounded, and 2,830 missing and captured, for a total of 10,944 out of 48,894 present for duty—22% casualties (compared to the Army of the Ohio's 12% and the Confederate Army of the Mississippi's 24%).

Its losses to enemy fire (its killed and wounded) were 17% of its total strength (compared to the Army of the Ohio's 11% and the Confederate Army of the Mississippi's 22%).

1st Division

Major General
John A. McClernand

John McClernand was a political general who owed his commission to the fact that he was a loyal Democratic congressman and newspaper editor from pro-Rebel southern Illinois—precisely the kind of anti-abolitionist opinion-maker that had to be kept loyal to the North in order to win a war with the South. He was also a friend of Abraham Lincoln.

His early life was much like Lincoln's, as he was a Kentucky-born, self-taught lawyer before he became a congressman. Being a favorite of the President excused McClernand from the usual school of instruction for political officers, which was to be placed in command of a regiment at the rank of colonel to learn the ropes. Rather, McClernand's first assignment was as a brigadier general in command of the "McClernand Brigade" of four Illinois regiments: the 27th, 29th, 30th, and 31st.

McClernand's greatest virtue was his willingness to fight. Especially at the beginning of the war, when few Northern generals dared to come to grips with the enemy, he was aggressive and brave in battle. He had been in the middle of the fighting at Belmont and at Fort Donelson, and in both, his personal presence on the battlefield had contributed greatly to Union success. Charles Dana wrote that he "behaved with the most conspicuous gallantry." Even his detractors among fellow generals, such as Lew Wallace and James H. Wilson, commented on his bravery. Wilson, later a severe critic, called him "an officer of undaunted courage" who "would be in the thick of the fight." He was one of few who disdained careful strategy and favored a policy of attacks followed by more attacks. He was, in fact, an able commander, especially for a politician-turned-general. However, he could be insubordinate and amateurish, as at Donelson when, without orders or authority, he made a futile attack against Redan No. 2, which had an entrenched force with strength equal to his own. A day later, when McArthur's brigade was added to the right of McClernand's line, McArthur said he was "without instructions," indicating a laxity in McClernand's battlefield control. At Shiloh, he would again demonstrate this fault.

By the time of the Vicksburg Campaign, Grant would call McClernand "unmanageable and incompetent." But while it is true that McClernand never read Hardee's Tactics, an example of McClernand's attention to detail was his instructions for the ascending of the Tennessee River before Shiloh. He carefully specified where each brigade was to land, how many skirmishers were to be set out, the size of the reserve, the mission of the cavalry, and the instructions for the artillery and baggage trains.

McClernand's biggest liability was that he was pompous, overbearing, impetuous, and rude. It was his incessant political maneuvering and scheming for more authority that was his downfall. McClernand wanted to be a war hero, knowing that war heroes tended to become presidents. Although he worked well with other generals in battle, when the fighting was over he would inevitably be found writing puffed-up versions of his own exploits to Lincoln in an attempt to vault himself over his superiors. This habit ultimately alienated him from Grant and every other general he worked with. Almost to a man they despised him, although in some cases their distaste was the result of career generals' prejudice against political generals. Admiral David D. Porter referred to him after the war as one of the "greatest charlatans in this or any other country." Grant finally removed him from command during the Vicksburg campaign.

With his Civil War military career ended, McClernand returned to Illinois and became district judge of the Sangamon District, 1870–73. He continued his interest in politics, and was president of the 1876 Democratic National Convention in St. Louis. McClernand died in Springfield, Illinois in 1900.

1st (McClernand's) Division at Shiloh

McClernand's 1st Division was the most veteran division on either side, composed almost entirely of troops that had "seen the elephant" in fighting at Fredericktown, Belmont, and Fort Donelson. It is ironic that these experienced brigades were led at Shiloh by woefully inexperienced brigadiers: Hare, Marsh, and Raith, all in brigade command for the first time.

The 1st Division was also the smallest division in the Army of the Tennessee, containing 6,941 Illinois and Iowa men in three brigades.

This was the division in Grant's army most amply supplied with artillery, with 20 guns in four batteries: McAllister's, Nispel's, and Timony's Illinois batteries and Burrows's Ohio battery. The 1st Division also had three companies of Illinois cavalry, which were useless in the ravine-crossed, heavily wooded terrain of Shiloh.

It is to McClernand's credit that he had sensed a surprise attack and had written to Grant on March 27 and Sherman on March 31, warning of an enemy assault. Both ignored him.

The 1st Division was camped across the Corinth Road to the north of Shiloh Church, with Hare's 1st Brigade camped farthest to the rear (that is, north), Marsh's 2nd Brigade in the middle, and, closest to the first fighting, Raith's 3rd Brigade, near the central crossroads of the Corinth Road with the Hamburg-Purdy Road.

On Sunday morning, around 9:00 a.m., after receiving a call from Sherman on the army's far right, McClernand demonstrated the same laxity of control that he had shown at Fort Donelson—he sent his brigades forward piecemeal into the gap between Prentiss and Sherman without tactical direction from above. As each brigade deployed on the morning of the battle, McClernand sent them forward with "a few brief, but burning words." However, without alignment, each arriving regiment advanced into Confederate fire coming from many directions, and many broke almost immediately.

McClernand's division formed for battle with Raith's brigade thrown forward to support Sherman's left. Marsh's brigade came up on Raith's left, and Hare's brigade came up along Marsh's left. The line ran straight west to east, parallel with the Hamburg-Purdy Road immediately to its rear, and connected Sherman's division with Prentiss's in the army's center. When the teeming lines of Confederates struck between 9:00 and 10:00 in the morning, McClernand's three brigades quickly lost two colonels commanding, two lieutenant colonels, and five majors. The line collapsed, and the division made its next stand at right angles to the first, running north to south and facing west. The division then retired again, to the camp of Hare's brigade. Here it rallied, made a countercharge, and drove the Confederates back.

McClernand's counterattack recovered his headquarters in the middle of his brigade camps around noon. However, the 1st Division held this advanced position only briefly before it was slowly driven back for the second time, until at 2:00 p.m. it was again in the field of Hare's camp. The division held this line until 2:30 p.m. It then retired across Tilghman Branch to a line at Cavalry Field, where at 4:30 p.m. it repulsed a charge made by Pond's brigade and Wharton's cavalry, and then retired to the Hamburg-Savannah Road, where, with its right thrown back, it bivouacked Sunday night at the right of Grant's army's last defensive line. On Monday morning the 1st Division advanced over the same ground where it had fought on Sunday, and at 4:00 p.m. reoccupied its now-pillaged camps on the field.

At Shiloh, McClernand and the 1st Division performed well under extremely difficult circumstances. He consulted closely with Sherman, who was complimentary of McClernand's "perfect concert" with his own division. That the Union right wing did not completely give way was due largely to McClernand's improvisations during the long first day. The only stain on the division's behavior came at the end of the day, when some elements of his command retreated, in what McClernand called "a tide of fugitive soldiers and trains," to the shelter of the gunboats at the landing.

At Shiloh, McClernand's 1st Division lost 285 killed, 1,372 wounded, and 85 missing and captured, totaling 1,742 out of 6,941 present for duty—25% casualties.

One indication of the spirit and fighting savvy of McClernand's division was its low rate of missing at Shiloh .5%, or one-tenth the 5% army average. Its losses to enemy fire (killed and wounded) were 24% of its total strength, the highest rate of losses to enemy fire of any division in Grant's Army of the Tennessee.

1st Brigade
Colonel Abraham M. Hare

Brigadier General Richard Oglesby, the brigade commander, was away on furlough, so 50-year-old Abraham Hare led the division's 1st Brigade at Shiloh as its senior colonel. It was not only Hare's first experience in brigade command, but his first experience in battle—his regiment, the 11th Iowa, had only been mustered in five months earlier.

He had shown interest in military matters in his native Ohio, where he had been a major of militia before he moved to Iowa. He was, however, not a soldier but a merchant, who had opened a hat business in Muscatine, Iowa. His claim to the colonelcy of the local regiment, the 11th Iowa, came from his eminence as among the wealthiest men of the town.

One of his men wrote appreciatively that Hare was "a very just and humane man always looking to the welfare of his men and never exacting more of them than was necessary for the welfare of the country." His ability as a leader of fighting men, however, went unremarked.

An observer described Hare as a "large, athletic man of bilious-sanguine temperament, and dark complexion. His hair, once black, is now streaked with gray; his eye, though mild, is penetrating. He is determined in purpose, and kind-hearted, a fact universally attested by the 'boys' of his regiment. He is cool, deliberate and fearless in battle, and unostentatious in manners." A wound suffered at the end of the battle's first day forced Hare's retirement from the army, and he eventually died back in Iowa in 1903.

1st Division, 1st (Hare's) Brigade at Shiloh

Col. Abraham C. Hare's 1st Brigade, at 2,214 men, was the largest brigade in the division. Aside from Hare himself never having seen a battle, his inexperience was compounded by absences among the regimental officers. One of his regiments was led by a captain, one by a major, and one by a lieutenant colonel. Only one regiment, the 13th Iowa, entered the battle with a colonel at its head.

The 8th and 18th Illinois regiments, however, were veteran, having fought side-by-side at both Belmont and Fort Donelson. The 8th Illinois was organized in the first two weeks of the war and got its first combat experience early, in two skirmishes in Missouri in the fall of 1861. At Fort Donelson, it had stood with the rest of Oglesby's brigade for three hours in the thickest of the fighting, losing 250 men, more than most entire brigades. At Shiloh it was almost leaderless, commanded by the captain of one of its companies.

The 18th Illinois regiment was a rugged group of men from the backwoods of southern Illinois, regarded in the army as a bunch of "desperate characters." Although hard fighters, the regiment was crippled by a power struggle between its hard-bitten Col. Michael Lawler and a group of roughnecks, and at Shiloh it was commanded by its major.

Neither of the Iowa regiments had seen combat. Both had arrived from Missouri on March 23, less than two weeks before the battle. The 11th Iowa were veterans of hard marching but little fighting in a harsh winter campaign in Missouri, and were commanded at Shiloh by the regiment's lieutenant colonel. The 13th Iowa had done unexciting garrison duty in Missouri in the previous winter months.

On the morning of battle, Hare's brigade was encamped in Jones Field. It was the last brigade to come up to the fighting line of McClernand's 1st Division, on the division's far left, connecting with Prentiss's 6th Division in the army's center. It moved from its camp at about 8:00 a.m. and formed up on the ridge between the Review Field and the Corinth Road, its left at the edge of Duncan Field, in the following order from left to right: 8th Illinois, 18th Illinois, 13th Iowa. (The 11th Iowa was detached from the brigade.)

In this position the three left regiments were attacked about 10:00 a.m. by Shaver's brigade of Hardee's corps. Some sources testify that one of Hare's regiments ran after firing just one volley, and that another retreated without firing a shot. Hare explained afterward that, seeing the enemy approaching in their front in great numbers, and "our troops on the right having given way, my regiments also broke and retired in confusion." The routed troops ran through Veatch's brigade, which had come up from Hurlbut's division to support their line. Hare eventually rallied them, but his regiments' retreat had left only unsupported artillery remaining on the first line of battle.

The entire division advanced and recovered its camps at noon. However, it soon retired again and did so continually throughout the afternoon.

The 13th Iowa participated in the repulse of Wharton's cavalry at 4:30 p.m. Here Col. Hare was wounded, ending his Civil War service, and Col. M. M. Crocker of the 13th Iowa took command of the brigade.

On Monday the brigade was attached to Tuttle's command, which served as a reserve for General Critttenden's division from the Army of the Ohio until about 3:00 p.m., when it was ordered to the front and charged the enemy southwest of Review Field. The 8th and 18th Illinois each captured one gun from the enemy.

At Shiloh, Hare's 1st Brigade lost 100 killed, 458 wounded, and 9 missing, for a total of 567 out of 2,214 present for duty—26% casualties.

2nd Brigade
Colonel C. Carroll Marsh

A 32-year-old native of Oswego, New York, Marsh had never commanded a brigade before Shiloh; however, he was a veteran of combat at the head of the 20th Illinois. He had led the regiment at the battle of Fredericktown, Missouri, the previous autumn, and had distinguished himself at Fort Donelson in February.

In 1853 he had moved to Chicago, Illinois, to study law. But the legal profession was overcrowded in the days before the American Bar Association was founded to establish standards, when anybody in Illinois could be a lawyer (which is how Abraham Lincoln became an Illinois lawyer with less than a year of schooling), and Marsh left law school after one year and went into business. He joined the Chicago Light Guard militia, renowned as one of the best-disciplined in the country, and rose to captain in that organization.

Due to his reputation with the Chicago Light Guard, Illinois Governor Richard Yates called Capt. Marsh to Springfield at the outset of the Civil War. Marsh hurried to the state capital and was given command of Camp Yates, where 7,000 recruits were soon drilling. He was made colonel of the 20th Illinois Volunteer Infantry Regiment when, despite being completely unknown to the men of the regiment, he was elected almost unanimously to its head. His character can be glimpsed in the letter he wrote his wife: "I feel in its full force the terrible responsibility that rests upon me. One thousand men under me to look after, care for, and protect; it is no small task, but I have put on the armor, and will bear it to the end, even though that end be my existence. . . . I feel that God who called me here, did it for some wise purpose, and if my country needs my life, her cause is sacred, and He who has numbered the hairs on my head will not permit me to die in vain."

Colonel Marsh and the 20th Illinois were transported to Cape Girardeau, Missouri, and attached to Col. Joseph B. Plummer's command before the battle of Fredericktown, where he "saw the elephant" at the first brigade-sized battle fought by units under Ulysses S. Grant's command.

At the head of his regiment, Marsh showed ability and resourcefulness. At Fort Donelson, Marsh's men were positioned on the right of the Union lines, where, on February 15, they were beaten back during the Confederate breakout attempt. Later that day, Marsh managed a counterattack which momentarily checked the Confederate sortie and saved an Illinois artillery battery from capture.

After the capture of Fort Donelson, Marsh was one of a select group of officers who presented Grant with an ivory-handled sword. The moment was bittersweet—Grant had just been temporarily removed from command of the army by Maj. Gen. Henry Halleck, commander of the Department of Missouri.

After Shiloh and the siege of Corinth that May, Col. Marsh was transferred to command the 3rd Brigade of the division, stationed at Jackson, Mississippi. He was appointed brigadier general in November, but never confirmed. He continued in brigade command until he resigned during the Vicksburg Campaign the next year. Marsh moved to moved to Santa Barbara, California, after the war and died in 1908.

1st Division, 2nd (Marsh's) Brigade at Shiloh

Colonel Marsh's 2nd Brigade of 1,847 Illinois men—the 11th, 20th, 45th, and 48th regiments—was the smallest and most veteran brigade in the Union army at Shiloh, all of its regiments having fought together at Fort Donelson. There, however, it had fought under a different brigade commander, Brig. Gen. W. H. L. "Will" Wallace, who at Shiloh had been elevated to command of the 2nd Division in Maj. Gen. C. F. Smith's absence.

The 11th Illinois was among the first called into service in the first weeks of the war, and in the fall of 1861 had skirmished in expeditions in Missouri. In its camps, under the instruction of "Will" Wallace, it was renowned for the excellence of its drill. At Fort Donelson, it lost 65% of its men, the heaviest losses of any Union regiment in that battle, and was so depleted that it would fight at Shiloh with only 239 men. It was ably commanded by its lieutenant colonel, Thomas E. G. Ransom, who would become known as one of the best and bravest officers of the war.

The 20th Illinois had been organized for ten months and had fought in two battles: Fredericktown in Missouri, and Fort Donelson. Its lieutenant colonel commanded in the absence of its Col. Marsh, now the acting brigade commander.

The men of the 45th Illinois were primarily lead miners from Galena. The regiment had suffered slight casualties at the battle of Fort Donelson. Its able colonel, John Smith, was the son of a Napoleonic officer.

The 48th Illinois, recruited from the backwoods of southern Illinois, had lost 17% casualties at Fort Donelson. The 48th was led, as at Fort Donelson, by Col. Isham Haynie.

Marsh became aware that the Confederate army was attacking only when a cannonball bounced through his brigade's camp. He formed his brigade and advanced south, toward the enemy, coming to a stop in the middle of McClernand's division's first line. Its left was at the northwest corner of the Review Field, and its right near the central crossroads of the Corinth Road and the Hamburg-Purdy Road. Lined up from left to right were the 20th Illinois, Burrows's Battery near the center, the 48th Illinois, and the 45th Illinois.

In this position the brigade was fiercely attacked from about 10:00 a.m. to 11:00 a.m., when it fell back in confusion about 700 yards and re-formed at right angles to the original division line, facing west. It held this position for a short time and then fell back again toward Pittsburg Landing and rallied at Jones Field.

In conjunction with other troops, it recaptured its camp at noon. In this advance the 20th and 11th Illinois, assisted by the 11th Iowa of Hare's 1st Brigade, captured Cobb's Confederate battery in a costly attack. The brigade retained possession of parts of its camp for about two hours, then retired slowly again to Jones Field, where it was engaged until 2:30 p.m., when it fell back to the army's final line, where the 20th, 45th, and 48th Illinois regiments united with remnants of Raith's 3rd Brigade and bivouacked Sunday night. The 11th Illinois, reduced to a captain and 80 men, bivouacked near the siege guns at the left end of this line, and was kept in reserve on Monday. The 20th, 45th, and 48th formed a part of Marsh's combined command and on Monday recovered their camps at about 3:00 p.m.

At Shiloh, Marsh's brigade lost 80 killed, 475 wounded, and 30 missing and captured, for a total of 585 out of 1,847 present for duty—32% casualties, the highest rate in the division.

3rd Brigade
Colonel Julius Raith

After the brigade's commander at Fort Donelson was wounded, the acting commander of the 2nd Brigade was Col. Leonard F. Ross of the 17th Illinois. He was on leave from the army, having just lost his wife, and so was not at Shiloh. Command passed to Col. J. S. Reardon of the 29th Illinois. On April 6, however, Reardon was sick, and Col. Julius Raith of the 43rd Illinois assumed command.

The 43-year-old Col. Raith (pronounced "Rite") had been born in Germany and at the age of 17 had emigrated to Illinois, opposite St. Louis, where he learned the trade of a millwright.

At 27 he was commissioned captain of a company of the 2nd Illinois Volunteers in the Mexican War and was distinguished at Buena Vista. After the war, he resumed constructing mills in St. Louis and Illinois, and became renowned for his expertise among mill owners and mechanics in the Northwest. When the Civil War broke out, Raith helped prominent Illinois German-American Gustave Koerner organize the 43rd Illinois, a German regiment, and Raith was appointed colonel by the governor of Illinois.

Raith Family Collection

On the morning of the Confederate attack, Col. Raith of the 43rd Illinois heard heavy firing, and had the regiment assembled, the tents taken down, the wagons loaded, and the regiment aligned on the colors. He sent Lt. Col. Engelmann to General McClernand to inform him of the approaching enemy. Engelmann was instructed to tell Col. Reardon, of the 29th Illinois, to assume command of the brigade, since General Ross had gone to Illinois on furlough. Colonel Reardon was sick, however, and the command of the brigade fell to Col. Raith, whose own regiment was the only one ready for action.

The staff officers of the brigade were a half-mile away at brigade headquarters. Beside one mounted officer of his own regiment, Raith had no assistance in turning out the other regiments of the brigade. To make matters worse, the camps of this brigade were closest to the initial fighting, sited east-to-west along the Hamburg-Purdy Road, just east of Sherman's headquarters near the Shiloh Church.

Caught in heavy fire on the first day at Shiloh, Raith was wounded by a minie ball in the leg above the knee and lay on the battlefield for 24 hours. Feeble and exhausted, he was placed on a steamer bound for the hospital at Mound City, Ill. His leg was amputated en route, and he died of tetanus.

1st Division, 3rd (Raith's) Brigade at Shiloh

Raith's 3rd Brigade consisted of four Illinois regiments—the 17th, 29th, 43rd and 49th—totaling 2,153 men. This had been Col. William R. Morrison's brigade at Fort Donelson, but he had been wounded in the hip in that attack and was still recovering at the time of Shiloh.

Although it was composed mostly of veteran regiments, three of whom—the 17th, 29th, and 49th Illinois—had fought at Fort Donelson, the brigade was hampered during the morning fighting at Shiloh by the sickness of its commander, confusion among its brigade staff, the absence of all four of its regiments' colonels, and the inexperience of its acting commander, the fourth-in-command, Col. Julius Raith.

The 17th Illinois, made up of central Illinois farmers, was one of the few regiments with experience in two battles. It had played a central role in Grant's army's first brigade-sized battle, the battle of Fredericktown on October 21, 1861, and in February 1862 at Fort Donelson. At Shiloh its colonel was on leave, and it was commanded by its lieutenant colonel, Enos Wood, for the first time.

The 29th Illinois were woodsmen from southern Illinois. After spending 1861 traipsing across southeast Missouri in pursuit of Jeff Thompson, the 29th had lost 18% of its men in its infernal baptism at Fort Donelson. At Shiloh, its original colonel was ill, and the regiment was commanded by Lt. Col. Charles M. Ferrell for the first time.

The 43rd Illinois, "The Koerner Regiment" of German-Americans, had joined the brigade soon after the battle of Fort Donelson. Considered excellent in drill, its service had been limited to guarding railroads in northern Missouri, and it had not yet fought a battle. At Shiloh, its Col. Raith was absent commanding the brigade, and command fell to Lt. Col. Adolph Engelmann, a veteran of the Mexican War.

The 49th Illinois, rural men from southeastern Illinois with only three months in service, had seen action at Fort Donelson. As there, it was commanded by its lieutenant colonel, Phineas Pease.

On Sunday morning, after finding out he was in command of the brigade, Col. Raith ordered Lt. Col. Engelmann to bring up the 49th Illinois, which was to the left of the 43rd, but the men of the 49th had only just seized their weapons when the enemy was upon them, and had no time to form a line of battle. Engelmann's 43rd Illinois for a time supported Waterhouse's Battery alone, and offered a stubborn resistance, leaving 36 men of the regiment dead in this first position, with many carried to the rear, severely wounded.

On McClernand's order, Raith moved the right of his brigade forward to Shiloh Church to support Sherman's left. In this position the brigade was attacked about 9:00 a.m. on its left flank by Wood's and Stewart's brigades and in front by Russell's and Johnson's, and was driven slowly back to the central crossroads at the Corinth Road and the Hamburg-Purdy Road, where it joined the right of McClernand's 2nd Brigade, commanded by Col. Marsh. Here, in a crossfire of Confederate artillery, Col. Raith was mortally wounded. When Marsh's and Sherman's troops gave way on either side of them, Raith's troops saw that they were outflanked on both the right and the left and became unnerved. About 10:00 a.m., McClernand ordered Raith's wavering regiments to fall back to a new line being prepared 600 yards to the rear. The withdrawal quickly turned to confusion, then to panic as the Confederates pursued them closely.

Enos Wood, the inexperienced lieutenant colonel who succeeded to the command of the brigade, could not hold the unit intact. After Raith went down, the brigade fought in pieces.

On Monday these regiments joined Marsh's command and advanced with him until the enemy left the field.

Raith's 3rd Brigade lost 96 killed, 392 wounded, and 46 missing at Shiloh, or 534 out of 2,153 present for duty—25% casualties. It was the lowest rate in the entire division.

2nd Division

Brigadier General
William H. L. Wallace

Brigadier General William H. L. Wallace was that rare phenomenon: a licensed lawyer and a man of few words. He was also a born soldier. An Illinois officer said of him, "I don't think him much of a hand for words or jokes. Think there is blood in him. . . . I like his style except his profanity. He is prompt, ready and exact—brief."

"Will" Wallace, 41 years old at Shiloh, was born in Ohio, but moved with his family to Illinois in 1834 at the age of 13. At 25, he had planned to study law with Abraham Lincoln, but the Mexican War intervened. He joined the 1st Illinois Infantry regiment and fought at Buena Vista, returning to Illinois after the war. He joined the practice of T. Lyle Dickey, who would be colonel of the 4th Illinois Cavalry at Shiloh, married Dickey's daughter Ann, and became district attorney in 1853.

When the Civil war broke out, Wallace volunteered as a private in the 11th Illinois, which was among the six Illinois regiments mustered in during the first week of the war. Shortly afterward he was voted colonel of the regiment. By the time of the battle of Fort Donelson eight months later, he was already known for his religious faith and his calm, fatalistic attitude toward combat. During that battle, at the end of a day when his brigade had been driven back with heavy losses, Wallace appeared riding slowly, one leg thrown casually over the horn of his saddle, leading 400 or 500 men to replenish ammunition before heading back into the fight. One general said Wallace looked like a "farmer coming from a day's hard plowing."

After his self-possessed performance under heavy fire at Fort Donelson, Will Wallace was promoted to brigadier general. A month later a new man was needed at the head of the 2nd Division, in light of the fact that its commander, Maj. Gen. Charles F. Smith, was incapacitated with the leg injury that would soon prove fatal. When Grant tapped Wallace to replace the universally respected Smith at the head of the 2nd Division, Wallace acknowledged that he lacked the credentials for the job.

Wallace had risen from Illinois lawyer to division commander in the space of one short year. One result of this steep rise was that he had only been in division command for two weeks at the time of the battle of Shiloh.

On the day of the battle, Wallace and his men manned much of what would be called the Hornets' Nest. There, as the remnants of Prentiss's 6th Division straggled into place on his division's left, Wallace oversaw Col. Tuttle's 1st Brigade to his left and Col. Sweeny's 3rd Brigade to his right. Grant had detached Col. McArthur's 2nd Brigade to a position hundreds of yards away on the army's left.

About 5:00 p.m., seeing that he was being surrounded, Wallace ordered his batteries to the rear and then attempted to move his infantry back to escape capture. Riding at the head of his troops through an exposed stretch of terrain nicknamed "Hell's Hollow," Wallace was struck by a bullet behind the left ear which exited his left eye. In the chaos of the retreat, he was left where he fell. Confederate soldiers covered him with a blanket against the overnight rain, and when the Union army retook the position in the morning, his brother-in-law, Cyrus E. Dickey, found him still breathing. He was carried to Pittsburg Landing, where his wife had arrived by steamboat to surprise him. She tended him as he was taken to Grant's Cherry Mansion headquarters at Savannah, where he died in her arms three days later, whispering, "We meet in heaven."

2nd (W. H. L. Wallace's) Division at Shiloh

Brigadier General "Will" Wallace's 2nd Division was a big division, containing 8,267 veterans from Illinois and Iowa in three brigades. It was well provided with artillery, having 18 guns in four batteries: Wood's Illinois battery and three batteries of the 2nd Battalion of the1st Missouri Light Artillery—Richardson's, Welker's, and Stone's. It was also supported by four companies of cavalry.

The 2nd Division formed the reserve of Grant's Army of the Tennessee. It camped in the rear, nearest Pittsburg Landing, and could reinforce any trouble spot as needed.

The division formed at 8:00 a.m. on the morning of the battle. Staff officer Lieutenant I. P. Rumsey wrote, "The division [was] ordered under arms, and soon after we were moving in column toward the front, with General Wallace at the head of the division, . . . to the Duncan Field, where we found a gap between General Prentiss' right and General McClernand's left, where General Wallace placed General Sweeney, commanding Third Brigade, on the right covering the Shiloh road and Duncan Field, and General Tuttle's First Brigade on the left, joining General Prentiss' right. Our Second Brigade, commanded by General McArthur, and Battery A, Captain Wood commanding, were diverted by General Grant and taken to the left to the support of General [Stuart], or to fill a gap between Generals Hurlbut and [Stuart]."

Grant ordered Wallace and Prentiss to "hold at all hazards" in their central position. Under Wallace's eye, the three Missouri batteries were placed on a ridge behind Tuttle's brigade. The Rebels of Shaver's Brigade, supported by artillery located in the Review Field, attacked Wallace in this position at about 9:30 a.m. At 10:30 a.m. the attack was renewed by the brigades of Shaver, Stephens, and Stewart, followed at noon by four determined attacks by Gibson's brigade. Confederate General Ruggles in mid-afternoon assembled ten batteries and two section of artillery on the west side of Duncan field, and sent Wood's, Anderson's, Stewart's, and Cleburne's brigades to reinforce Shaver in yet another attack upon Wallace's front. At the same time the Union divisions of McClernand, Sherman, and Hurlbut retired, allowing the enemy to gain Wallace's flanks and rear. In the 2nd Division's subsequent retreat, Wallace was mortally wounded and entire regiments that did not receive orders to retire in time were captured. The rest of the division, under Col. Tuttle, retired to the army's last defensive line, to the right of the siege guns.

On Monday, the division was too shattered to play a large part in the battle; it is indicative of its condition that a colonel was the ranking officer in the division. The infantry, under acting commander Col. Tuttle, acted as a reserve to Crittenden's division of the Army of the Ohio until about noon, when it advanced to the front line on Crittenden's right and participated in the fighting late in the day.

At Shiloh, Wallace's 2nd Division lost 270 killed, 1,173 wounded, and 1,306 missing and captured, for a total of 2,749 out of 8,408 present for duty—33% casualties.

Wallace's missing and captured were a whopping 48% of his casualties at Shiloh, largely as a result of poor communication by General Prentiss in the last minutes of the defense of the Hornets' Nest.

Its losses to enemy fire (its killed and wounded) were 17% of its total strength, slightly below the 18% median for killed and wounded among the divisions in Grant's Army of the Tennessee.

1st Brigade
Colonel James M. Tuttle

Tuttle, 38 years old at Shiloh, was a native of Ohio but emigrated to Farmington, Iowa, at the age of 13. He tried his hand at farming and shopkeeping and became prominent enough in Farmington to be elected sheriff. When the Civil War came, he raised a company and was commissioned lieutenant colonel of the 2nd Iowa Infantry, which was led by Mexican War veteran Samuel R. Curtis. Curtis was quickly made a brigadier general and transferred, which in September 1861 made Tuttle colonel of the regiment.

During the campaign in the summer of 1861 and most of the winter of 1862, Tuttle's 2nd Iowa operated all over northern Missouri, from St. Joseph in the west to St. Louis in the east, and the slow-talking Tuttle gained a reputation for toughness. In February 1862 at the battle of Fort Donelson, Tuttle led the 2nd Iowa in one of the most gallant, reckless and successful charges of the whole war, making it renowned in the army as the first to pierce the enemy's lines. General Halleck named the 2nd Iowa "the bravest of the brave," and it was given the honor of marching first into the fort after the Confederate surrender. Tuttle himself remained with the regiment even after being wounded.

An observer wrote, "In size Tuttle is above the medium, with broad, square shoulders, and weighing 190 pounds. He has a sanguine, bilious temperament; light, florid complexion; and gray eyes. His mental and physical organism seem to be in perfect sympathy; for he is slow of speech, and slow in action. He is like General Grant—slow and sure. Lacks confidence in his own ability. But he is stubborn, and his deliberate opinions are not easily shaken."

On April 5, the day before the Confederate attack at Shiloh, brigade commander Brig. Gen. Jacob Lauman was given command of a brigade in the new 4th Division of the Army of the Tennessee, and Tuttle, as senior colonel, was given command of the brigade.

As he had at Fort Donelson, Tuttle shared his men's dangers, and went among his men to reassure them. "His presence was a tower of strength to us," wrote one of his officers, "and wherever 'Yaller,' the colonel's horse could be seen, confidence was there."

Tuttle was promoted to brigadier general two months later, on June 9, 1862, in recognition of his distinguished performances at Fort Donelson and Shiloh. He commanded a division for much of the war, and unsuccessfully ran for governor of Iowa on the Democratic ticket while still with the army. He ended up in a district command, but resigned in 1864 amid charges of profiteering, bribery, and collusion. He died away in Des Moines, Iowa in 1892.

2nd Division, 1st (Tuttle's) Brigade at Shiloh

Colonel James M. Tuttle's 1st Brigade, 1,804 strong, was all Iowans—the 2nd, 7th, 12th, and 14th regiments—all well led and veterans of Fort Donelson, where all but the 12th Iowa had fought together under Jacob Lauman, making it one of the most cohesive brigades coming into the battle of Shiloh. The 12th was transferred from Cook's brigade soon after the capture of Fort Donelson.

Tuttle's own 2nd Iowa regiment had been in service for almost a year, most of it spent guarding railroads in northern Missouri. At Shiloh, with Tuttle tapped to lead the brigade, command of the 2nd Iowa fell to the lieutenant colonel, a lawyer.

The largely German 7th Iowa was one of the few regiments hardened by experience in two battles. The men were "the heroes of Belmont" after losing a full 58% of their number there. At Fort Donelson they stormed the works immediately behind the 2nd Iowa. The regiment was led by veteran soldier Lt. Col. James C. Parrott, four times wounded at Belmont, who had recovered in time to lead his men again at Fort Donelson.

The 12th Iowa had only been in service for four months, but had seen fighting at Fort Donelson. At Shiloh the regiment was led by its able original colonel, a West Point graduate. The 14th Iowa was similar to the 12th Iowa in that it was only two months out of its training camps, but had seen action at Fort Donelson, and was led by its original colonel, a veteran soldier and adventurer.

Bringing his brigade from their camps near the Tennessee River, Tuttle deployed his four regiments on and near the Sunken Road at the north end of Duncan Field in the following order, from left to right: 14th Iowa, 12th Iowa, 7th Iowa, and 2nd Iowa, with the right reaching the Corinth Road. About 9:30 a.m., Confederate batteries opened fire on Tuttle's brigade. This was soon followed by an infantry attack coming through the thick brush on the left. At about 10:30 a.m., the Rebels of Stephens's small brigade attacked across Duncan Field. Fire from Tuttle's men halted them when they reached the middle of the field. Stephens pulled back, then made a second, similarly forlorn attack. Another attack, this time by Shaver's brigade, was stopped before it started. About noon Gibson's brigade attacked Tuttle's position, and made four determined but unsuccessful charges, lasting until after 2:00 p.m., when Gibson withdrew and Stephens made his third attack.

General Ruggles then assembled the Confederate grand battery on the west side of Duncan Field and concentrated the fire of 50 to 60 guns upon Tuttle and the batteries in his rear. At the same time, Ruggles sent Wood, Anderson, and Stewart to reinforce Shaver in a renewed attack at the front. While meeting this attack, at 5:00 p.m., division commander W. H. L. Wallace ordered Tuttle to withdraw his brigade. Tuttle had held his position for about six hours. The 12th and 14th Iowa, late in receiving the order to retire, were captured. Tuttle, with the 2nd and 7th Iowa, retired to the siege guns on the army's last defensive line. There he took command of the division after the mortal wounding of General Wallace.

On Monday, Tuttle commanded the division, minus four captured regiments—two from his own and two from Sweeny's brigade. It acted as a reserve to Crittenden's division of the Army of the Ohio until about noon, when it advanced to the front line on Crittenden's right and participated in the fighting toward the end of the day.

At Shiloh, Tuttle's brigade lost 39 killed, 143 wounded, and 676 missing and captured, for a total of 858 out of 1,804 present for duty—48% casualties.

2nd Brigade
Brigadier General John McArthur

Tall, brawny, and iron-willed, the 35-year-old John McArthur was a celebrity among the Chicago military set before the war, and was one of the few brigade commanders at Shiloh with battle experience at that level, which he had acquired at Fort Donelson.

McArthur was a native of Scotland. Although an excellent scholar, he chose to learn the blacksmith's trade in his father's shop until he was 23, when he moved to Illinois and got a job as the foreman of the Excelsior Iron Works. He also displayed a military bent, and when the Chicago Highland Guard militia was formed, he joined and was later elected captain.

From the beginning of the war effort in Illinois, McArthur was consistently in the vanguard and among the elite. He was elected colonel of the 12th Illinois Infantry regiment and assigned to Cairo in the first month of the war. When the Confederate army invaded Kentucky in September 1861, Grant sent McArthur's 12th Illinois to guard Paducah, Kentucky, as one of the two best-equipped regiments in the District of Cairo. By the end of 1861, McArthur was commanding a brigade. At the battle of Fort Donelson in February 1862, he displayed such courage, coolness, and daring at the head of his brigade—moving, in a crisis, to fill a gap in the right of the Union line without waiting for orders from a tardy McClernand—that he was promoted to brigadier general on March 21, two weeks before Shiloh. However, he was arrested soon after, probably for excessive drinking, and relieved of his duties. He was restored to his command by Will Wallace, the new division commander, on the morning of April 6 when the first shots of the battle of Shiloh rang through the division's camps.

After Shiloh, when Wallace died of his head wound, McArthur was placed in command of the 2nd Division. He would develop into one of the ablest generals in the Union armies in the Western Theater.

After the war, McArthur returned home, but his ironworks failed. He became a Chicago postmaster, but a bank failure cost his office over $70,000. He became the director of Chicago's public works, but the Great Chicago Fire happened during his tenure. Despite McArthur's misfortunes, he stayed active in veterans' and Scots' organizations until his death in Chicago, May 15, 1906.

2nd Division, 2nd (McArthur's) Brigade at Shiloh

The 2nd Brigade of the 2nd Division was known as the "Highland Brigade" after its Scottish leader, John McArthur. It was a big brigade, with 2,296 troops in five regiments—the 9th and 12th Illinois, the 13th and 14th Missouri, and the 81st Ohio. It had only recently been cobbled together, and it is an indication of its lack of cohesion that on the first day at Shiloh it was broken up and deployed at three different places on the battlefield.

The 9th and 12th Illinois were solid. Both were among the six original Illinois Civil War regiments. It was the 9th and 12th that General Grant hand-picked in September 1861 to take to Paducah, Kentucky, to seize that important town. They had fought together under Col. McArthur in some of the heaviest fighting at Fort Donelson, holding the Union far right during the Confederate breakout attempt. Both were ably led.

The 13th and 14th Missouri, however, were polyglot, multi-state regiments. The 14th was a sharpshooter regiment in the mold of "Berdan's Sharpshooters" back East, not trained to be put in a firing line with conventionally trained regiments. These two regiments had also fought at Fort Donelson, but with other brigades.

The 81st Ohio was another regiment recruited for sharpshooting with special rifles, but when the exigencies of the war intervened, it was conventionally armed and sent to northern Missouri, where it had guarded railroads since late September 1861. It was without combat experience, only added to the brigade at Pittsburg Landing.

Wallace's first orders to the brigade, at 7:30 a.m., scattered its regiments and sent them to different parts of the field. They were not united again until after the battle was over. The 13th Missouri went to Sherman; the sharpshooting 14th Missouri and the green 81st Ohio went to the army's far right to guard the Snake Creek bridge. General McArthur would personally oversee only two of his regiments. With the veteran 9th and 12th Illinois and Willard's Battery, he moved directly south along the Hamburg-Savannah Road to the support of Col. Stuart on the Union left.

McArthur formed his demi-brigade on Stuart's right rear just east of the Peach Orchard, in a heavily wooded ravine. He placed the 50th Illinois—which had inadvertently detached itself from Sweeny's brigade on the march to the front—on the left, the 12th Illinois in the center, and the 9th Illinois on the right. In this position McArthur sustained himself against the Confederates of Jackson's Brigade until about 2:00 p.m., when Jackson was reinforced by Bowen's Brigade. McArthur himself was wounded in the foot and compelled to fall back with his command. His control, however, was unstinting: missing were just 1.8% of his men—a very low figure.

At Shiloh, the 2nd (McArthur's) Brigade lost 99 killed, 470 wounded, and 11 missing, for a total of 580 out of 2,548 present for duty—23% casualties.

3rd Brigade
Colonel Thomas W. Sweeny

"Fighting Tom" Sweeny was Regular Army, an exuberant career soldier. Sweeny's many wounds attested to the fact that he led extravagantly from the front. His men testified loudly to his popularity, his inspiring figure, and his enthusiasm for battle.

Born in Cork, Ireland, 46 years before Shiloh, he emigrated to the U.S. at age 12 and was apprenticed to a printer. When he was a young man he joined the Baxter Blues, a military organization in New York City, and, at 26, at the outbreak of the Mexican War, enlisted in a New York regiment. Sweeny would prove to be especially unlucky when it came to avoiding enemy projectiles.

Fighting under General Winfield Scott at the battle of Cerro Gordo, Sweeny was wounded in the groin by a spent ball, but remained on the field. During the battle of Churubusco, he was hit by a bullet in the right arm above the elbow, but, again, continued to lead his men until he was assisted off the field from exhaustion and loss of blood. His arm was amputated. For his heroics, his fellow servicemen nicknamed him "Fighting Tom," and he received the brevet of Captain from the Governor of New York and a silver medal from New York City. After the Mexican War, Sweeny served in the U.S. 2nd Infantry. With the regulars, he fought Indians in the Yuma War from 1850–1853, where he was severely wounded in the neck by an arrow.

When the Civil War began, Sweeny was in charge of the arsenal at St. Louis, which contained munitions enough to arm and equip 60,000 men, together with 40 tons of powder. When 3,000 Confederate sympathizers gathered to force him to surrender the arsenal, he declared that he would sooner blow it up. It remained in Union hands.

Sweeny was second-in-command in the capture of the Rebel Camp Jackson outside St. Louis in May 1861 and assisted in organizing the pro-Union Missouri Home Guards. He was appointed brigadier general of the Home Guards on May 20, 1861, and was at the head of 300 of them at the battle of Carthage on July 5, 1861. At the head of 1,800 Home Guards at the battle of Wilson's Creek on August 14, 1861, he cemented his reputation for combativeness. Before the battle, when retreat was being discussed, he growled, "Let us eat the last bit of mule flesh and fire the last cartridge before we think of retreating." One of his men wrote,

"He had one arm off, and was a picturesque sight on a horse. He was a typical Irishman, full of fun, strict in discipline, and with a kind word for everybody. We all like him very much." At Wilson's Creek, he was hit in the right thigh by a ball that remained there the rest of his life, and took six months to heal.

When Sweeny recovered in February 1862, he was made colonel of the 52nd Illinois. His regiment arrived at Fort Donelson ten days later, after the fort's surrender. Sweeny and his regiment conducted 6,000 Rebel prisoners to Camp

Douglas at Chicago, Illinois, and then proceeded to Pittsburg Landing, where they arrived on March 20. There, the regiment was brigaded with the 3rd Brigade, 2nd Division, and, as ranking colonel, Sweeny was put in command of the brigade. Sweeny was a dynamic leader in combat, but at Shiloh most of the men in his brigade barely knew him.

Sweeny was promoted to brigadier general on November 29, 1862, and rose to division command in the Western armies later in the war, playing an especially prominent role in the Battle of Atlanta. Afterward he became involved in Irish nationalist issues, and died in 1892 in Long Island, New York.

2nd Division, 3rd (Sweeny's) Brigade at Shiloh

The 3rd Brigade of the 2nd Division was a recently improvised brigade, a catch-all consisting of the 7th, 50th, 52nd, 57th, and 58th Illinois and the 8th Iowa.

The 7th Illinois was the first Illinois regiment organized in the Civil War. The 7th and 50th Illinois had been brigaded together at Fort Donelson, where the brigade was commanded by the 7th's Col. John Cook. Cook had been recently promoted to brigadier general and detached from the army, and the 7th's lieutenant colonel was absent sick, so at Shiloh the 7th Illinois was commanded by a major.

The 50th Illinois, whose colonel was a country doctor, had spent the winter patrolling railroads in northern Missouri and was only lightly engaged at Fort Donelson.

The 52nd Illinois had only been organized for five months, and had missed the fighting at Fort Donelson. It did not arrive at Pittsburg Landing until March 20. Its colonel was Tom Sweeny, who, as senior colonel, was immediately raised to command the newly formed brigade, which left the raw 52nd Illinois in the command of a major.

The 8th Iowa, which had spent the winter in freezing camps in Missouri, arrived at Pittsburg Landing on March 21. The 57th Illinois, only three months removed from civilian life, was still equipped only with altered flintlock muskets. It arrived at Pittsburg Landing on March 26. The green-as-grass Chicago city boys of the 58th Illinois had arrived at Pittsburg Landing on March 29, little more than a week before the battle.

From its camps near Pittsburg Landing on the morning of April 6, Sweeny's 3rd Brigade followed Tuttle's 1st Brigade south along the Hamburg-Savannah Road. When the column turned right to follow the East Corinth Road toward the Union right, the 50th Illinois mistakenly attached itself to McArthur's 2nd Brigade regiments, which were continuing along the Hamburg-Savannah Road toward the Union left.

The bulk of the brigade that proceeded toward the Union right became further fragmented upon reaching the front. The 8th Iowa Infantry was detached to connect the left of Tuttle's brigade to General Prentiss's division, going into line on the Sunken Road, but it was tardy in deploying, only reaching its position at noon. The remainder of Sweeny's brigade, going into line between Tuttle's brigade on the left and McClernand's division on the right, did not have room to deploy at full length.

Because of the limited space, the fighting line of the brigade was manned only by the 58th and 7th Illinois. The 58th extended Tuttle's right on the Sunken Road, straddling the Corinth Road, with the 7th Illinois on the 58th's right, connecting with the left flank of General McClernand's division. Brigade commander Sweeny, knowing his 52nd Illinois's inexperience and command vacuum better than anybody, held that regiment in reserve, and detached them to the Union right at mid-afternoon. Likewise, he put the 57th Illinois in reserve behind the right of Tuttle's line.

When the Confederates attacked, Sweeny's short front line shared in the successful repulse of several attacks against Tuttle's command. In the midst of the heavy fighting for Duncan Field, a pair of Confederate rounds found Sweeny. One round struck him "in the fleshy part of his remaining left arm" and another hit him in the foot. Sweeny's horse, even more unlucky than its rider, was riddled with eight bullets. "Almost fainting from loss of blood," wrote a newspaper correspondent, "he was lifted upon another horse and remained on the field."

A large part of Sweeny's brigade was captured with Prentiss in the Hornets' Nest, but Sweeny, though wounded, escaped to Pittsburg Landing. One of his colonels later complained that Sweeny let his brigade "go to pieces," but Sweeny's right flank had been uncovered in the late afternoon by Sherman and McClernand's retreat.

At Shiloh, the 3rd (Sweeny's) Brigade lost 127 killed, 501 wounded, and 619 missing and captured, for a total of 1,247 out of 3,571 present for duty—35% casualties.

3rd Division

Major General Lew Wallace

Wallace was a political general who owed his commission and rapid rise to the fact that he was the son of a former Indiana governor and Democratic state senator. Recognizing the political value of a distinguished war record, he traded on his slim military credentials—he had gone to Mexico with the 1st Indiana Volunteers in the Mexican War, but had missed the fighting—and recommended himself to his friend, Indiana Governor Oliver Morton, for the post of Indiana adjutant general at the start of the war. Instead, Morton made him colonel of the 11th Indiana regiment. After brief service in western Virginia, he was promoted to brigadier general of volunteers on September 3, 1861, and given the command of a brigade under the command of Brig. Gen. Charles F. Smith at Paducah, Kentucky.

His relationship with Smith, a universally respected career soldier, was poisoned by Wallace's conviction that Smith was a Southern sympathizer. In their first campaign, however, under Ulysses Grant at Fort Donelson, Wallace was given a chance to distinguish himself. At the start of the movement against the fort, Grant had signaled his lack of regard for Wallace by leaving him behind to guard the captured Forts Heiman and Henry. (Wallace wrote his wife that he was filled with rage at being left in the rear.) After two days of fighting at Fort Donelson, however, needing all his available troops, Grant sent for Wallace. Upon Wallace's arrival at Grant's headquarters on February 14, Grant created a new 3rd Division and put Wallace, as the ranking available commander, at its head, in charge of the newly-arriving Union regiments and batteries. On that day, Wallace led his new command in a counterattack that ended a Confederate break-out attempt on the Union right flank. In the heady aftermath of Grant's brilliant victory, Wallace was promoted to major general, making him, on the eve of the battle of Shiloh, the youngest major general in the Union army.

Having seen combat for the first time so recently, however, it may be that Wallace was overmatched by his responsibility at the head of the Third Division. His lamentable performance on the approach Shiloh put his Fort Donelson success in shadow. His non-appearance at the battle on Sunday made him an easy scapegoat for the army's near-disaster on the first day. However, Wallace later demonstrated ability in his defense of Cincinnati during Kirby Smith's invasion in September 1862 and his defense of Washington, D.C., at the battle of Monocacy in 1864. After the war he further retrieved his reputation by writing the bestselling novel Ben Hur, though he was never fully able to raise the shadow of Shiloh from his record. He died in Indiana in 1905.

3rd (Lew Wallace's) Division at Shiloh

Lew Wallace's 3rd Division contained 7,564 veterans in three brigades. It was a mid-sized division in Grant's Army of the Tennessee at Shiloh. Leadership of the brigades was suspect, since none of the three brigade commanders were generals. Two of the colonels, however, Morgan L. Smith and John M. Thayer, were excellent, and would soon rise.

The 3rd Division had been created on February 15, 1862, in the middle of the battle of Fort Donelson, and was uneven in its battle experience. It contained some veteran troops as well as many new, inexperienced regiments. Its men were mainly from Ohio and Indiana.

The 1st Brigade was division commander Lew Wallace's own brigade, transferred from C. F. Smith's spit-and-polish 2nd Division after Fort Donelson.

The 2nd Brigade had been created from late-arriving troops at Fort Donelson. They, like the 1st Brigade, had "seen the elephant" in the bitter, frostbitten struggle for the fort.

Most of the regiments of the first two brigades, then, whether they had been organized for a year or only a few weeks, were battle-tested at Fort Donelson. Charles Whittlesey's 3rd Brigade, however, was green. It included the 20th and 76th Ohio, who, though they had been in Wallace's 3rd Division at Fort Donelson, had been held in reserve there, and had seen no fighting. The three other regiments were just arrived from Ohio.

Twelve guns in two batteries and two companies of cavalry were attached to the 3rd Division. Neither the batteries nor the troopers had seen fighting.

Wallace's division, with its headquarters at Crump's Landing, was separated from the main body of Grant's army, which was about four miles to the south at Pittsburg Landing. In addition, Wallace's division was itself in pieces: Col. Smith's 1st Brigade was on the Tennessee River at Crump's Landing; Col. Thayer's 2nd Brigade was two-and-a-half miles west at Stoney Lonesome; and Col. Whittlesey's

3rd Brigade was even further advanced, five miles west of the landing at Adamsville.

On the morning of April 6, hearing the sounds of the main body under attack, Wallace concentrated his three brigades in a central position at Stoney Lonesome. There, if, as he thought, the attack against Pittsburg Landing was only a diversion and his isolated division was the main Confederate target, Sherman could come to his aid along the Shunpike Road, an improved road which ran to Stoney Lonesome directly from Sherman's position at Shiloh Church. Wallace conferred with Grant that morning at Crump's Landing and told him of his concentration underway toward Stoney Lonesome. Grant told him to hold that position until he received further orders.

About 9:00 a.m., as he disembarked from his river steamer at Pittsburg Landing and beheld the chaos in his army's rear, Grant became convinced that his main body, anchored there, was indeed the target of the Confederate attack. He told his chief of staff, Captain Rawlins, to send an officer with an order to Wallace to bring his division.

At 11:30 a.m., that officer arrived at Stoney Lonesome with Grant's order to join the main body of the army. Wallace later claimed that Grant's orders were unsigned, hastily written, and vague. Confusion stemmed from the fact that there were two routes by which Wallace could move his unit to the front, and, Wallace contended, Grant did not say which one to take. Wallace chose to take the Shunpike Road, which was in better condition and which would lead him to reinforce Sherman's initial position, at Shiloh Church.

Wallace allowed his men a half-hour to eat, then at noon put them on the Shunpike Road toward the battle. At 2:00 p.m., an officer from Grant arrived to hurry Wallace along, and told him that Sherman had been pushed back. Wallace realized that if he continued his present course, he would come in on the left rear of the Confederate army, and would be separated from the main body of the Union army, which was fighting for its life.

Wallace decided to turn back and follow a connecting route to the River Road, which would deliver him on the right of the Union army in its retreated position. Because the 3rd Brigade at the tail of his column was so green, however, Wallace was loath to execute a simple about-face. This would have put the 3rd Brigade in the van coming onto the battlefield. Rather, Wallace chose to march the head of his column back along the column's length to preserve what he thought was the most advantageous order of arrival, with his favorite brigade—the 1st, his old command—in the lead. In doing so, Wallace lost additional precious time. To make matters worse, the route connecting the Shunpike Road with the River Road was waterlogged and Wallace's approach was painfully slow. Wallace finally arrived at Grant's position at about 7:00 p.m., too late for the fighting on Sunday.

On Monday, Wallace's division was the first to attack from the extreme right of the Union army, with Smith's 1st Brigade on the left, Thayer's 2nd Brigade in the center, and Whittlesey's 3rd Brigade on the right. The remainder of Grant's reduced, battle-weary divisions waited for Wallace's division to move forward, and then they went forward en echelon on his left. Things went well until Sherman's and McClernand's men were stalled at the Water Oaks Pond. At that point, Wallace grew tentative. Rather than striking the exposed left flank of the Rebel defenders, he worried that he himself was isolated from the rest of the Union army, and he felt further stalled by the difficulty of resupplying his division with ammunition. However, for most of the Monday fighting, Wallace steadily moved the Rebel army back by continually threatening their exposed left flank.

After the battle, to deflect the criticism in the North over the horrendous casualties and the evidence of surprise by the Confederate army at Shiloh, both Grant and Halleck put blame on Wallace's tardy approach. Wallace was removed from his command in June and reassigned to the backwater of the Cincinnati defenses.

At Shiloh, Wallace's 3rd Division lost 41 killed, 251 wounded, and 4 missing, for a total of 296 out of 7,564 present for duty—4% casualties, by far the lowest rate of losses to enemy fire of any division in Grant's Army of the Tennessee.

1st Brigade
Colonel Morgan L. Smith

Smith, a 40-year-old native New Yorker, left home at 21 and began a nomadic adulthood. He moved to New Albany, Indiana, and became a school teacher. Then, for five years, he enlisted in the U.S. Army under the alias of Martin L. Sanford. From 1850 until the outbreak of the Civil War, he worked as a riverboat man on the Mississippi and Ohio rivers.

He possessed a gift for leading men, however, because when the Civil War began, Smith recruited an entire 1,000-man regiment from the rough, rowdy riverfront elements of St. Louis. This became the 8th Missouri Infantry, with Smith as their elected colonel. Smith gained a reputation as a strict disciplinarian—necessary to mold the riverfront mob into a fighting unit. First assigned to combat enemy guerrillas around St. Louis, Smith's regiment was later sent to Paducah, Kentucky and placed under Brig. Gen. C. F. Smith's command.

In one of the improvisations in the command structure during Grant's February 1862 expedition to capture Forts Henry and Donelson, Smith was

placed at the head of a brigade. He immediately showed a flair for battle, displaying reckless bravery in his brigade's assault on Fort Donelson on February 15. After the battle for the fort, Smith was one of only four colonels Grant recommended for promotion to brigadier general, calling him an "old soldier of decided merit." Smith would receive his promotion two months later.

In his memoirs, Grant said of Wallace's tardy 7:00 p.m. arrival on the Shiloh battlefield that if Smith had been in command, the 3rd Division would have arrived at noon. Later, Sherman said of Smith, "His perfect self-possession, coolness under fire, and good judgment in action manifested a special fitness for the military profession. … He served during the rest of the war as a division commander, and I always esteemed him as one of my best practical officers." Sherman, too, later remarked on Smith's grasp of command: "I asked for [Morgan's 8th Missouri] and Gen. Grant assigned it to my division, and I gave [Smith] the command of a brigade. … He was perfectly familiar with the drill from the company up to a division, and at Memphis, in 1863, his was the model division of the army."

After the war, Morgan Smith was appointed U.S. Consul General in Honolulu, in what were then the Sandwich Islands. He declined the governorship of the Colorado Territory because he disliked holding office, and became a counsel in Washington, D.C., for the collection of claims. In 1874 he died suddenly in Jersey City, New Jersey, on a trip in connection with his collection business.

3rd Division, 1st (Smith's) Brigade at Shiloh

Morgan L. Smith's 1st Brigade was a small one, numbering 1,998 men in only three infantry regiments—the 11th and 24th Indiana and the 8th Missouri. It had been Maj. Gen. Lew Wallace's brigade, and command had passed to Smith after Wallace's promotion to division command on February 14, 1862, at Fort Donelson.

The 11th Indiana and the 8th Missouri had been brigaded together under the command of just-promoted Brig. Gen. Wallace on September 11, 1861, at Paducah. These two regiments had spent seven months together and fought side by side at Fort Donelson.

Wallace had assembled the crack 11th Indiana from the 10 best militia companies of the 130 in the state and named himself colonel of the regiment, the first organized in Indiana for the war. He trained his elite 11th Indiana in Zouave tactics.

The 8th Missouri was a rugged group of St. Louis dock workers, mostly Irish, recruited and trained under the firm hand of Smith. Named "The American Zouave Regiment," they had already fought several skirmishes in Missouri in the summer of 1861 before they were sent to Paducah in September. With the ascension of Smith to brigade command, the 8th was led at Shiloh by its lieutenant colonel, who had been absent at Fort Donelson and tended to quarrel with fellow officers.

The 24th Indiana was the newcomer, transferred from duty in Missouri and added when the brigade gathered at Fort Henry before ascending the Tennessee River to Crump's Landing. It had spent the winter in Missouri, and had not fought a battle.

General Wallace regarded the 1st Brigade as his best. It was this brigade that he insisted on keeping at the head of his column as it approached the battlefield at Shiloh on Sunday. For its movements on Sunday, see the 3rd Division account above.

On Monday morning, Smith's 1st Brigade was on the left of Wallace's division, which was on the far right of the combined Union armies. It was the first brigade to move forward, with the rest of the division following en echelon. The brigade formed in Perry Field, with the 24th Indiana on the left, the 11th Indiana on the right, and the 8th Missouri in reserve. At about 6:30 a.m. it advanced across Tilghman Branch ravine and at 8 a.m. entered the field of Hare's brigade camp. It crossed the field in a southwesterly direction, driving back the Confederate forces from there through the Crescent Field and to McDowell's brigade camp, where it bivouacked Monday night. Wallace used it continually all day to flank each successive Confederate line. Although it was more in harm's way than Wallace's 2nd and 3rd Brigades to its right, its low casualties reinforce the idea that it was used more for maneuver than for combat.

At Shiloh, Smith's Brigade lost 18 killed and 114 wounded, for a total of 132 out of 1,998 present for duty—7% casualties.

2nd Brigade
Colonel John M. Thayer

Thayer was born on a humble Massachusetts farm in 1820 to a family who took great pride in the fact that all the males in the family had served in the colonial militia or the American army. Although not an intellectual, he was admitted to Brown University in 1837, and taught elementary school between class terms to earn tuition. He also served as a lieutenant in the local militia. He graduated with honors and in 1841 started a 13-year law career in Massachusetts.

Thayer felt the tug of opportunity in the West, and in the early 1850s made his way to Nebraska, which at the time was a wild frontier, fraught with hostile Indians. Thayer became one of the founders of Omaha, realizing that its site on the Missouri made it an ideal gateway to the West. When the Pawnee nation staged an uprising, the Nebraska territorial legislature commissioned Thayer, already respected as a leading citizen, as a brigadier general. Thayer rewarded their trust, soundly defeating the Pawnees in a battle in which the settlers were outnumbered 1,500 to 200. The experience gave Thayer military experience which would prove valuable in the coming war.

When the war came in 1861, Thayer raised the 1st Nebraska Infantry regiment. Made colonel of the regiment, he marched them to Missouri to fight Confederate irregulars there during the fall and winter. In February 1862, Thayer's gritty defense during the Confederate breakout attempt at Fort Donelson demonstrated the same stalwart unflappability under fire that he had shown against the Pawnees. Grant's report after the battle singled Thayer out for praise, and he continued at the head of his brigade as Grant pushed his army up the Tennessee River toward Shiloh.

Thayer continued to rise in rank. Made brigadier general in the fall, he would be commanding a division before the year was out. He was brevetted major general at the end of the war.

After the war, Thayer helped accomplish Nebraska statehood. He was elected as one of Nebraska's first two U. S. senators, serving from 1867 to 1871. President

Grant then appointed him Governor of the Territory of Wyoming in 1875, where he served until 1878. He was elected governor of Nebraska, serving two full terms from 1886 to 1892. He died of old age in 1906 in Lincoln, the state capital.

3rd Division, 2nd (Thayer's) Brigade at Shiloh

Thayer's brigade numbered 2,236 men in four regiments—the 1st Nebraska, the 58th and 68th Ohio, and the 23rd Indiana.

The 1st Nebraska and the 58th and 68th Ohio had been brigaded together at Paducah, Kentucky, in preparation for the battle for Fort Donelson and were thrust into the path of the Confederate break-out attempt on February 15.

The 1st Nebraska had been Thayer's regiment, and when Thayer was lifted to the head of the brigade before Fort Donelson, command of the regiment fell to its lieutenant colonel.

The 58th and 68th Ohio were new regiments, only two months old. Due to the urgent Call for Troops in February during the Forts Henry and Donelson expedition, each interrupted its instruction to join the fighting at Fort Donelson, where they were coddled, kept out of heavy action.

The 23rd Indiana was a recent addition to the brigade. In February, it had embarked with Smith's Paducah troops on the Forts Henry and Donelson expedition, but was left behind to guard Fort Henry during the fighting at Fort Donelson, and now had something of a chip on its shoulder. Though the regiment was without battle experience, its colonel was a Mexican War veteran hand-picked by Governor Morton.

For Thayer's brigade's movements on Sunday, see the division account above.

Monday morning it formed en echelon in the right rear of Smith's 1st Brigade, with the 1st Nebraska on the left, the 23rd Indiana on the right, and the 58th Ohio in reserve. It followed the movements of Smith's brigade throughout the day. Whittlesey's 3rd Brigade likewise followed to the right rear of Thayer's. For most of the Monday fighting, Thayer's brigade, with the rest of the division, moved the Rebel army back by continually threatening their exposed left flank.

The 68th Ohio did not fight at Shiloh; it guarded the ordnance and supply trains.

At Shiloh, Thayer's brigade lost 20 killed, 99 wounded, and 3 missing, for a total of 122 out of 2,236 present for duty—5% casualties.

At Shiloh, the 23rd Indiana lost 7 killed, 35 wounded, and 1 missing in its first fight, for a total of 43 out of 633 present for duty—7% casualties.

3rd Brigade
Colonel Charles Whittlesey

Whittlesey was not a soldier but a 53-year-old scholar, a renowned geologist from northern Ohio who spent much of his time in the Lake Superior region for his studies. He had studied geology at West Point, which is why, after spending the previous 25 years as a geologist, he was suddenly in demand as a military officer.

Whittlesey had become an assistant geologist of Ohio in 1837, and participated in the geological survey of the state conducted in the late 1830s. During the survey, he discovered numerous Native American earthworks. The people who constructed these earthworks became known as the Whittlesey Focus, in honor of the man who discovered the remains of their civilization. Whittlesey spent the intervening years continuing his geological work for the Federal and state governments, as well as for private businesses.

With the outbreak of the Civil War, Whittlesey became the assistant quartermaster-general for Ohio troops. He also participated in the western Virginia campaign in the summer of 1861, serving as the chief engineer for General George McClellan's Ohio military units. Following this campaign, Whittlesey helped design the defenses of Cincinnati, and in December 1861 he was commissioned colonel of the 20th Ohio Infantry.

Whittlesey, it seems, didn't like soldiering. Less than two weeks after the battle of Shiloh, on April 19, he sent in his resignation. He said that the critical condition of his wife's health and his own disabilities, which threatened to soon unfit him for service, compelled him to leave the army.

Whittlesey returned to his geological explorations of Lake Superior and the upper Mississippi basin. Returning also to his literary interests, in 1867 he founded the Western Reserve and Northern Ohio Historical Society, of which he was president until his death, in Cleveland, in 1886.

3rd Division, 3rd (Whittlesey's) Brigade at Shiloh

This was a newly organized, all-Ohio brigade, and none of its regiments had seen combat. It was composed of the 20th, 56th, 76th, and 78th Ohio, all recently arrived with Grant's army. The 76th and 78th had not even completed their training when they were rushed forward to join the army.

In March 1862, Whittlesey's four regiments were gathered in camps at Crump's Landing, and on March 31 the newly brigaded regiments were moved five miles westward to Adamsville, the division's forward position. (For the movements of the brigade on Sunday, see the division account above.)

Monday morning the brigade formed the extreme right of the Union line, en echelon in the right rear of Thayer's 2nd Brigade—the most protected position in the division as it wheeled to the left. On the left, closest to Thayer, was the 78th Ohio. On the right was the 76th Ohio, anchored on the swamps of Owl Creek. The 20th Ohio was in reserve until it crossed Tilghman Branch, when it took position on the right of the brigade. Retaining this formation, the brigade advanced, swinging to the left until 11:00 a.m., when it was moved behind and to the left of the rest of the division in support of Stuart's brigade of Sherman's division. The 76th remained here, and the other two regiments were shuttled back to the division's right, the 20th in the front line, the 78th in reserve. The last engagement before the Confederate retreat was with a two-gun section of artillery, whose shelling inflicted 11 casualties on the 20th Ohio.

In all, the fighting on Monday cost the brigade only 2 killed, 32 wounded, and 1 missing, the least of any engaged brigade in the Union army.

4th Division

Brigadier General Stephen A. Hurlbut

Stephen Hurlbut, 47, seemed always at the center of controversy. His birthplace was unusual for a Union officer: the Cradle of the Rebellion—Charleston, South Carolina. Unusual for a war leader, too, was his education by his Unitarian minister father. However, at the outbreak of the Seminole War Hurlbut enlisted in a South Carolina regiment and was elected adjutant.

At the age of 30 he moved to Illinois to start what would be a successful law practice, and was many times elected a state legislator. But he always maintained his interest in the military—during the 1850s he commanded an Illinois militia company.

Soon after the Civil War began Hurlbut raised a company, but lost the election for colonel of the 15th Illinois regiment in May 1861. This disappointment was followed only days later, however, by an appointment to brigadier general, a purely political gesture by his friend Abraham Lincoln, who on the same day gave Grant, Prentiss, and McClernand their appointments. General George McClellan in Cincinnati ordered Hurlbut to prepare a regiment, go to Missouri, and take responsibility for the vulnerable railroads there. At this point, Hurlbut's bête noire introduced itself: he got roaring drunk. He wasted time and money in dissipation, and his military duties suffered. Officers around him were disgusted and ridiculed him openly to the politicians, the men who had made him, including Lincoln. Hurlbut, though, being an expert drinker, was also an expert at avoiding the consequences. He promised those in power that he would remain sober.

Meanwhile, a number of Illinois regiments were marching into northern Missouri under Hurlbut's command. There were not enough to prevent Rebel guerrilla raids on the railroads, however, and Hurlbut began to drink more heavily as his frustration grew. His ineptitude became obvious to everyone, and on September 7, 1861, his superior, General John Pope, arrested him for misconduct and furloughed him, sending him back to Illinois to await trial. The scandal was in all the papers. The episode came to an end only when Lincoln himself restored Hurlbut to command in late December.

Hurlbut reported first to the camp of instruction in Paducah under Sherman, and drilled Sherman's new recruits faithfully and skillfully for six weeks, rehabilitating his reputation. In mid-February, he reported to Grant at Fort Donelson. On February 21, Grant—a man who also had to live down a drinking problem—gave Hurlbut command of the newly formed 4th Division. Hurlbut was realistic about his improbable resurrection, saying, "I know full well that no regiment in my old division desired to be under my command when we met at Donelson." Nevertheless, Hurlbut was soon thrust to the van. On March 17 his division was the first to occupy ground inland from Pittsburg Landing, on the west bank of the Tennessee River, and within two weeks the rest of Grant's new Army of the Tennessee had joined him there.

In the three weeks before the battle of Shiloh, sensing no danger, Hurlbut returned to the bottle. On March 22, Isaac Pugh, colonel of the 41st Illinois, wrote to his wife, "Genl Hurlbut is a drunkard & is drunk all the time when he can get any thing to get drunk on." Then, in the days leading up to the battle, Hurlbut reversed course and became convinced that an attack was imminent. Two days before the battle, on April 4, hearing rumors that Sherman was being threatened, Hurlbut actually ordered the long roll to be beaten, and led a column to the aid of Sherman. Sherman sent an irritated dispatch ordering him to turn back, and Hurlbut was derided by his own troops as they slunk back to their camps.

Although he was a drunken politician ridiculed by his men, with no experience as a division commander and also none in battle, Hurlbut was a quick study, according to Sherman. He was an excellent drillmaster, and shone in the heat of combat. At Shiloh, Hurlbut detached Veatch's 2nd Brigade to go to the Union right to support Sherman and McClernand, and thus only oversaw his 1st and 3rd Brigades on the Union left, at the Peach Orchard, but he displayed admirable control over their movements. One soldier reported, "Conspicuous in his resplendent general's uniform—complete with its yellow sash, epaulets, sword, and scabbard—Hurlbut ignored a shell that exploded within ten feet of his gray charger and screaming rifle ball that struck a tree only a few feet from his head. A stern warning from one of his staff officers to avoid overexposing himself to enemy fire prompted an undaunted Hurlbut to reply, 'Oh, well, we generals must take our chances with the boys.'"

Hurlbut's performance in defense at Shiloh was to be his military zenith. After Shiloh and the long march to Corinth, he was placed in backwater commands. However, he was a competent general when sober, and rose to the head of a department by the end of the war. He was relieved from command at Memphis in mid-1864, in favor of Cadwallader C. Washburn, for his failure to contain the incurions of Forrest's cavalry, only to see Forrest raid Memphis itself after his departure, forcing his successor to flee from a hotel down an alleyway in his nightshirt. Thus Hurlbut's notable comment: "They removed me from command because I couldn't keep Forrest out of West Tennessee, and now Washburn can't keep him out of his own bedroom!"

In his postwar years, Hurlbut, though he continued to battle charges of drunkenness and corruption, won two terms to Congress and was named minister to Colombia and Peru. He died at the ministry in Lima, Peru, in 1882.

4th (Hurlbut's) Division at Shiloh

The 4th Division was a mix of veterans and inexperienced troops from Illinois, Indiana, and Kentucky. It was the first of three divisions (the 4th, 5th, and 6th) hastily organized for Grant's army in February and March 1862 between the battles at Fort Donelson and Shiloh.

On March 14, General Sherman, leading his division on its raid up the Tennessee River to burn the Memphis & Charleston Railroad bridge over Yellow Creek, noticed the importance of Pittsburg Landing as he steamed past it. When one of his transports was fired on by Confederate artillery as it passed the landing, Sherman sent back a request to headquarters at Savannah that a division be sent to the landing "as a precautionary measure." Hurlbut's division was dispatched, and when Sherman's division floated back down the river after the failure of the "high-water raid" on the Yellow Creek bridge, they found the 1st and 3rd Brigades of Hurlbut's division floating on their transports anchored at Pittsburg Landing. Both divisions went ashore to stay, Hurlbut's disembarking first. Thus began Grant's army's concentration at the site of the battle of Shiloh, now only three weeks distant. Hurlbut's remaining brigade, Veatch's 2nd, would land three days later, on March 18.

Hurlbut's 4th Division numbered 7,825 men in three brigades of infantry, commanded by Cols. Williams and Veatch and Brig. Gen. Lauman. Lauman had been recently promoted after showing ability at the head of a brigade at Fort Donelson.

The infantry was supported by three artillery batteries and two battalions of Ohio cavalry, none of which saw combat until the cavalry skirmished with curious nearby Confederates in the days before Shiloh.

On Sunday, April 6, at 7:30 a.m., in response to a plea for support from Sherman, Hurlbut sent Veatch's 2nd Brigade to the army's right. Shortly afterward, another request for help came from Prentiss, and by 8:00 a.m., Hurlbut was at the head of Williams's 1st and Lauman's 3rd Brigades, with the divisional artillery, marching down the Hamburg-Savannah Road toward the left center of the Union line.

Finding Prentiss falling back, Hurlbut put his division in line at the Peach Orchard field, Williams's brigade on the south side, Lauman's brigade on the west side, the batteries behind them. In this position he was attacked by Chalmers' and Gladden's brigades, which were pursuing Prentiss's division, and by Robertson's, Harper's, and Girardey's batteries.

Hurlbut held his position at the Peach Orchard until about 1:30 p.m., when he was attacked by Breckinridge's Reserve Corps. Finding that Stuart's 5th Division brigade was falling back on his left, Hurlbut retired to the north side of the field with Williams's brigade, and moved Lauman's brigade from the right to the suddenly unprotected left flank. This was a crucial moment for the Union Army of the Tennessee. Hurlbut was now the left of the army, and if the left were turned, the Confederate attackers would have nothing between them and Pittsburg Landing. The way would be cleared for Confederate victory according to A. S. Johnston's original plan to sever Grant's army from Buell's approaching reinforcements and drive it into the swamps of Owl Creek, where it could be crushed.

But here Hurlbut maintained himself until 3:00 p.m., when he was again forced to retire, this time to the left of his camps. At about 4:00 p.m. Hurlbut found that his left was again being turned. He fell back to the siege guns at the army's last line and re-formed. Veatch's 2nd Brigade rejoined the division and all participated in the final action of the day.

On Monday, Williams's and Veatch's brigades formed on McClernand's left, while Lauman's brigade reported to Sherman. All were engaged until the Confederates retired from the field.

At Shiloh, Hurlbut's 4th Division lost 317 killed, 1,441 wounded, and 111 missing and captured, for a total of 1,869 out of 7,825 present for duty—24% casualties.

Its losses to enemy fire (killed and wounded) were 23% of its total strength—along with McClernand's 1st Division, the highest rate of any division in Grant's Army of the Tennessee.

1st Brigade
Colonel Nelson G. Williams

As a young man from Utica, New York, Nelson Williams showed an early interest in soldiering and went to West Point for one year, but had to drop out because of bad math scores. He moved to New York City, where he went into the importing business. Still seized with wanderlust in middle age, in 1855 he moved again, to Dubuque, Iowa, and opened a mercantile house, then bought a farm.

He tendered his services early in the Civil War but was for a few weeks unsuccessful in receiving a command. Finally, in mid-summer, aided by his friends, he was made colonel of the 3rd Iowa, which had already been deployed in northern Missouri guarding the railroads. When he joined the 3rd Iowa, Williams was a complete stranger to the regiment. He had an overbearing manner, and when he showed a willingness to enforce strict discipline, the men quickly developed a warm hatred for him.

One journalist echoed the men's first impression: "In person, he is short, and heavy set, with full chest and large, square shoulders. He is not attractive in his personal appearance.

"As a commanding officer, I judged him to be precise and exacting; and I have since learned that this was his character. While in command of his regiment, he was tyrannical, and, by a majority of both the officers and men, sincerely hated."

Williams was also the target of criticism from above after his first firefight at Shelbina, Missouri, on September 4, 1861. After retreating before a superior force of the pro-Confederate Missouri State Guard, Williams was unfairly arrested by the man who would be his commanding officer at Shiloh, General Stephen Hurlbut.

When Williams was restored to command in November, his problems with his men recommenced. Immediately upon his return, he arrested the officers he recognized as his personal enemies. They in turn brought charges against Williams for conduct unbecoming an officer, and he was again put under arrest, this time by General Halleck. Williams spent more time in the stockade awaiting his court martial, and the 3rd Iowa chafed as they continued guarding track in northern Missouri while glory was being won at Fort Donelson in Tennessee. At his trial, Williams was acquitted and again restored to command, and with the cabal of enemy officers absent, Williams made peace with his regiment, though they could never love him. Fellow brigadier Jacob Lauman wrote home shortly before Shiloh that Williams was "thoroughly disliked and distrusted."

In March, Williams and the 3rd Iowa were summoned to join Grant's army for its expedition up the Tennessee River, and Williams, as senior colonel, was put in charge of the 1st Brigade of General Stephen Hurlbut's new 4th Division, containing regiments recently arrived with Grant's army, none of whom knew Williams.

Hurlbut had by this time gained faith in the 55-year-old colonel. Williams, however, left an incomplete record, being incapacitated in his first moments under fire at Shiloh, his only battle. In November 1862, seven months after Shiloh, Williams resigned his commission and returned to his farm. In 1869, President Grant appointed him deputy collector of customs in New York City. He died of heart disease in Brooklyn in 1897.

4th Division, 1st (Williams's) Brigade at Shiloh

Williams's 1st Brigade contained the 28th, 32nd, and 41st Illinois regiments, and the 3rd Iowa, numbering 2,323 men.

Few men in the brigade had seen heavy fighting. Only the 41st Illinois had fought a pitched battle, at Fort Donelson. The 3rd Iowa had skirmished frequently with Confederate Missouri State Guard troops in northern Missouri, and some companies in the 32nd Illinois had fought with Confederates when they arrived at Pittsburg Landing. All were commanded by colonels except the 3rd Iowa, which was led at Shiloh by its major.

Williams's brigade was camped across the Corinth Road, a mile from the river. On Sunday morning, the brigade moved out on the Hamburg-Savannah Road and formed line of battle along the south side of the Peach Orchard in the following order, from left to right: 41st Illinois, 28th Illinois, 32nd Illinois, and 3rd Iowa. In this position Williams's men were attacked by skirmishers from Chalmers's brigade and by artillery fire. At this early point, a solid shot struck Williams's horse in the breast, exiting just behind the saddle, killing it instantly. The colonel also took the shock and had to be carried off the field. He remained completely paralyzed for weeks, and the debilitating effects of the injury ended Williams's military career. Williams would have a persistent pain in his ears and diminished vision in his right eye for the rest of his life as a result of his Shiloh blow.

Chalmers's brigade was withdrawn and Williams's replacement, Col. Isaac C. Pugh, retired the brigade to the center of the Peach Orchard, where it was attacked about 1:30 p.m. by Statham's and Stephens's brigades, and at 2:30 was driven back to the north side of the orchard. The 32nd Illinois was transferred to the left of the brigade east of the Savannah-Hamburg Road, and lost its Lt. Col. Ross, killed. As the left of the line was driven back, Col. Pugh again retired the brigade, this time to the Wicker Field, where he held his line until 4:00 p.m., when Hurlbut ordered the brigade to retire to the army's last line, alongside the siege guns near Pittsburg Landing, where it remained in line Sunday night.

The 3rd Iowa, occupying the right of Hurlbut's line, remained behind, connected with Prentiss's left at the Hornets' Nest until about 5:00 p.m., when it retired along the Corinth Road just before the Confederates closed their lines behind Prentiss. Commanded at this point by a first lieutenant, the regiment joined with the 13th Iowa in the last action of the day, and then reported to Pugh.

On Monday, the brigade formed on McClernand's left and helped to thwart a Confederate counterattack that threatened to separate the remnant of Grant's army from Buell's army advancing slowly on its left. With the rest of Grant's army, the brigade's advance ground to a halt by mid-day.

At Shiloh, Williams's brigade lost 112 killed, 532 wounded, 43 missing, for a total of 687 out of 2,407 present for duty—29% casualties.

2nd Brigade
Colonel James C. Veatch

James Clifford Veatch seemed out of his element in an army camp. He was an indoorsman, a 42-year-old lawyer who served as an Indiana state legislator and county auditor.

He had led a privileged childhood in Elizabeth, Indiana, on the Ohio River opposite Louisville, Kentucky. His father had been a member of the Indiana House of Representatives, and Veatch augmented his public school education with study under private tutors. He studied law, established a private practice in Elizabeth, and was the auditor of Spencer County, Indiana from 1841 until 1855. He was serving in the state legislature when the Civil War began.

At the start of the war Veatch volunteered for service in the Union army. Despite the complete absence of a military background, besides forebears who had fought in the Revolution, Governor Morton appointed him colonel of the 25th Indiana Infantry. He suffered from digestive and heart ailments, and led the regiment at Fort Donelson at the same time he was suffering from rheumatic heart trouble.

Though Veatch's was an entirely political appointment, Morton's confidence in him was not misplaced. On the morning of the battle of Shiloh, when General Hurlbut sent an aide to Veatch with orders to take his brigade to Sherman's support, the brigade was reported to be marching within ten minutes. Through it all, Maj. John W. Foster noted that "Colonel Veatch acted with great courage. He was always with his brigade in the thickest of the fight." Veatch had two horses killed under him on the first day.

Three weeks after Shiloh, on April 28, 1862, Veatch was appointed brigadier general of volunteers. The next October, he was wounded in battle, and was assigned to a quiet post at Memphis. He was eventually returned to combat command with the Army of the Tennessee, which indicates fellow officers' faith in his ability. He rose to command of a division of infantry, but after his return from an absence due to illness during the Atlanta Campaign, he was sent off to a non-combat command in the Gulf Coast before the critical actions around Atlanta commenced.

After the war, Veatch moved back indoors. He became Indiana Adjutant General in 1869, and was active in local veterans' and fraternal organizations until his death in 1895.

4th Division, 2nd (Veatch's) Brigade at Shiloh

The 2nd Brigade numbered 2,583 men in four regiments: the 14th, 15th, and 46th Illinois, and the 25th Indiana. The unit was a recent creation—none of the regiments in Veatch's 2nd Brigade had been brigaded together before.

Veatch's own 25th Indiana was the only regiment in the brigade with battle experience, having stormed the works at Fort Donelson. The 46th Illinois was also at that battle, but was barely engaged.

The 14th and 15th Illinois considered each other "brother" regiments, a relationship that grew from close contact and shared experiences in Missouri in 1861. The regiments of the brigade were well led, the 15th and 46th Illinois by full colonels, the 15th Illinois and 25th Indiana by able lieutenant colonels.

On Sunday morning, General Hurlbut sent Veatch's brigade to reinforce McClernand, and it moved out along the Corinth Road and formed in line behind Hare's brigade of Sherman's division. Veatch's brigade then moved to the right and, about 9:00 a.m. deployed about 30 yards behind Marsh's brigade in the order from left to right: 25th Indiana, 14th Illinois, 46th Illinois, 15th Illinois. When Marsh's men broke, about 10:30 a.m., Veatch's regiments became engaged. With Marsh's men running through their lines, "Everything was confusion around us, a perfect storm of shell and bullets," wrote an Illinois captain. Officers were especially hard hit, and, without supports to either flank, Veatch's regiments lost order. On the brigade's right, the 15th, then the 46th Illinois regiments headed for the rear. By 11:00 a.m., the entire brigade was in retreat.

The 25th Indiana and 14th Illinois fell back 200 yards and re-formed along the road that ran east and west from Review Field past McClernand's headquarters. A little later they retired to the right of Hare's brigade, where they held their position until after noon, when they fell back to another of McClernand's improvised lines. There, they repulsed Pond's brigade at 4:30 p.m. Veatch's brigade—minus the 46th Illinois—then rejoined Hurlbut in the last Union line on Sunday.

The 15th Illinois lost all its field officers and several captains at the brigade's first position and retired at 11:00 a.m. to the Jones Field, where it was joined by the 46th Illinois in supporting Barrett's Battery. These two regiments joined McDowell's left in the advance at noon and continued in line until 1:00 p.m., when they retired—the 15th Illinois to join Hurlbut, the 46th Illinois to its camp for dinner. Later the 46th joined Marsh's command on the Hamburg-Savannah Road on the army's right, and assisted in the final action of the day. It was with Marsh's command on Monday.

The rest of Veatch's brigade began Monday in reserve. The 14th and 15th Illinois and 25th Indiana, under Col. Veatch, formed the left of the Army of the Tennessee with the remnants of Tuttle's brigade. They joined McCook's right until about 11:00 a.m., when they crossed the Corinth Road near Duncan Field and were engaged in Review Field. They were in the front line until the Confederates retired.

At Shiloh, Veatch's 2nd Brigade lost 130 killed, 492 wounded, and 8 missing, for a total of 630 out of 2,722 present for duty—23% casualties.

3rd Brigade
Brigadier General Jacob G. Lauman

Jacob Lauman, 49, was a hero of the battle of Fort Donelson, and of Belmont before that, and he had just been rewarded with his brigadier general's star on March 21. Lauman, in fact, was disappointed with his new assignment at the head of Cruft's brigade. He was jealous of "Will" Wallace, who had been promoted to brigadier on the same day as him, but who had just received command of Charles F. Smith's 2nd Division.

Born in Taneytown, Maryland, Lauman grew up in nearby York, Pennsylvania. In 1844, at the age of 31, he moved to Burlington, Iowa, and became a successful businessman. At the outbreak of the Civil War, Lauman threw himself into recruiting military companies, and on July 11, 1861, Governor Kirkwood made him colonel of the 7th Iowa Infantry.

After its training, the 7th moved to the southeastern "boot-heel" of Missouri, and there served under General Grant. Lauman and his regiment saw their first action at Belmont on November 7, where both were distinguished for hard fighting—the regiment lost more than 400 casualties and were known as "the heroes of Belmont," and Lauman, though a novice at war, was conspicuous in his energy and leadership. He received a serious wound in his left thigh when a minie ball entered from the front and passed close to the femur. After the battle, he was commended for gallantry by Grant.

Lauman recovered in time to lead a brigade in the battle of Fort Donelson three months later. There, the gallantry of his regiments made him again a hero. Facing the daunting earthworks, Col. Tuttle of the 2nd Iowa begged him for permission to lead a charge. Lauman demurred. "Why, sir, you can't go up there; didn't I try it yesterday?"

Colonel Tuttle became insistent: he would charge the works, he said, even if he lost the last man of his regiment.

Lauman replied, "Oh, sir! You'll soon get that taken out of you." But he relented, and after the assault of the 2nd Iowa gained the top of the works and covered them all in glory. Lauman, the military amateur, became a believer that there was nothing that brave men could not accomplish if they put their will into the task.

The bald brigadier with thick curly side hair was not physically imposing. An observer wrote, "Lauman is of only middle size. His person is slender, and his weight about 140 pounds. He has a nervous, excitable temperament, and a mild, intelligent countenance. As a military leader, he is brave to a fault, but he lacks judgment. He would accomplish much more by intrepidity than by strategy; and, if his intrepidity failed him, he might lose every thing."

After his new brigade command assignment at Pittsburg Landing, Lauman was unhappy at being separated from his original regiment. He and his staff still walked to the 7th Iowa's campsite to eat meals.

At Shiloh, despite Lauman's being a newcomer to his entire brigade, his command deployment remained intact throughout the battle, and his missing were less than one percent of his casualties—a low figure that bespoke firm control. His strong showing at Shiloh added luster to his excellent performances at Belmont and Fort Donelson, and Lauman was posted at Memphis, eventually rising to division command. After a disastrous assault in the Vicksburg Campaign, however, he was suddenly dismissed when his superior accused him of wanton disregard of orders that led to heavy loss. His belief that there was nothing that brave men could not accomplish had served him ill.

Lauman would suffer two strokes within a year (1863-1864), the first relatively mild, but the second severe. He was still in Union service, but was unable to return to the field or perform his duties on any level. He was mustered out in August of 1865. The luckless Lauman would be confined to his bed for much of the rest of his life, able to walk only with assistance. After developing almost complete paralysis in his left side, he died in February 1867.

4th Division, 3rd (Lauman's) Brigade at Shiloh

The men of Lauman's 3rd Brigade—the 17th, 31st, and 44th Indiana, and the 25th Kentucky—had been together since November 1861 at Camp Calhoun, near Owensboro, Kentucky.

The brigade was commanded by Col. Charles Cruft, and had come into Grant's army whole, on February 14, 1862, when it debarked from its river transport at the climax of the battle of Fort Donelson.

The brigade was on loan from General Buell's Army of the Ohio, where it had been designated the 13th Brigade. On February 9, it had boarded the transport and steamed down the Green and Ohio rivers to Paducah, then up the Cumberland River to Fort Donelson. There, Cruft's brigade was placed in Lew Wallace's 3rd

Division and marched behind the length of Grant's army to the right of the army's line. Grant immediately redesignated the brigade as the 1st Brigade of his newly created 3rd Division.

The men of the brigade threw themselves immediately into the heaviest of the fighting. Under the gallant leadership of Col. Cruft, they withstood the fury of the climactic Rebel breakout attempt while McClernand re-formed his shattered brigades in their rear.

Cruft's loaned brigade, now experienced in combat, remained with Grant, who never returned it to Buell. However, although it remained with Grant, the brigade would not remain under Col. Cruft. On April 5, the day before the battle of Shiloh, command of the brigade was transferred to Brig. Gen. Jacob Lauman.

The 1,522 men of Lauman's 3rd Brigade camped on the south side of Dill Branch, its right at the Hamburg-Savannah Road. At about 8:00 a.m. on Sunday, it moved south to the nearby west side of the Peach Orchard field and formed line with its right in the woods near the head of Tilghman Branch. The order of its regiments from left to right was: 17th Kentucky, 25th Kentucky, 44th Indiana, 31st Indiana. About 9:00 a.m. Lauman's small brigade found itself confronted by 15 fresh Confederate regiments, nearly 10,000 men. It was attacked through the timber on its right by Gladden's Brigade, closely followed in succession by attacks upon its whole line by Stephens's Brigade and the right of Gibson's Brigade. According to Hurlbut's report after the battle, Lauman held his position for three hours.

About 2:00 p.m. the brigade was transferred a short distance to the left and formed in open woods just east of the Hamburg-Savannah Road, the 31st Indiana in reserve behind the left flank. Lauman's regiments held this position "a full hour," according to General Hurlbut. When the brigade was flanked on its left by an overwhelming Confederate force, Hurlbut found himself without reinforcements to send to Lauman, who coolly recognized that he could neither hold his advanced position nor retreat without losing his remaining troops and batteries. In desperation, Lauman ordered the 44th Indiana to attack. Rallying his battalion with the Mexican War battle cry "Remember Buena Vista!," the regiment's major led the charge. Hurlbut, expecting the annihilation of Lauman's whole command, thought the act "A gallant but rash movement!" Somehow, the "rash movement" worked and the Confederate forces broke and fled. According to Hurlbut, "this gave him time to draw off his force in order and comparative safety." Lauman and his intact brigade retired with Williams's brigade to the siege guns.

On Monday Lauman's brigade reported to Sherman and served with him until the close of the battle.

At Shiloh, Lauman's 3rd Brigade lost 70 killed, 384 wounded, and 4 missing, for a total of 458 out of 1,751 present for duty—26% casualties.

5th Division

Brigadier General
William T. Sherman

"A 'bundle of nerves,' all strung to the highest tension," was how one newspaperman described William Tecumseh Sherman. Known as "Cump" to his friends, Sherman at 42 was a restless, talkative, West Point-trained adventurer.

Sherman was an upper-crust Ohioan, born in Lancaster near the state capital of Columbus. His father, an Ohio Supreme Court judge, died when Sherman was nine, and Sherman was adopted by a family friend, Ohio senator Thomas Ewing. Senator Ewing secured an appointment for Sherman to West Point, where he was a bright student but a nonconforming cadet. He was one of few West Point graduates of that time who did not fight in the Mexican War, being assigned to duties in the Gold Rush area of California instead.

Sherman quit the army in 1853 to become a San Francisco banker. After five harrowing, unsuccessful years as a speculator in San Francisco real estate, he practiced law in Leavenworth, Kansas for a year, and then moved to Baton Rouge, Louisiana, to become superintendent of the state's military college, later to become LSU. When the Civil War threatened, he resigned and returned to the North, taking a position as president of a St. Louis streetcar company. When the war started, he offered his services to the Union army, and was summoned to Washington on June 7, 1861.

In July Sherman commanded a brigade at First Bull Run and in August was named brigadier general. Being an Ohioan, he was sent to the West and raised to the command of the Department of the Cumberland on October 8, but he was relieved a month later in the shadow of accusations that he had gone insane under the pressure of holding the Ohio River line. His friend General Henry Halleck held him in a backwater post in Missouri for three months, and when Grant moved to attack Forts Henry and Donelson in February 1862, Halleck reinstalled Sherman in Grant's old post as head of the District of Cairo, stationed in Paducah, Kentucky. He was the only West Point-trained professional soldier among the six leaders of Grant's divisions.

Sherman put his division on steamboat transports in Paducah and steamed up the Tennessee River, ultimately disembarking at Pittsburg Landing on March 18. Grant placed him in command of his army's concentration there. This was Sherman's first operation in command of a division, and he made the mistake of scattering its camps. Sherman's collapse of confidence in October was still fresh in his own mind, and perhaps to compensate, he now scoffed at the scouting reports that Rebels were gathering in the vicinity, and showed unconcern when he heard news of Confederate troops in the wooded approaches to Shiloh Church.

Once the bullets started flying, however, Sherman was in his element: "The coolest man I saw that day," according to a man who saw him, even though he was hit twice on Sunday—a bullet seriously wounded his right hand, and a spent ball bruised his shoulder. Sherman's calm steadied his command.

By the end of the war, Sherman's fame would be second only to Grant's.

After the war, President Grant in 1869 made Sherman Commanding General of the United States Army, in which position he served until 1883. Much of his attention was given to making the Great Plains settlers safe from Indians. He died in 1891 in New York City of erysipelas of the face after a bad cold.

5th (Sherman's) Division at Shiloh

Numbering 8,580, Sherman's 5th Division was the largest division in Grant's Army of the Tennessee. It was composed of new regiments just arriving from their home states, and was as solidly Ohioan as the 1st Division was Illinoisan. When Halleck appointed his friend Sherman commander of the District of Cairo on February 14, 1862, he promised Sherman that as soon as he had collected enough troops for a division, he would be allowed to lead them in the field.

The division that Sherman organized at Paducah during February was woefully inexperienced. Eight of the Ohio regiments were so new they had only received their weapons within the previous two weeks. The 53rd Ohio received its rifles on the same day it boarded the steamer to go upriver to Pittsburg Landing.

On March 6–8, Sherman's new division—four fresh brigades with three batteries of artillery and about 450 cavalrymen—started up the Tennessee River on 17 steamboats. Sherman had no illusion about the fighting material at his command. "My division was made up of regiments perfectly new," he wrote, "nearly all having received their muskets for the first time at Paducah. None of them had ever been under fire or beheld heavy columns of an enemy bearing down on them." The men, he said, "had as much idea of war as children."

The four brigade leaders were all colonels recently lifted from regimental commands, and were no more expert at war than their men. John A. McDowell had been a civil engineer and railroad executive for the last decade. David Stuart was a disgraced Chicago lawyer. Ralph P. Buckland was a 50-year-old Ohio politician. Jesse Hildebrand was 61 years old and had operated stagecoaches while he dabbled in the militia.

The 5th Division's steamboats reached Fort Henry on March 11 and continued their ascent of the Tennessee River, reaching Savannah on the next day. On the morning of March 14, General C. F. Smith, acting commander of the Tennessee River Expedition, gave Sherman's division a mission to go further up the Tennessee and raid southward to cut the Memphis & Charleston Railroad east of Corinth. By noon that day, Sherman's men boarded 19 transports and steamed to the mouth of Yellow Creek, where they disembarked that evening in a downpour. The deluge flooded out the Yellow Creek raid, and the 5th Division floated back downriver to Pittsburg Landing on March 16, disembarking again on March 18 to establish its camps along the Hamburg-Purdy Road with its center at Shiloh Church. Stuart's brigade was sent two miles to the east, at the extreme left of what would be the army's campground, placed near the intersection of the Hamburg-Purdy Road and the Hamburg-Savannah Road.

On the Sunday morning of the battle, the division formed in front of its camps, where Hildebrand's 3rd and Buckland's 4th brigades became engaged at 7:30 a.m. on the Union army's right. These two brigades, with support from Barrett's, Waterhouse's, and Behr's batteries, and reinforced on the left by Raith's brigade of McClernand's 1st Division, held the line against seven piecemeal frontal attacks by four Rebel brigades until about 10:00 a.m., when Sherman attempted to fall back to the Hamburg-Purdy Road. In this movement his 3rd and 4th Brigades became disorganized and retreated a mile to the Hamburg-Savannah Road, with only parts of regiments remaining in line.

At the moment that Hildebrand's brigade melted away, Barrett's and Waterhouse's batteries held Sherman's left flank alone, repulsing Confederate attacks with canister. Waterhouse's Battery's lack of practice was evident, however. As they limbered to retreat, because of Waterhouse's drivers and horses "not having sufficient drill," according to a nearby Federal officer, "they were unable to limber up all their pieces in time" and the battery lost three guns to the advancing Confederates, and a fourth disabled piece which was soon ditched.

On Sherman's far right, McDowell's 1st Brigade, after its fallback from its original line, became engaged in Crescent Field until about 2:00 p.m.

At the retreat of McDowell's brigade, Behr's battery retired to the Hamburg-Purdy Road and Corinth Road crossroads. The battery was met there by Sherman, who ordered Behr to unlimber his guns. As he spoke, Capt. Behr was struck by a bullet and fell dead from his horse. To Sherman's dismay, the German gunners panicked when Behr fell, and they fled in disorder, abandoning five cannon without firing a shot.

Sherman, in his report, outlines his rearward movement in the following hours: "[A]bout 4 p.m. it was evident that Hurlbut's line [on the army's left] had been driven back to the river; and knowing that General Lew Wallace was coming with reinforcements from Crump's Landing, General McClernand and I, on consultation, selected a new line of defense, with its right covering [the Snake Creek] bridge by which General Wallace had to approach. We fell back as well as we could, gathering in addition to our own such scattered forces as we could find, and formed the new line. ...I had a clear field, about two hundred yards wide, in my immediate front, and contented myself with keeping the enemy's infantry at that distance during the rest of the day. In this position we rested for the night."

Sherman, in his report, also describes his division's condition at the end of the day: "My command had become decidedly of a mixed character. Buckland's brigade was the only one that retained its organization. Colonel Hildebrand was personally there, but his brigade was not. Colonel McDowell had been severely injured by a fall off his horse, and had gone to the river, and the three regiments of his brigade were not in line. The 13th Missouri, Col. Crafts J. Wright, had reported to me on the field, and fought well, retaining its regimental organization; and it formed a part of my line during Sunday night and all Monday. Other fragments of regiments and companies had also fallen into my division, and acted with it during the remainder of the battle."

On Monday, Sherman's mixed force was engaged on the left of Lew Wallace's fresh 3rd Division all day, but, wearied by the previous day's fighting, moved slowly.

At Shiloh, Sherman's 5th Division lost 325 killed, 1,277 wounded, and 299 missing and captured, totaling 1,901 out of 8,580 present for duty—22% casualties.

Sherman's losses to enemy fire (killed and wounded) were 19% of its total strength, slightly above the 18% median for divisions in Grant's army.

1st Brigade
Colonel John A. McDowell

The portly McDowell, 36, was the son of a former mayor of Columbus, Ohio. He was also the younger brother of General Irvin McDowell, the unlucky Union commander at First Bull Run. At central Ohio's Kenyon College he studied tactics, and in 1846 was the first captain of the Kenyon Guards, a militia company formed by students, which became famous for its discipline and drill.

In his fifteen years between college and the Civil War, McDowell demonstrated a restless heart. He studied law for two years, then joined the 2nd U.S. Dragoons in California for two years. In 1850, he left the military and ran successfully for mayor of Monterey, California. He then returned east and settled in Keokuk, Iowa, where he became City Engineer, then chief engineer of an Iowa railroad.

When the Civil War began, McDowell's outgoing personality aided him in recruiting an entire regiment drawn from ten Iowa counties. It became the 6th Iowa Infantry, and he was made its colonel on July 17, 1861. He saw no fighting with the 6th Iowa, however; it guarded the Pacific Railroad in the winter of 1861–62, before being sent to Pittsburg Landing.

When McDowell's 6th Iowa reached Pittsburg Landing on March 16, it was assigned to the 1st Brigade of Sherman's 5th Division, and McDowell, as senior colonel, was made commander of the brigade.

An observer sketched him thus: "McDowell is a large man, and well proportioned, but a little too fleshy to look comfortable. He is above six feet in height, and erect; has a good-natured countenance. Usually he seems kind and approachable, but, when aroused, the flash of his eye makes him look, as he really is, a most formidable opponent. He has large self-esteem, a good education and fine social qualities. His conversational powers are remarkable. He is fond of merriment, to be convinced of which you have only to look on his shaking sides: he laughs, like Momus, all over.

"McDowell has fine ability, but is naturally, I believe, inclined to be a little lazy. He is a close observer, and forms positive opinions. His experience in the army destroyed his faith in field artillery.

"As a soldier, McDowell excelled as a disciplinarian and tactician: he was a splendid drill-master, a fact attested by his regiment, which was one of the best drilled in the volunteer service."

However, McDowell soon demonstrated his lack of battle experience and the fact that he had only been in brigade command for three weeks. Like his superior,

General Sherman, he had ignored the signs of the enemy gathering in his front in the first days of April. When he heard the first crackle of musketry on Sunday morning, he was not sure where his brigade pickets were stationed. His brigade lost 11% of its casualties missing in the battle, indicating laxity in deployment. Personal bravery makes up for any number of sins in a military leader, however, and he was always in the thick of the fight.

McDowell would be recommended for a brigadier's star by General Sherman, who described him as a "good kind hearted Gentleman," but he was never promoted. He resigned his colonel's commission in 1863 and left the army, returning to Iowa where he eventually disappeared from the public record.

5th Division, 1st (McDowell's) Brigade at Shiloh

McDowell's 1st Brigade consisted of the 1,930 men in the 40th Illinois, 6th Iowa, and 46th Ohio regiments.

In Paducah, Sherman had organized the 40th Illinois, 46th Ohio, and Morton's Battery into a brigade commanded by the 40th's colonel, Stephen Hicks. Hicks had a bad habit of antagonizing Sherman, however, and Sherman "fired" him as brigade commander on March 16 by attaching the 6th Iowa to the brigade, whose colonel, John McDowell, was senior to Hicks. McDowell—as unready as he was—took command of the brigade, and the insubordinate, surly Hicks went back to his regiment.

McDowell's brigade of three regiments was camped on the Hamburg-Purdy Road on the extreme right of the Union army, its right on the high ground near Owl Creek, in the order from left to right: 40th Illinois, 46th Ohio, 6th Iowa. At the first alarm Sunday morning, two companies of the 6th Iowa, with one gun of Behr's battery, were on guard at the bridge over Owl Creek. About 8:00 a.m. the brigade was advanced to the brow of the hill overlooking Shiloh Branch, the 40th Illinois going to the right of Buckland's brigade.

In the first hours of the battle, McDowell's brigade was unscathed, with the brunt of the attack being taken by Buckland and Hildebrand to its left.

McDowell was ordered at 10:00 a.m. to retire to the Hamburg-Purdy Road, and move to the left to connect with Buckland's brigade near the crossroads with the Corinth Road. In obedience to this order the brigade moved by the left flank, but found that the Confederates occupied the road between it and Buckland's right. McDowell then retired and put his brigade in line on the west side of Crescent Field facing east, where he engaged and drove back the enemy advance. Following orders from Sherman, McDowell's brigade then retired again into

Sewell Field facing south, where it connected with McClernand's 1st Division at 11:30 a.m. It then advanced with elements of McClernand's division to the center of Marsh's brigade's camp. Here the 6th Iowa was transferred from the right to the center of the brigade and the 13th Missouri placed between the 40th Illinois and the 6th Iowa, with the 46th Ohio slightly in rear and to the extreme right of the line.

At about noon the brigade was attacked on its right flank by Trabue's brigade, and faced its first heavy fighting of the day. In an engagement that lasted until 1:30 p.m., the 6th Iowa had 52 killed, and the 46th Ohio recorded 246 killed and wounded. Here, McDowell, in the thick of the fight, was thrown from his horse and disabled. Increasing pressure on his exposed right flank caused McDowell and his brigade to retire to the landing at about 2:30 p.m.

On Monday, the 6th Iowa and 40th Illinois were attached to Garfield's brigade of the Army of the Ohio, and remained with him until Wednesday, but were not engaged.

At Shiloh, McDowell's brigade lost 136 killed, 439 wounded, and 70 missing and captured, for a total of 645 out of 1,930 present for duty—33% casualties.

2nd Brigade
Colonel David Stuart

For David Stuart, the Civil War was a golden opportunity to redeem his ruined reputation.

Stuart had been a Michigan congressman and a high-powered Chicago attorney, but a divorce case he had been arguing had exploded into scandal when it came to light that he had carried on an illicit affair with his client. When the war began, Stuart, desperate to reclaim his good name, sought to raise a regiment, but the public outcry was so loud that the governor denied him permission. Not to be denied, the high-powered Stuart got permission through the War Department.

His father had been in the Lewis and Clark Expedition, established the trading post at Astoria, Oregon, and was known as a "frontier potentate, whose will was law."

David Stuart was given a privileged liberal arts education worthy of a potentate's son, at Phillips Academy, Andover, Oberlin, and Amherst. He started a hugely successful law career in Detroit, and was named City Attorney, then elected Prosecuting Attorney in Wayne County. A biographer wrote, "No one ever stood higher at the bar of Detroit than he did. With the manners and the courtesy and high breeding of an accomplished gentleman, an address singularly fascinating and agreeable, Stuart became idol of the Democratic party." He was elected to Congress from Michigan in 1852.

The restless Stuart, however, didn't even wait until the end of his term to move to Chicago, in 1855. There he became a railroad lawyer and friend of Senator Stephen Douglas.

After Fort Sumter, with the blessing of the War Department he raised an entire brigade of two regiments, to be named after Senator Douglas. Because of Stuart's notoriety as a result of the divorce scandal, many opposed the equipping of his men. Despite all his detractors, however, on October 31 Stuart was elected colonel of the second of his two regiments, his hard-won creation, the 55th Illinois Infantry, which he nicknamed the "2nd Douglas Regiment." (The 1st Douglas Regiment was the 42nd Illinois, which was destined never to be paired with its sister regiment.)

David Stuart was a natural leader. For one thing, he had the loudest voice any of his men had ever heard. However, he liked the sound of it overmuch. Lucien Crooker, the 55th's regimental historian wrote, "One pronounced trait in Stuart's character was a penchant for making speeches on every possible occasion. In the light of later experience Stuart's orations now seem extravagant, if not ludicrous."

In fact, Stuart was completely without instruction in the art of war. Crooker reported, "Colonel Stuart took little part in actually drilling the regiment, and herein was his first mistake, inasmuch as he failed to keep abreast or ahead of the rank and file in the acquirement of a knowledge of tactics; and when on occasion he sought publicly to exercise the functions of his high office, his lack of technical training generated a species of contempt always fatal to the respect due a field officer.

"Another characteristic of Col. Stuart early began to manifest itself. This was his unbounded faith in the military skill and inspiration of the lieutenant colonel [Swedish army veteran Oscar Malmborg] and distrust of his own ability in that direction. As to the former, most of the regiment and its officers, for good reasons, differed with him; and as to the latter, a little self-reliance, coupled with moderate industry, would soon have brought all to his feet in respectful admiration of his unquestioned ability.

"At this time began an arbitrary system of transfer and promotion regardless of the rules of the service or the rights of individuals, which was persistently pursued by the colonel during his entire career, as best suited his personal views and ends. This was unutterably unjust and subversive of subordination, for it deprived the non-commissioned officers and privates alike of the just right to promotion within their own companies, and according to rank and worth. Stuart in this regard, as in others, 'Sowed the wind and reaped the whirlwind.'"

By February, according to this recruit, "Many of the line officers were chafing under the unstable policy of the colonel, and the ill-tempered abuse of the lieutenant colonel."

The 55th was unfortunate, too, in its lack of suitable weapons, which had been made unavailable in the public uproar over Stuart's recruitments.

On February 27, the inexperienced and maladroit Stuart assumed command of Sherman's 2nd Brigade as senior colonel. When Sherman disembarked his division at Pittsburg Landing on March 18, he assigned Stuart to camp two miles from the other three brigades, on the opposite side of the Shiloh plateau. This poor decision ensured that Stuart would receive no word of help or advice from his superiors. Then, the day before the battle, the four pieces of artillery assigned to Stuart were transferred to the 2nd Division. If it came to fighting, he would be fighting on his own.

Stuart was appointed brigadier general the following November, but in March 1863, the U.S. Senate failed to confirm his appointment, and he resigned the next month. Stuart went back to Detroit to resume his law practice, where he died in 1868.

5th Division, 2nd (Stuart's) Brigade at Shiloh

Stuart's 2nd Brigade numbered 1,939 men in three green regiments: the 55th Illinois and the 54th and 71st Ohio.

The colonel of the 55th Illinois was Stuart himself, absent commanding the brigade, so the regiment was led by Lt. Col. Oscar Malmborg. Malmorg was hated by his men, who chafed under his ill-temper and abuse.

The 54th Ohio, though untested in battle, was trained in Zouave tactics and led by its able original colonel, T. Kilby Smith.

The 71st Ohio was untrained and led by Rodney Mason, a political hack installed by Ohio's governor. He was rotund and inept. The regimental historian of the neighboring 55th Illinois called him "That globule of adipose pomposity." The officers in the regiment detested him: "They cannot ask him a civil question without getting a cursing for an answer," said one.

Stuart's brigade was camped at the junction of Hamburg-Purdy Road with the Hamburg-Savannah Road in the order from left to right: 55th Illinois, 54th Ohio, 71st Ohio, with a company from each regiment on picket, one at the Lick Creek ford and two on the Bark Road. On Sunday morning about 8:00 a.m., the pickets gave warning of the approach of the enemy.

Stuart formed his brigade in line, but finding that he was exposed to artillery fire from batteries on a bluff south of Locust Grove Branch, and obeying orders to guard the Lick Creek ford, he moved at 10:00 a.m. to his left, placing the 54th Ohio on his left behind McCullar's Field, the 55th Illinois in the middle, and the 71st Ohio on his right at Bell Field.

Chalmers's Confederate brigade faced Stuart on the bluff south of Locust Grove Branch and, after clearing Stuart's camps with his artillery, moved across the creek and attacked the 54th Ohio and 55th Illinois in position. After a short conflict Stuart withdrew to a ridge running due east from his headquarters. The 71st Ohio was here attacked by the right of Jackson's brigade.

As a historian of the 71st Ohio reported, "At the first appearance of the enemy Col. Mason put spurs to his horse, basely deserting his men. And about this time an enemy regiment made a rush at them and this, in connection with the conduct of Col. Mason, precipitated a wild stampede to the rear, the men throwing away their arms in the flight, the Confederates at the same time firing into the disorganized mass. Adjutant Hart, of the 71st, succeeded in getting 17 of the men to rally with the 55th Illinois, who were on their left, and they fought both days gallantly through the battle." Stuart reported he could not locate the 71st Ohio for the duration of the battle. Most of its men had run pell-mell to the shelter of Pittsburg Landing, trying in vain to keep up with their worthless colonel, without having received or delivered one volley. Another part of the regiment under the major passed down a ravine to the Tennessee River, where they were picked up by a gunboat.

The 54th Ohio and 55th Illinois, with their right exposed by the flight of the 71st Ohio, now panicked and began to run, but here Stuart had his shining moment, according to one of his men: "The conduct of Colonel Stuart was magnificent. He spurred his horse beyond the vortex of the disorder which surrounded him, and, like a chief of ten thousand, faced the throng of excited and disorganized men, and with eyes flashing, and voice ringing through the woods like a trumpet, commanded them to halt. His superb magnetism impressed itself upon the multitude instantly. If Stuart had then died, he would have been canonized in the hearts of his men. Suddenly the men stopped."

About 800 of the brigade—500 from the 55th Illinois and 300 from the 54th Ohio—turned about and faced the enemy. In the confusion of the rout, Stuart was wounded in the shoulder and passed command of the brigade to the 54th Ohio's Col. Thomas Kilby Smith.

The two suddenly-stout regiments successfully resisted the half-hearted attacks of Chalmers until 2:00 p.m., when their ammunition was exhausted and they were obliged to fall back to Pittsburg Landing. There that evening they were engaged in resisting Chalmers's last attack.

On Monday, Col. T. Kilby Smith, with his 54th Ohio and the 55th Illinois, joined Sherman's command and fought on the right next to Lew Wallace's fresh 3rd Division all day.

At Shiloh, Stuart's brigade lost 80 killed, 380 wounded, and 90 missing, totaling 550 out of 1,939 present for duty—28% casualties.

3rd Brigade
Colonel Jesse Hildebrand

Jesse Hildebrand at 61 was the oldest brigade commander in the Army of the Tennessee, but he came with substantial credentials. He was well known as having been the most active militia general in southern Ohio for many years, and at a time when southern Ohio was drained of recruits and attracting new men was difficult, he filled the roster of his regiment, the 77th Ohio, within 60 days.

Hildebrand's life had followed an eccentric arc. He was born in 1800 on Pennsylvania's Cornplanter Indian Reservation, where his father was the sawmill operator. His family moved to southeast Ohio about 1820, and there, for 25 years before the war, Hildebrand operated stagecoaches while he officered the militia.

At Shiloh, Hildebrand had only been in brigade command for a few weeks, and he was ill on the day of the battle. He was, however, aware of the enemy in the vicinity before the rest of the division.

As a sexagenarian militia general, Hildebrand knew little of modern tactics, but he compensated by demonstrating to his men how to be fearless of bullets. A huge man, riding an enormous black horse, Hildebrand was a striking figure on the battlefield. When the teeming Rebel line came into view at Shiloh, one soldier wrote, he was "as cool and collected as if leading a parade," galloping about with "reckless gallantry." At one point he rode his horse between the opposing battle lines to steady his men.

Hildebrand's brigade managed to defend its front for two hours against seven uncoordinated Confederate attacks. However, Hildebrand had no staff to assist him, and his brigade broke, unhinging Buckland's position. A nearby artillerist with Barrett's battery wrote later that, after his command dissolved, Hildebrand "sat down on a log near me and cried like a child at the cowardice of his men." Hildebrand joined McClernand's staff as an aide for the rest of the battle.

His remaining career with the army was short. In August, he was ordered with his regiment, the 77th Ohio, to Illinois to guard a prison at Alton, and he would die of disease there a year later.

5th Division, 3rd (Hildebrand's) Brigade at Shiloh

Hildebrand's 3rd Brigade numbered 1,833 untested Ohioans in three regiments: the 53rd, 57th, and 77th Ohio. All three regiments had been mustered in during January and February 1862, and had little chance to train before being brought to Paducah to join Sherman's division.

The brigade's regimental command was a further weakness. The rotund, inept colonel of the 53rd was elderly and without any military experience, so that when they arrived in their Shiloh camps, they had never drilled. The 57th's colonel was sick, so the regiment was led by its lieutenant colonel, a 26-year-old classical studies scholar. Hildebrand insisted on retaining command of his 77th at the same time he commanded the brigade.

Hildebrand's 3rd Brigade was camped with its right, the 77th Ohio, at Shiloh Church; the 57th on the left, and the 53rd Ohio far forward, in Rhea Field and separated from the 57th by a small, marshy stream.

About 7:00 a.m., the brigade formed to meet the Confederate attack, with the 57th and 77th in advance of their camps in the valley of Shiloh Branch. The woebegone Col. Jesse J. Appler of the 53rd Ohio, when threatened by the first Confederate wave, mistakenly formed the regiment's line north to south, presenting its left flank to the Rebel onslaught.

While in this position, the brigade was attacked by Cleburne's and Wood's brigades. When the attack fell upon the exposed left flank of the 53rd Ohio, its confused commander attempted to change its front and form a new line. His nerves at the breaking point, Appler cried out at the height of the attack, "Retreat and save yourselves!" At this, almost the entire regiment ran to the rear in disorder, fleeing all the way to Pittsburg Landing. Two companies, under a captain, remained and joined the nearby 17th Illinois of Raith's brigade, in McClernand's division. The departed eight companies were re-formed at Pittsburg Landing by the regiment's major and supported Bouton's Battery in McClernand's last line. On Monday they advanced with Marsh's command.

The 57th and 77th were reinforced by Raith's brigade of McClernand's division and held their position for some time. Finally, however, after the 53rd, then the 57th regiment broke and ran on the 77th Ohio's left, the domino effect reached the 77th. They "ran like sheep," according to one artillerist with Barrett's Battery. . . . Some of our company drew revolvers on the cowards, but nothing could keep them to their posts."

In his report after the battle, General Sherman regretted that "My Third Brigade did break much too soon, and I am not yet advised where they were on Sunday afternoon and Monday morning." However, he evidently faulted the individual regiments, because he commended Hildebrand himself in the next sentence: "Colonel Hildebrand, its commander, was as cool as any man I ever saw, and no one could have made stronger efforts to hold men to their places than he did. He kept his own regiment, with individual exceptions, in hand an hour after Appler's and Mungen's regiments had left their proper field of action."

At Shiloh, Hildebrand's 1st Brigade lost 70 killed, 221 wounded, 65 missing, for a total of 356 out of 1,833 present for duty—19% casualties.

4th Brigade
Colonel Ralph P. Buckland

Ralph Buckland was a native Ohioan, a 50-year-old career lawyer and politician with absolutely no military experience. That this might be a deficiency didn't seem to occur to him. On the battlefield, as everywhere else, he was cool and self-assured. Perhaps he was inured to hardship by raising eight children.

He attended Tallmadge Academy, studied law at Kenyon College, and was admitted to the bar at the age of 25. Nine years later, he was the law partner of future president Rutherford B. Hayes. Buckland was elected mayor of Fremont, Ohio, from 1843 to 1845, was a delegate to the Whig National Convention in 1848, and was twice elected to the Ohio State Senate as a Republican, serving from 1855 to 1859.

When the war broke out, Governor William Dennison appointed Buckland to recruit volunteers in Sandusky County in northern Ohio, and in January 1862 Buckland was appointed colonel of the 72nd Ohio. Buckland's regiment left for the war on January 24, 1862, and within six weeks he was ascending the Tennessee River as the commander of the 4th Brigade in Sherman's 5th Division of the Army of the Tennessee.

As the 4th Brigade made their camps near Pittsburg Landing, many of the men were ill from being packed together for weeks on the steamboats and from drinking river water. Morale in the brigade was low. Away from home, sick and fearful, knowing that Buckland was a political appointee with no military experience, they grumbled about their commander's lack of credentials. Buckland himself was acutely aware of his lack of military training, and said so in a letter to his wife: "As I have said before my greatest fear [is] that I shall commit some great blunder by which men will be sacrificed and our success endangered. But I shall do the very best I know at whatever risk to myself."

When his moment of truth came on Sunday morning, Buckland gave the order to advance, but his men hesitated. Buckland immediately rode toward one of the color bearers, grabbed the staff, and escorted both the color bearer and the flag to the front while the rest of the brigade cheered and advanced with him. After repulsing seven uncoordinated Confederate attacks, Buckland's brigade retired, by Sherman's order, after Hildebrand's brigade broke on its left. Buckland, however, could not prevent his regiments from disintegrating as they moved rearward.

After the battle, Sherman wrote, "Colonel Buckland managed his brigade well. I commend him to your notice as a cool, intelligent, and judicious gentleman, needing only confidence and experience to make him a good commander." Buckland was promoted to brigadier general in July 1862, three months after Shiloh, with his commission approved on November 29, 1862. He continued in brigade command until 1864, when he retired from the army to run for Congress.

Buckland was elected U.S. Representative from Ohio twice, serving from 1865 to 1869. He then resumed his law practice, and served as an executive with the Union Pacific Railroad from 1877 to 1880. He died of an aneurysm in 1892.

5th Division, 4th (Buckland's) Brigade at Shiloh

Buckland's 4th Brigade numbered 2,107 Ohioans in three regiments: the 48th, 70th, and 72nd Ohio. These were all brand-new regiments, formed in January and quickly forwarded to Sherman in Paducah. Local politicians commanded all three regiments, with only Col. Sullivan of the 48th Ohio having some military experience in the Mexican War.

Buckland's brigade was camped with its left at Shiloh Church in the order from left to right: 70th Ohio, 48th Ohio, and 72nd Ohio. It formed for battle about 200 yards in front of its camps, where it withstood the attacks of Cleburne's, Anderson's, and Johnson's brigades until 10:00 a.m. The attacks were uncoordinated, and the odds were not overwhelming: about 3,000 Confederates against Buckland's 2,100. Buckland suffered lightly, at first less than 150 casualties. In this position, when the lieutenant colonel commanding his rightmost regiment, the 72nd Ohio, went down with a mortal wound, Col. Buckland rode over and personally commanded the regiment.

When Buckland's right flank was threatened by Pond and Trabue, Sherman ordered Buckland to fall back to the Hamburg-Purdy Road. In making this movement the brigade became disorganized and scattered. Buckland later wrote, "We formed line again on the Purdy road, but the fleeing mass from the left [Hildebrand's brigade] broke through our lines, and many of our men caught the infection and fled with the crowd. Col. Sullivan and myself kept together and made every effort to rally our men, but with very poor success. They had become scattered in all directions."

On the left, the colonel of the 70th Ohio with a portion of his regiment joined Raith's brigade of McClernand's division and fell back with it to Jones Field, where it joined McDowell's 1st Brigade. The 70th was engaged with McDowell's brigade until 1:00 p.m., when that brigade retired to the Hamburg-Savannah Road. The adjutant and 40 men of the 70th Ohio joined the 11th Illinois and fought with it until night. The 48th and 72nd Ohio regiments retired to the Hamburg-Savannah Road, where Col. Buckland reorganized his brigade and was engaged in the 4:30 p.m. fighting.

On Monday Buckland's 4th Brigade was reunited. With what was left of Stuart's brigade and other mixed units it formed Sherman's line that advanced to the east of McClernand's camp, and from there southwesterly to Shiloh Church, where the brigade reoccupied its camps about 4:00 p.m.

At Shiloh, Buckland's brigade lost 36 killed, 203 wounded, and 74 missing, for a total of 313 out of 2,107 present for duty—15% casualties.

6th Division

Brigadier General
Benjamin M. Prentiss

Benjamin Prentiss, 42, was an imposing, quarrelsome bull of a man with a blue blood pedigree that went back to the Mayflower colony. He spent his early childhood in Virginia, where his education included a private military school. He and his father migrated to Missouri on the Mississippi River when Benjamin was 16, and they went into the cordage business—rope-making. Five years later, in 1841, they moved across the river to Quincy, Illinois, and continued their business there.

With the rise of the Mormon troubles in west Illinois in 1844, Prentiss joined the militia and developed a fascination with military life. At the opening of the Mexican War in 1846, he enlisted in the 1st Illinois Infantry and served as first lieutenant and later as captain of Company I, which he commanded under General Zachary Taylor at the battle of Buena Vista.

Upon his return to Illinois in 1848, Prentiss practiced law and developed a political life that culminated in an unsuccessful run for Congress in 1860. Meanwhile, he remained active in the militia, where he rose to the rank of colonel, and at the outbreak of hostilities in 1861, he was one of the first to answer Lincoln's Call for Troops, volunteering his hometown militia company, the Quincy Rifles.

Prentiss's company mustered in with the 10th Illinois Infantry, which elected him their colonel. The 10th was sent to Cairo, and the regiments there, brigaded together in the first month of the war, were allowed to choose their own brigadier, again by vote. With his political skills and his bullish persona, Prentiss got more votes than his rival, West Pointer John Pope, and was elected brigadier of the three-month troops. Prentiss thus became Illinois's first general.

Prentiss was soon joined by three other politically appointed brigadier generals, among them U.S. Grant. Grant was sent into the southeastern Missouri "boot heel" in August of 1861 at the same time Prentiss arrived with his brigade from Cairo, precipitating an argument over who outranked whom. Prentiss mistakenly thought he had that honor, and he was mistakenly seconded by their superior, General Fremont, another political appointee who knew very little about the intricacies of military seniority. By the time the imbroglio was sorted out and Grant correctly installed as senior officer, Prentiss had tendered his resignation—it was not accepted—and put himself under arrest, leaving Grant to appoint someone else in his place in southeastern Missouri. General Prentiss was named to a command in northern Missouri. The encounter left both Grant and Prentiss with a jaundiced view of the other.

Prentiss left Missouri on March 26, 1862, after being named commander of Grant's 6th Division at Pittsburg Landing, with directions to organize arriving troops into brigades. He arrived on April 1 and took command of one brigade under Col. Everett Peabody and another, partially organized, under Col. Madison Miller. Prentiss found his division's camps placed forward of the other five divisions in Grant's army.

Peabody's brigade of four regiments was encamped on the west side of the Eastern Corinth road, 400 yards south of the Barnes Field. Miller's brigade's three regiments were in camp on the east side of the Eastern Corinth road. Hickenlooper's 5th Ohio Battery and Munch's 1st Minnesota Battery and two battalions of 11th Illinois Cavalry had been assigned to the division and were camped in rear of the infantry. Other regiments on their way up the river had been ordered to report to General Prentiss, but had not arrived. The 16th Iowa arrived at Pittsburg Landing April 5 and sent its morning report to General Prentiss in time to have it included in his report of present for duty that day, but it was not fully equipped and its last boatload did not disembark until the morning of April 6, when the reunified regiment was detached to reinforce McClernand after he was attacked.

Although Prentiss's faulty timing in the retreat from the Hornets' Nest in the late afternoon cost the capture of not only his own division but much of "Will" Wallace's 2nd Division, the captured Prentiss was promoted to major general. After being exchanged, he was assigned to a command in Arkansas, and reinforced his own high estimation of his ability by a victory at the battle of Helena in the summer of 1863, defeating an attacking force of twice his size. Perhaps bitter about being assigned to a backwater command, he resigned from the army later that year.

After the war he moved to Bethany, Missouri, where he served as Federal postmaster, before dying at the age of 81.

6th (Prentiss's) Division at Shiloh

Prentiss's 6th Division was created on March 22, 1862, only two weeks before the battle of Shiloh. At the time of the battle, it contained 7,545 inexperienced troops in two brigades, made up of unassigned troops arriving at Pittsburg Landing. They were supported by Munch's and Hickenlooper's batteries, and 627 cavalrymen in two battalions. Most of Prentiss's men, with the exception of some Missouri regiments, were raw recruits, without training and lacking discipline. Of the 10 regiments assigned to the 6th Division, only four had served in the field and only one had fought in a battle. On the morning of the battle of Shiloh, three of the division's regiments were not yet in camp; they were still at Pittsburg Landing.

There was no room on the Shiloh plateau for the camps of Prentiss's raw troops near the landing, so they were forced to make their camps on the outskirts of the army, nearest the enemy, where they would feel the full brunt of a Confederate attack.

The other Union generals in council doubted that the Confederates were massed in the vicinity in the hours before the battle, but at his own request General Prentiss was permitted to send a small group forward to find out whether the enemy was there in force.

The battle began at 4:45 a.m. on Sunday morning when Prentiss's reconnoitering party, three companies of the 25th Missouri, ran into the Confederate advance and slowly retreated toward its camp, where it was reinforced by four companies of the 16th Wisconsin and five companies of the 21st Missouri. These troops were then reinforced by the whole of Col. Peabody's brigade and held the line until 8:00 a.m., when they fell back to Prentiss's line of camps, closely pursued by the Confederates.

Here Prentiss's division—with Miller's brigade on the left, Hickenlooper's and Munch's batteries in the center on either side of the Eastern Corinth Road, and Peabody's brigade on the right—was attacked by the brigades of Gladden, Shaver, Chalmers, and Wood. Prentiss had no experience in division command, and had not seen a battle since the Mexican War. However, he did a creditable job in avoiding the complete collapse of his division in the chaos of the early hours of the battle. When Prentiss's line collapsed at 9:00 a.m., he established a second position at the Sunken Road—later known as the Hornets' Nest—at the center of the Union army, between Hurlbut's 4th Division on his left and Will Wallace's 2nd Division on the right. Here Prentiss was joined by the roughly 575 men of the 23rd Missouri arriving from Pittsburg Landing. That put Prentiss in command of about 1,100 soldiers, a relatively small chunk (12 percent) of the approximately 8,850 Federals defending this central position of the Shiloh plateau.

General Grant told Prentiss to hold the line "at all hazards," which he did for hours against at least seven uncoordinated attacks by Shaver, Stephens, and Gibson. At 4:00 p.m., Hurlbut's division withdrew, and the now unopposed Confederate brigades on Prentiss's left pivoted to envelop him. Prentiss continued to resist the attacks until about 5:30 p.m., when he was finally forced to surrender himself and his remaining men. Much of Wallace's division on Prentiss's right was also captured.

At Shiloh, Prentiss's division lost 236 killed, 928 wounded, and 1,008 missing and captured, or 2,172 out of 7,545 present for duty for a total of 29% casualties. Losses to enemy fire (Prentiss's killed and wounded) were 15% of its total strength, which is less than the 18% median suffered by the other divisions in Grant's army. This salient fact tends to discredit the narrative set forth by David W. Reed in his seminal *The Battle of Shiloh and the Organizations Engaged*, and advocated by many historians thereafter, that the Hornets' Nest was the scene of the battle's heaviest fighting.

1st Brigade
Colonel Everett Peabody

Harvard-educated Everett Peabody started working in the railroad business in Massachusetts before moving to St. Joseph, Missouri, to work for the Hannibal & St. Joseph Railroad. He became the Chief Engineer of the Memphis & Ohio Railroad in the mid-1850s, and in the decade before the Civil War was renowned as "the best field engineer in the West." At 31 years old, he was intimidating at six feet one and 240 pounds—stern, headstrong, and argumentative, with the short temper of a man used to getting his own way.

When the Civil War broke out, one of his friends wrote to James H. Lane of Kansas acclaiming Peabody, asserting that nobody in bitterly divided northern Missouri could better aid the Union cause. Peabody was appointed major in the 13th Missouri, and then, on

September 1, 1861, he was appointed its colonel. He was twice wounded and captured in the battle of Lexington, near Kansas City, that month. Following his exchange and the reorganization of his old regiment as the 25th Missouri, Peabody joined Grant's Army of the Tennessee at Pittsburg Landing, becoming senior colonel and commander of Prentiss's 1st Brigade.

Peabody was a competent man, perhaps too outspoken for the liking of his superiors, but he did have the confidence of the men who served under him. Although Peabody was new to command of a brigade, it was he who sent out the patrol whose aggressive reconnaissance discovered the approach of the Confederate army. In the chaos that followed the opening of the Confederate attack, Peabody spent most of the morning in a search for Prentiss. After returning to the front line, he attempted to rally his men and make a stand, but was killed after only a few minutes.

6th Division, 1st (Peabody's) Brigade at Shiloh

Peabody's 1st Brigade numbered 2,790 men in four regiments: the 21st and 25th Missouri (Peabody's old regiment), the 16th Wisconsin, and the 12th Michigan. All were led at Shiloh by colonels except Peabody's 25th Missouri, which was led at Shiloh by its lieutenant colonel, the mayor of Kansas City. The 25th was also the only regiment in the division that had ever seen a battle, at Lexington, Missouri, in September 1861. The biggest question mark was the 12th Michigan, led by Col. Francis Quinn, who the governor of Michigan said was "the worst colonel I ever saw."

This brigade of four regiments was camped on the west side of the Eastern Corinth Road, about one-half mile south of the Hamburg-Purdy Road, in the order from left to right: 16th Wisconsin, 21st Missouri, 12th Michigan, and 25th Missouri.

When on Saturday, April 5, Peabody received reports that enemy troops were in the woods nearby, he did not scoff or sit still, as did other brigade commanders. He sent out five companies on a reconnaissance the next morning.

Three companies of the 25th Missouri under Maj. James E. Powell set out at 3:00 a.m. on Sunday to reconnoiter. Moving southwest from camp, they encountered Confederate pickets near the southeast corner of Fraley Field and were fired upon at 4:55 a.m. After an engagement of over an hour, Powell fell back before the advance of Wood's brigade to the Seay Field, where he was reinforced by Col. Moore with the 21st Missouri and four companies of the 16th Wisconsin. Colonel Moore took command, but was soon severely wounded. Lt. Col.

Woodyard of the 21st Missouri assumed command and was engaged about one hour, when he fell back to Rhea Field and was there met by Col. Peabody and the remainder of the brigade. Peabody held the Confederates in check until 8:00 a.m., when he fell back to his camp. Here he was attacked by Shaver's brigade and the right of Wood's brigade. With his brigade near collapse, Peabody, wounded four times, was attempting to rally his men when he threw up his hands, reeled in the saddle, and fell dead from his horse, a bullet having entered his upper lip and passed to the back of his head. The 1st Brigade was forced to abandon its camp at 9:00 a.m.

Two hundred men of the 21st Missouri, surviving the rout through their camp, joined Prentiss and elements of the 18th Missouri, 12th Michigan and 18th Wisconsin regiments in what became known as the Hornets' Nest. These units delayed the Confederate attacks on the rest of Grant's army until 5:30 p.m., when Prentiss surrendered.

On Monday, the remainder of the brigade took part in Grant's counterattack.

At Shiloh, Peabody's brigade lost 113 killed, 372 wounded, and 236 missing and captured, for a total of 721 out of 2,790 present for duty—26% casualties.

2nd Brigade
Colonel Madison Miller

Madison Miller, 51, was a successful Missourian, a perfect example of high-ranking officers in the first year of the war who, with only brief experience in war, were expected to lead men in combat because they had been leaders of men in politics and business. He had served as mayor of Carondelet, Missouri, was elected to the Missouri General Assembly in 1860, and had been president of the St. Louis & Iron Mountain Railroad. He also had military credentials, with experience as a captain of the 2nd Illinois Infantry in the Mexican War, where he had been wounded at the battle of Buena Vista.

His initial service in the Union army was as captain of a company in the 1st Missouri Infantry, and he was especially mentioned for gallantry in the battle of Wilson's Creek in August 1861. In September 1862, the 1st Missouri was reorganized as an artillery battalion, and Miller was made captain of a battery. In February 1862, he went from captain of artillery to colonel of the 18th Missouri Infantry following the removal of its previous colonel, W. James Morgan, for his harsh treatment of Missouri civilians.

Miller was captured at the Hornets' Nest, and he resigned upon his release, citing ill health. However, he later commanded a brigade in Missouri. After the war he was active in the railroad business and real estate before dying away in 1896 at the age of 85 in St. Louis.

6th Division, 2nd (Miller's) Brigade at Shiloh

The 2nd Brigade numbered 2,509 men in three regiments: the 61st Illinois, 18th Missouri, and 18th Wisconsin. They were all new and untested.

Miller's brigade had three regiments in camp, with a fourth assigned and reported but not yet in camp. The regiments were camped between the Eastern Corinth Road and Locust Grove Branch in the following order from left to right: 18th Wisconsin, 61st Illinois, and 18th Missouri.

Miller's brigade was formed for battle Sunday morning at 7:30 a.m. to the left of Peabody's 1st Brigade, on the south edge of Spain Field. Capt. Andrew Hickenlooper's 5th Ohio Battery unlimbered in the northwest corner of the field, east of the Eastern Corinth Road. Also anchoring Miller's right was Capt. Emil Munch's 1st Minnesota Battery, placed astride a country road.

Gladden's brigade launched an attack on Miller's line at 8:00 a.m., which Miller's men repulsed. General Prentiss personally repositioned Miller's defensive line. Gladden was reinforced by Chalmers's brigade for second Rebel assault at 8:30, and this time, after suffering only a few casualties, Miller's brigade fled panic-stricken through its camps.

Colonel Miller, with parts of the 18th Wisconsin and 18th Missouri, about 300 men, formed with Prentiss at the Sunken Road, and remained with him until captured at 5:30 p.m. The 61st Illinois passed through Hurlbut's line and stayed in reserve behind that division all day Sunday, except for about an hour when it relieved another regiment in the front line.

In his report after the battle, Prentiss put Miller at the top of his list of commendations, citing his "distinguished courage, coolness, and ability."

At Shiloh, Miller's brigade lost 67 killed, 311 wounded, and 352 missing and captured, for a total of 730 out of 2,509 present for duty—29% casualties, 15% from enemy fire.

Army of the Ohio

Major General Don Carlos Buell

Don Carlos Buell, 44 years old, was a supremely capable organizer and administrator, much in the mold of his mentor and friend, Army of the Potomac commander General George McClellan. He was stern in expression, formal, even icy, in manner, cautious and deliberate by nature, and intellectually rigid—qualities that estranged him from his subordinates. Like McClellan, he was also remarkably brawny, and Buell sometimes displayed his upper-body strength by clasping his wife by the waist, picking her up off the floor, holding her straight out in front of him, and then sitting her on a mantle.

His early years were spent on his father's farm near the Ohio River town of Marietta. When Buell was five his father died of cholera, and when his mother remarried three years later, she sent him to live with his uncle, a prominent farmer and merchant in Lawrenceburg, Indiana, another Ohio River town about 250 miles to the west. His uncle's business contacts eventually helped secure Don Carlos an appointment to West Point.

Buell graduated an unremarkable 32nd out of 52 cadets in West Point's Class of 1841. Appointed second lieutenant in the infantry, he first served in Florida during the Second Seminole War in 1841–42, and then in garrison duty at Jefferson Barracks near St. Louis. There, Buell was court-martialed for cutting off part of an enlisted man's ear with his sword in a fight. The incident earned Buell a reputation as a hard-headed disciplinarian, a reputation that would follow him for the rest of his career.

Buell saw action during the Mexican War (1846–48) in major battles at Monterrey and Churubusco, where he was wounded. He emerged from the war with a promotion to major after being brevetted for bravery three times.

Buell spent the next 13 years as an administrator in adjutant generals' offices in various departments across the United States, and rose to the rank of lieutenant colonel. He married a southerner in 1851 and became an owner of slaves from his wife's family.

The outbreak of the Civil War found Buell living in far-off California, serving as adjutant of the Department of the Pacific. He was soon summoned to the seat of war. Promoted to brigadier general of volunteers in May 1861, he was recalled to Washington, D.C., in August, and in September took the field as a division commander in the Army of the Potomac, at General McClellan's request. (Divisions were the largest command units at the time. Their commanders reported directly to the army commander.) Buell was McClellan's kind of man: an expert at organization and a proven professional soldier with conservative Democrat political views. Through September and October 1861, Buell helped McClellan organize and train the Army of the Potomac.

Buell's career breakthrough came soon, as a result of two unconnected changes in the Union high command. On November 5, in Washington, D.C., General McClellan took over as General-in-Chief from Winfield Scott, and on November 9, in Louisville, Kentucky, General Sherman buckled under the pressure of commanding the Department of the Ohio and was dismissed. McClellan installed Buell in Sherman's position.

Only six months into the war, times had changed when the hiring of commanders was concerned. Radical Republican favorites had prosecuted the war in the beginning, but by now Lincoln's hiring strategy had changed to signal to Democrats—the national majority party—that the war was not a Republican war, but one in which all Americans, and indeed, all the world, had a stake. Thus, a sudden glut of Democrats appeared at the heads of Union departments and armies.

Buell did not have the charisma of McClellan. He would never ride pell-mell down his lines holding his cap in the air and hear the roar of tens of thousands of his men cheering themselves hoarse at the sight of him, as McClellan did. But he shared much with his friend besides his politics. Both were West Point-trained Regular Army veterans, compact, barrel-chested men of immaculate appearance, both tireless workers, cool professionals, competent managers, efficient organizers, and believers in stringent discipline. Unfortunately, Buell's stringency shaded over into inflexibility—he could never accept that his volunteers, no matter how many hours he drilled them, could never copy the machine-like maneuvers of the Regular Army regiments, nor the Regulars' unquestioning obedience to authority. His men thought Buell a martinet—scowling, arrogant, and aloof. He did, however, have the correct conservative social views for the Kentucky theater: he considered crushing the rebellion more important than abolishing slavery. Thus, McClellan thought, he would not be seen as an enemy by Kentucky slaveholders—after all, his own family owned slaves.

Once installed, Buell began to fashion his Army of the Ohio in his own careful style. However, politicians' goals for Buell's army immediately clashed with his own purely military objectives. Lincoln insisted on a march into eastern Tennessee, where Union-loving enclaves were begging to be liberated, but Buell refused on logistical grounds. The roads were too narrow and muddy, he pointed out, and his supply wagons were too few. Even if an army could reach eastern Tennessee, how could he sustain it there? Buell insisted instead that the capture of Nashville was the proper goal.

To this end, he patiently recruited, organized, and trained his Kentucky army, which he named the "Army of the Ohio," through the months of November and December 1861 and January 1862. When, in February, Grant broke through the Confederate defensive line at Forts Henry and Donelson, Buell was able to walk into Nashville without firing a shot, a triumph of maneuver. He was promoted to major general the next month.

After the Shiloh campaign, Buell's army would be forced to countermarch back into Kentucky to block an advance by Bragg's Confederate army, a period of maneuvering which ended in the indecisive battle of Perryville. After Perryville, Buell's tardiness in pursuit of Bragg would bring about his removal from command of the Army of the Ohio by Federal military authorities on October 24, 1862.

After the war Buell was an executive in the iron industry while penning rather critical views, in the Century Magazine, of Grant's performance at Shiloh. He died in Kentucky in 1898 at age 80.

In the weeks after Fort Sumter and Lincoln's Call for Troops in mid-April 1861, volunteers raised in the Northern states boarded trains and headed for the flashpoints at the extreme ends of the nation's battlefront—Washington, D.C., which was surrounded by slave territory in Virginia and Maryland; and Cairo, Illinois, built on a dagger of land thrust between the slave states of Missouri and Kentucky, and dominating the meeting-point of the great highways of the West, the Mississippi and Ohio rivers.

In the vast middle was created, on May 3, 1861, the Department of the Ohio, which included Illinois, Indiana, and Ohio. In the summer months of 1861, most Illinois recruits were directed to Cairo or Missouri, where a bloody, drawn-out guerrilla war threatened to collapse the western end of the national front. Indiana and Ohio troops, under the direction of General George McClellan, headquartered in Cincinnati, attacked Virginia from the west, where it fronted the

Ohio River. Tiny battles in western Virginia did little to change the war's strategic picture except to lift their victorious leader, McClellan, into command of the army in Washington, D.C., where the nation's early attention was directed.

Along the 300-mile Ohio River front between Missouri and western Virginia sprawled the border state of Kentucky. In reaction to Lincoln's Call for Troops, other border states—Virginia, Arkansas, North Carolina, and Tennessee—declared they would join the Confederacy, which had until then consisted only of deep-South Cotton States. On May 7, the day Tennessee seceded, Lincoln instructed Brig. Gen. Robert Anderson, the recent "Hero of Ft. Sumter" and a native Kentuckian, to recruit the four regiments requested from Kentucky in the Call for Troops.

However, on May 20, Kentucky—in the tradition of its Great Compromiser Henry Clay, and Senator John J. Crittenden, author of the recent Crittenden Compromise— made a formal declaration of neutrality, refusing to take sides with either the North or the South. Lincoln knew he must be careful lest Kentucky go the way of Virginia, Arkansas, North Carolina, and Tennessee. He confided his feelings about his native state to a friend in a letter: "I think to lose Kentucky is nearly the same as losing the whole game." To this end, Lincoln wrote soothing letters to Kentucky leaders. assuring them he would not violate their neutrality.

Lincoln did act, however, though stealthily. On May 28 he formally named Fort Sumter's Anderson to command the Department of Kentucky, consisting of the part of Kentucky within 100 miles of its northern border, the Ohio River. Clandestine recruiters soon crisscrossed Kentucky, appointed either by President Lincoln, Brig. Gen. Anderson, or Secretary of War Cameron. Prominent loyal Kentuckians, commissioned to recruit four Kentucky regiments, established two camps just north of the Ohio River: Camp Clay in Ohio near Cincinnati in May, and Camp Joe Holt in Indiana across the river from Louisville, Kentucky, in June. Both camps drew Kentuckians eager to join the Union Army.

Lincoln's patient treatment of Kentucky, although criticized in the North, was soon rewarded. A promising signal came on June 20, 1861, when, in a special congressional election, Unionist candidates won nine of Kentucky's ten congressional seats. On July 1, Lincoln responded by authorizing Kentuckian Naval Lieutenant William "Bull" Nelson to organize three more Kentucky regiments, and he gave Nelson a secret mission to distribute 10,000 muskets and six artillery pieces to the Kentucky Home Guards, which were pro-Union militia units.

A second political signal was given on August 5, when in a Kentucky state election Unionists won overwhelming, veto-proof majorities. The next day, Lt.

Nelson established Camp Dick Robinson, the first Union base south of the Ohio River, in the heart of the rich Kentucky Bluegrass region around Lexington. Thousands of men, many who had previously been members of the loyal Kentucky Home Guards, flocked to its tents.

In addition, on August 15 Lincoln expanded the Department of Kentucky to include all of Kentucky and Tennessee, and named Robert Anderson to head this new creation, now named the Department of the Cumberland. Lincoln allowed Anderson to choose four brigadier generals, and Anderson named trusty Regular Army men: Don Carlos Buell, George H. Thomas, Ambrose Burnside, and William T. Sherman.

Three weeks later came the end of Kentucky neutrality, brought on by one of the great blunders of the war: the Confederate invasion of Kentucky. On September 3, 1861, thinking—incorrectly—that Union troops were about to seize Columbus, a key post on the Mississippi River, Confederate troops in west Tennessee under Generals Gideon Pillow and Leonidas Polk moved north into Columbus and seized it first. Governor Morton of Indiana warned Secretary of War Cameron, "The war in Kentucky has commenced."

General Anderson moved his headquarters from Cincinnati to Louisville, the target of a likely Confederate push northward along the logistically crucial Louisville & Nashville Railroad. But he received no reinforcements from Secretary Cameron, who was still ordering all new regiments either to General Fremont in St. Louis or General McClellan in Washington. Anderson, with only the half-trained recruits in his Ohio River camps, telegraphed Cincinnati for troops, crying, "Kentucky has no armed men whose services I can command." It was at this darkest hour that the Army of the Ohio was born.

On September 18, 1861, Anderson learned that a Confederate army under Brig. Gen. Simon Bolivar Buckner had boarded trains in Nashville and rolled north on the Louisville & Nashville Railroad as far as Bowling Green, halfway between Nashville and Louisville. Anderson, in despair, sent his newly appointed second-in-command, Brig. Gen. William T. Sherman, south on the railroad, leading the ill-prepared volunteers of the Louisville Legion and the Louisville Home Guard militia, to Muldraugh Hill, high ground about 30 miles south of Louisville, to block Buckner's advance. By October 1, Sherman had collected two brigades at Muldraugh Hill, and had enough confidence to advance from there to the Nolin River, about 20 miles further south, where he established Camp Nevin.

Only five months removed from the drama of Fort Sumter, this proved too much for General Anderson. He summoned Sherman to Louisville on October 5 and told him "he [Anderson] could not stand the mental torture of his command any longer, and that he must go or it would kill him."

Sherman took command of the Department of the Ohio on October 8. He only lasted a month. He dared do nothing beyond strengthening his twin forward positions, Camp Dick Robinson and Camp Nevin.

Sherman worried that two known Confederate armies, Buckner's at Bowling Green—now under the renowned General Albert Sidney Johnston—and Felix Zollicoffer's in eastern Kentucky, would combine and overwhelm any outpost, most likely George Thomas's at Camp Dick Robinson. On October 16, Secretary of War Cameron, on a fact-finding mission to the West, came to visit Sherman in Louisville. Sherman listed the dangers on his stretch of the Union front between Fremont in the West and McClellan in the East, and warned that, "if Johnston chose, he could march to Louisville any day." Sherman produced a United States map and demonstrated to Cameron that McClellan in the East covered a front of less than 100 miles with 100,000 men, and that Fremont in the West covered a front of about 100 miles with 60,000 men, but that he, Sherman, in the center, was expected to cover a front of over 300 miles with 18,000 men. He finished by saying that "for the purpose of defense, we should have 60,000 men at once, and for offense, would need 200,000."

Sherman's estimate was, in fact, prophetic of the size of the army it would take to capture Atlanta in 1864. But in 1861, uttering this number was Sherman's undoing. Cameron called 200,000 men "insane," and it leaked to the press. Soon newspapers referred to "insane Sherman." Sherman's own behavior gave weight to the story. Believing himself to be "far outnumbered" by the Rebels—Sherman thought there was an effective Rebel force of at least 55,000 in the state, according to one who was at the Cameron interview—and believing that his own positions were teeming with spies, he wrote later that his concerns "broke me down," and that he contemplated suicide. On November 4 he asked to be relieved, not yet a month after taking command. On November 9, General McClellan turned Sherman's command over to his friend, General Don Carlos Buell.

McClellan abolished Sherman's Department of the Cumberland and made Buell the commander of an enlarged Department of the Ohio, one that included the earlier territory of Ohio, Michigan, and Indiana, and added Sherman's Kentucky and Tennessee. (McClellan subtracted the part of Kentucky west of the Cumberland River where Grant and C. F. Smith were operating, and transferred it to General Halleck in St. Louis.)

Buell was appalled at the disarray in the command he inherited—"Sherman was a disorganizer," wrote one observer who sympathized with Buell. Besides grouping the Camp Nevin regiments into four brigades under fellow Ohioan Brig. Gen. Alexander McCook, Sherman had not attempted to fashion an army out of his scattered command. Buell set to work, like McClellan in Washington two months earlier, to build an army out of a mishmash of regiments. Buell's initial organizational solution, however, was eccentric, out of step with the systems used to the east, west, and south. He created 16 brigades, and numbered them in order, from the "1st Brigade" to the "16th Brigade," to indicate that they were all directly subordinate to him. New brigades were created about every other week, and the brigade numbers would rise into the twenties before Shiloh. On December 2, 1861, Buell's titled his creation the "Army of the Ohio" for the first time, and created five divisions, numbered 1st through 5th, each with about three brigades supported by artillery and cavalry.

Buell had an especially acute shortage of qualified officers for his new divisions and brigades. Every army in the war battled this shortage—the United States was fortunate in that it had no enemies on either border. Except for a handful of examples, the business of soldiering in the decades leading up to the Civil War had never offered much in the way of prestige in America. Because Kentucky had been neutral, and because there had been no fighting in the state for the first five months of the war, troops from northern states fronting the Ohio River had been sent away to salient points east and west, and the short supply of experienced officers had been sent east and west with them—the present general-in-chief and commander of the Army of the Potomac, George McClellan of Ohio, being a prime example.

To make matters worse for Buell, an extra political requirement further shortened the list of generals considered for command in Kentucky. To demonstrate the lessons learned from the earlier mistake of importing radical Republicans to command in Missouri, and because, as a conservative Democrat, he himself felt no abolitionist ambitions, McClellan instructed Buell to choose officers acceptable to Kentuckians, men who would assuage the fears of Kentucky's slave owners and show that the Union army there had no intention of disrupting their local institutions. Such officers would preferably be men from Kentucky or southern Illinois, Indiana, and Ohio. Buell himself, a Democrat born and raised in Ohio River towns and a slave-holder by marriage to an Alabamian wife, was the model.

The division commanders followed this model: William Nelson and Thomas L. Crittenden were Kentuckians; Ormsby Mitchel was a Cincinnatian born in Kentucky; George Thomas was a Virginian; and Alexander McCook an Ohioan from an Ohio River county. Directly beneath them, among the first 11 brigade commanders Buell appointed, there were no "yankees," in the sense that the word had at the time; that is, men from New England. Instead, five—Rousseau, Wood, Johnson, Boyle, and Ward—were from Kentucky; three—Sill, Ammen, and Cruft—were from the Ohio River valley; and Carter was from Tennessee. Only Turchin, from Russia, and Hascall, from northern Indiana, were outsiders.

The practice of appointing "none but Southern and Western officers" was "a stroke of good policy," according to one of them, Richard W. Johnson. However, it inevitably degraded the quality of the officer corps in Buell's army. Only two of the new brigadiers, Johnson and T. J. Wood, were active Regular Army men, and the men in the ranks felt the lack of good officers and were galled by it. "We have, all of us, large confidence in Genl Buell," wrote one captain, "though the brood of Brig Genls under him in Kentucky do not inspire much respect or confidence."

The 1st Division, under Brig. Gen. George H. Thomas, the ablest of Buell's division commanders, was at Camp Dick Robinson, near Danville in the heart of the rich Kentucky Bluegrass region. Nelson named the camp after Richard Robinson, the man who owned the land. This set a precedent, and the practice of naming new camps after the land's owner was followed. The 2nd Division's Camp Nevin, established by Brig. Gen. Lovell Rousseau on October 9, was on land owned by David Nevin, a known secessionist. However, his farm was located on a crucial site that dominated at once the main highway, the Louisville & Nashville Railroad track, and the Nolin River, so Rousseau occupied it and made sure Nevin got the humiliation of having a Union camp named after him. (The 3rd Division erected Camp John Quincy Adams not after the former president but after the local farmer, whose name was John Quincy Adams.) At Camp Dick Robinson, the 1st Division would not only guard Kentucky's most populous region, but also be in a position to block any Confederate advance on either Cincinnati or Louisville. The regiments of the 1st Division had been training since September, preparing to march southeast to the aid of the eastern Tennessee Unionists, a pet project of President Lincoln. In its central Kentucky posts, Thomas's 1st Division numbered about 13,000 men in January 1862.

The 2nd Division represented the army's center, 50 miles south of Louisville on the north-south Louisville & Nashville Railroad. Buell had determined that this would be his axis of advance when the time was ripe. McCook's 2nd Division numbered about 11,000 men in January 1862.

In mid-December 1862 the new 3rd Division was forwarded to the army's most advanced position, at Munfordville, 25 miles forward of the 2nd Division at Camp Nevin. The 3rd Division consisted mainly of regiments being withdrawn from western Virginia, where they had fought in small battles under General

Rosecrans, and from eastern Kentucky, where they had been training under General Nelson. Brig. Gen. Ormsby Mitchel's 3rd Division counted 8,000 men in January 1862.

When Buell established the 4th Division in early December, its headquarters were at Maysville, on the upper Ohio River, making it the easternmost division guarding the army's left flank. But Buell ordered the 4th Division immediately to Camp Wickliffe, south of Louisville and directly between the headquarters of the 1st and 2nd Divisions, ready in case either of those main posts should be attacked. Nelson's 4th Division numbered about 8,000 men in January 1862.

Buell posted Brig. Gen. Thomas L. Crittenden's 5th Division to the west in Calhoun, Kentucky, in advance of Owensboro on the Ohio River southwest of Louisville. This division consisted of troops that had been organizing in Owensboro and Henderson, Kentucky. The 5th Division would guard the Army's right flank, and numbered about 5,000 at the start of 1862.

In mid-December the Confederate force at Bowling Green had made no aggressive moves in the two months it had been there. On December 17, finally satisfied that the Rebels there had no intention of attacking him, Buell had McCook advance Johnson's 6th Brigade, two regiments of Rousseau's 4th Brigade, and a battery 20 miles south to protect the bridge on the Green River. There they established Camp Wood at Munfordville (on a farm owned by the 5th Brigade's General Thomas J. Wood's father). They would soon be joined there by Ormsby Mitchel's new 3rd Division.

On December 24, Buell ordered Wood, one of his two Regular Army-trained brigadiers, to Bardstown, Kentucky, situated just in the rear of the army's forward line, to establish a camp of instruction for the torrent of arriving recruits. On January 7 and 8, 1862, these troops were combined to make the 19th, 20th and 21st Brigades. The latter two were organized into a new 6th Division on February 11, 1862, with Wood at the head.

Buell was, according to one observer, "too much of a regular, so that when he came to command a great volunteer force he looked for and strove in vain to attain the perfectness in appointment, organization, drill, and all that routine duty to which he had been accustomed in the old army." Buell believed in instilling discipline by rigorous, constant, repetitive drill. According to his instructions, his regiments practiced close order drill several hours a day to produce men who would obey authority without thinking. The newest recruits constantly marched and performed the "manual of arms." The more experienced troops practiced by companies, learning to form lines and columns. The result was that his Army of the Ohio regiments were, over the next few months, well trained in close order drill—but little else. Almost never were they allowed to take target practice to improve their skill with weapons. Almost never did regiments practice together in brigade maneuvers.

Perhaps because of the absence of any drill at levels larger than regimental, the men grew justifiably proud of their individual regiments and found their identity in them. As a result, there were successes in small actions where individual regiments were involved. When, on December 17, the 32nd Indiana was sent forward to repair a bridge over Green River destroyed by Rebels, there was a sharp fight entirely to the credit of the Hoosier soldiers, where they fought to a standstill a larger Confederate force of infantry, artillery, and cavalry. Soon known as the battle of Rowlett's Station, the stand by the 32nd Indiana was trumpeted in the national press.

In January 1862, before his brigade commanders had learned to coordinate their regiments' movements on a battlefield, Buell undertook his army's first short campaign. Being a military man in the mold of George McClellan, Buell was unwilling to make any move without being absolutely certain of its success. After months in the camps, however, his army was decimated by disease, and its men were chafing at the inaction. "Our army is large enough for an advance," wrote a soldier in the 49th Ohio, "but it looks as if this was a peaceful war against the rebels.... Let the war be prosecuted with vigor." Another vented his frustration in a letter to his hometown newspaper: "Winter is upon us, and yet no battle has been fought; no victory tells of the bravery of our men, and no trophies tell of the daring exploits." The feeling intensified after Grant's army brought on the battle of Belmont; in comparison with them, one of Buell's men called the Army of the Ohio "Old Maids. . . . Ready but not wanted."

Under growing pressure from Washington to make a move to liberate the Unionist residents of eastern Tennessee, and aware of the grumbling among troops loitering in disease-ridden camps, Buell in January 1862 reluctantly ordered Thomas's 1st Division in the Bluegrass region to advance southeast and give battle to a small Confederate force camped north of the Cumberland River. On January 19, the ensuing infantry firefight, called the battle of Mill Springs, was a confused affair in dark woods in a driving rain, and showed the lack of proficiency on both sides in coordinating maneuver above the regimental level. The Confederates, however, lost their commanding officer, Brig. Gen. Felix Zollicoffer, early in the action and recoiled, retreating all the way to Carthage, Tennessee, and leaving all their heavy equipment behind.

Though the battle exposed the weakness of command and control above the regimental level in the Army of the Ohio, it was hailed by a Northern press starved for news of a victory. Also, the small battle had consequences far larger than the meager forces which had fought it: it completely collapsed the right flank of the Confederate line in Kentucky. Buell was not emboldened to follow up his victory in eastern Kentucky, however. The weather was bad, he protested. The roads were muddy. He lacked supply wagons.

The real reason for Buell's case of "the slows" was that he had his heart set on an assault on Nashville by the great bulk of his army, the three divisions he had massed north of Bowling Green. The Confederates under Johnston were also massed there in opposition, in what Buell was convinced were great numbers. Buell could not allow himself to believe the truth: that his army outnumbered the entire Confederate force along the whole of the Kentucky line, from Polk's men in Columbus to Zollicoffer's survivors in eastern Kentucky. Buell consumed the next few weeks dashing off telegraphic dispatches to the army's high command, hoping to convince Major General Henry Halleck, in charge of the Department of the Missouri to the west, to make a coordinated attack down the Mississippi River that would paralyze any troops that might be rushed to the support of Bowling Green. Halleck balked; he had ideas of his own in which Buell would play the supporting role.

As the higher-ups piled dots upon dots and dashes upon dashes trading telegrams about who would make the primary thrust and who would support whom, the winter weeks passed in tedium for the men in the camps. Buell's 2nd Division historian called it "a time of deep mud, incessant toil and weary exhaustion." The impasse was shattered by Ulysses S. Grant at Cairo, who, in early February, loaded his men on steamboats and attacked Fort Henry, the gateway to the upper Tennessee River Valley in the heart of the South. Grant followed his success there with an overland attack resulting in the successful capture of nearby Fort Donelson, the key to the Cumberland River Valley. The fall of Forts Henry and Donelson completely collapsed the entire Confederate line in Kentucky. On Buell's front, with Union troops able to steam quickly up the Cumberland River, Johnston's Confederate force at Bowling Green had to retreat quickly to Nashville to avoid capture.

With the prize of the Tennessee capital now before him, and with new prodding from General-in-Chief McClellan added to the constant prodding from Halleck, Buell mobilized. On February 10, after Fort Henry fell, he sent Nelson's 4th Division and Crittenden's 5th Division on steamboats to aid Grant in the coming battle for Fort Donelson. He set most of the rest of his army in motion toward Bowling Green, with Mitchel's 3rd Division in the vanguard. (Buell judged Mitchel would be quicker than McCook to move, so he ordered the former officer to pass through McCook's forward position and move to the front of the column.) On February 14 Mitchel approached Bowling Green and found the bridge over the Barren River there destroyed and the tail of the Rebel column barely visible on the horizon, marching southward.

Buell now ordered almost his entire army into pursuit on the roads and rivers toward Nashville. Thomas's 1st Division, which had been at Somerset, Kentucky, after the battle of Mill Springs, now moved rearward by forced marches to Louisville, where it was put on steamers for Nashville. Nelson, with two 4th Division brigades already steaming up the Cumberland River to reinforce Grant at Fort Donelson, was now ordered further up the Cumberland to the Tennessee capital, where he would be joined by his third brigade under Col. Bruce, which was marching south from Bowling Green with Buell's main body. Wood's 6th Division in the army's rear was put on trains for Bowling Green, where it was given the task of repairing the Louisville & Nashville Railroad, which had been ripped up by the retreating Confederate army.

Buell arrived at Nashville in the vanguard with Mitchel's 3rd Division on February 24, 1862, only to find that the steamboats bearing Nelson's 4th Division had beaten them to the Tennessee capital. Between February 24 and March 10, all the pieces of Buell's army arrived, and Army of the Ohio was united—for the first time—in a ten-mile circle of camps around Nashville.

While the men lounged or drilled in their Nashville camps, the pace of events in the Western Theater leapt ahead. In the first week of March, General Halleck in St. Louis ordered an ascent of the Tennessee River by Grant's 37,000-man army at Fort Donelson to strike at the railroad connections near Corinth, Mississippi. Since he could not be sure of Buell's support, Halleck conceived Grant's army's strike as a quick raid. Grant's men, briefly under the command of Brig. Gen. C. F. Smith, boarded steamboats and ascended the Tennessee while Halleck and Buell bickered. The standoff between the two generals was ended on March 11, when President Lincoln published his "War Order No. 3," whose intent was to get the maddeningly inert Union armies moving south. In the East, George McClellan was removed as General-in-Chief, and in the West, a new Department of the Mississippi was created for Henry Halleck that included everything west of a north-and-south line drawn through Knoxville, Tennessee, which included Buell's command. Buell would now be taking orders from Halleck. Grant's strike up the Tennessee would not be a brief raid but a full-scale invasion.

And it would be joined by the Army of the Ohio.

The Army of the Ohio at Shiloh

In mid-March, Halleck ordered Buell to "Move your forces by land to the Tennessee as rapidly as possible. You must direct your march on [Savannah, Tennessee], so that the enemy cannot get between us." Buell agreed with the idea of moving his army overland to join Grant rather than taking river transports: "It can move in less time, in better condition, and with more security to our operations than by the river," he wrote Halleck. "It will have also the advantage of driving out the scattered force of the enemy on this side of the [Tennessee] river, and operate powerfully on the minds of the people."

As dearly as he wanted to make his martial show, however, Buell's army was ill-prepared for this march of more than a hundred miles in late winter. Having been camp-bound since their inception, the regiments had not yet learned the art of long campaign marches, especially through the rain, sleet, snow, and knee-deep mud of March, across Tennessee's most barren scrub forests. And they had no pontoon train, having sent it ahead to Savannah by boat, so they would have to stop and build bridges across any unbridged rivers.

Too, Buell could not move with his whole force; he must also provide for the defense of what he had already won. To that end:

He created a new 7th Division under Brig. Gen. George W. Morgan from troops he had recently sent to the Cumberland Gap area under Samuel P. Carter, plus the 18th Brigade, recently withdrawn from eastern Kentucky. The 7th Division's orders were to defend Cumberland Gap and, if possible, strike into Eastern Tennessee.

He detached Mitchel's 3rd Division to move straight south from Nashville into Alabama and strike the Memphis & Charleston Railroad, the east-west spine of the Confederacy, and there block any forces from the East coming to the support of the Rebel army gathering at Corinth, Mississippi.

He detached Brig. Gen. William T. Ward's 16th Brigade and ordered it back to Bardstown, Kentucky, to guard the approaches to Louisville and Cincinnati.

He organized a 23rd Brigade under the command of Col. William W. Duffield and sent it to garrison Murfreesboro, 30 miles southeast of Nashville.

He left a brigade-sized force in Nashville under Brig. Gen. Ebeneezer Dumont.

Also at this time, he made a few organizational changes, as follows:

He transferred Brig. Gen. Jeremiah Boyle's 11th Brigade from the 1st Division to the 5th Division. He transferred Col. Milo Hascall's 15th Brigade from the 4th to the new 6th Division. He attached Col. Bruce's 22nd Brigade, recently organized in January 1862, to the 4th Division to replace the 15th Brigade. And he would soon detach Brig. Gen. James S. Negley's 7th Brigade from the 2nd Division and leave it to garrison Columbia, Tennessee.

After leaving Negley's brigade behind, Buell had, in all, detached half his 73,000-man army to guard his rear, leaving him the 37,000 men of the 1st, 2nd, 4th and 6th Divisions to march to join Grant for the assault on Corinth.

Buell started his army's long march from Nashville to Savannah on March 15. He sent off his cavalry first, hoping by a quick dash to prevent the Confederates from burning the bridges over Rutherford Creek and the Duck River, near Columbia, about 40 miles to the southwest. McCook, as senior division commander, claimed the vanguard. His 2nd Division set off the next day along the Central Alabama Railroad line toward Columbia. Over the next two weeks, McCook was followed by Nelson's 4th, Crittenden's 5th, Wood's 6th and Thomas's 1st Division.

All soon were stopped at the Duck River, where the cavalry had found the bridges already collapsed in flames into the river, which was swollen by spring rain and running 40 feet deep. It took considerable time for Buell's inexperienced army to improvise a group of engineers to rebuild the bridge. Buell decided to take the time to rebuild the bridge completely, having been advised by dispatches brought by couriers from Grant, "There is no need of haste; come on by easy marches." Buell, too, assumed that Grant's army was camped at Savannah, on the eastern, protected side of the Tennessee River from the Confederate army collecting in Corinth. He was unaware that Grant's divisions were exposed on the vulnerable western bank at Pittsburg Landing.

Bull Nelson was the only leader in the Army of the Ohio who fretted over the delay at Duck River. When the river level dropped far enough to allow fording, he told Jacob Ammen, one of his brigadiers, "Damn you, get over, for we must have the advance and get the glory." Nelson's men obediently put their clothes on the ends of their bayonets and plunged in. The bridges were finished soon after, on March 29, ending a two-week delay, and the other divisions followed Nelson's, which had a good 12- to 15-hour lead. Crittenden's division came second, followed by McCook's, Wood's, and Thomas's, which did not cross until April 2. The enormous wagon train traveled between Wood's and Thomas's divisions, placing the latter so far in the rear that it would still be 40 miles away when the battle at Shiloh began.

After a week's hard marches—a week during which the Confederate Army of the Mississippi was also moving, stealing toward Pittsburg Landing from Corinth—Nelson's three brigades—Ammen's 10th, Hazen's 19th, then Bruce's

22nd—arrived at Savannah on the afternoon of April 5. Grant had provided no transports to convey them the six miles up the Tennessee River to Pittsburg Landing, so Nelson's division camped in Savannah that night.

When, the next morning, they heard the opening of the first day's battle of Shiloh, Nelson's men were still on the wrong side of the river. It took all day for Nelson's three brigades to follow a swampy river wagon-path, with the help of a local guide, to a site from which they could be ferried directly across the Tennessee River to Pittsburg Landing. The lead regiment, Grose's 36th Indiana of Ammen's brigade, was gotten across in time to take part in the last fighting on Sunday, before the rest of Ammen's brigade came up from the landing. Ammen's men, being the first to arrive, were placed nearest the river. Bruce's and Hazen's brigades did not get over the river until after dark, with Bruce put into line on the right of Ammen, and Hazen on the right of Bruce. Crittenden's 5th Division, which had come by steamboat from Savannah, also arrived that night, about 11:00 p.m., and was put into line to the right of Nelson's division.

Wood's and McCook's divisions arrived at the landing the next morning, so that at the resumption of the battle on Monday, the Army of the Ohio occupied the left of the Union line, extending in a semicircle from the Tennessee River, north of Dill Branch, to the north side of the Corinth Road, one mile from Pittsburg Landing, with Nelson's division on the left, Crittenden in the center and McCook on the right. On McCook's right were the surviving pieces of Grant's army under Sherman and McClernand, with Lew Wallace's division—arrived on the battlefield the night before—extending the Union line to Owl Creek. Buell personally led Crittenden's division.

The divisions of the Army of the Ohio moved forward, preserving their relative positions in line, and became engaged about 8:00 a.m. They advanced slowly until about 2:00 p.m., when Wood's division was put in place just as the final retreat of the Confederates began. In the forward movement McCook's division kept to the Corinth Road, with Crittenden's division following the direction of the Eastern Corinth Road. This separated the divisions so that at about 11:00 a.m., Veatch and Tuttle, from Grant's army, were moved into the interval and became engaged in the Review Field. At 2:30 p.m. the Confederates retired from the field, and the Army of the Ohio bivouacked on a line extending from Stuart's camps through Prentiss's camps to near Shiloh Church.

General Buell brought 17,918 men of the Army of the Ohio onto the battlefield at Shiloh before the Confederate withdrawal. Of these, 241 were killed, 1,807 were wounded, and 55 were missing or captured at the end of the day—12% casualties (compared to the Army of the Tennessee's 22% and the Confederate

Army of the Mississippi's 24%). Losses to enemy fire (the killed and wounded) were 11% of the total (compared to the Army of the Tennessee's 17% and the Confederate Army of the Mississippi's 22%).

The Army of the Ohio's casualties indicate that the heaviest fighting was on the left, nearest the Tennessee River, with Hazen's brigade conspicuous. Nelson's division on the left lost 15% of its men to enemy fire while Hazen's brigade lost 23%, and both Crittenden's division in the center and McCook's division on the right lost 12%.

2nd Division

Brigadier General
Alexander McCook

Alexander McDowell McCook, at 40, was the highest ranking officer of the "Fighting McCooks," 15 men from one Ohio family, 14 of whom were officers who fought for the Union in the Civil War. Alex McCook had been groomed for high command. He graduated from West Point in 1842, taking five years to complete the four-year course of study. He then spent his pre-war life in the 3rd Infantry Regiment of the Regular Army, fighting Indians in the West before returning to West Point to teach infantry tactics in 1858.

McCook was a shooting star in the Civil War's first half-year. Whisked from his classroom, he was given command of the 1st Ohio Infantry on April 16, 1861, fought at its head at the battle of Bull Run on July 21, was promoted to brigadier general on September 3, and was called to Kentucky to command the 2nd Division of the Army of the Ohio on November 9.

There was a political component to McCook's high post in Kentucky, since McCook's views before the war were Southern and Democratic. Even now, slaves were not safe within his lines; they were simply secured, and if the owner applied he could take them away. These politics fit perfectly with the hiring policy of the Army of the Ohio in Kentucky.

During his short tenure, Sherman had shown confidence in McCook by putting him in charge of the army's forward position at Camp Nevin. McCook had shown administrative skill by fashioning provisional brigades from his regiments there. It was, in fact, the misfortune of Alexander McCook that, amid the almost universal military ignorance of the officers at the beginning of the Civil War, his skill at organization was mistaken for greatness. When it became clear that McCook was less than great, his fall would be the harder for it.

As 1862 began, there was already stifled laughter. McCook had been known as "Gut" for his rotundity ever since his West Point days. General Sherman called him "a juvenile." Fellow Ohioan Lt. Col. John Beatty derided McCook as a "chucklehead," "deficient in the upper story." One journalist gibed that no one could see McCook "without thinking of the biggest boy in school." As McCook's lack of capacity for large commands became more noticeable, others remarked on it, like the captain in the 93rd Ohio who wrote that McCook "don't look to be equal to the position he holds; he seems to have drawn a lucky card." To make matters worse, McCook was arrogant and preening. One observer remarked that McCook was awfully proud of being "General McCook."

At Shiloh, McCook did not make himself conspicuous. He showed adequate control of his division, using his reserves to protect his flanks, and advanced his division at the same rate as the other commands.

A year and a half after Shiloh, McCook would be relieved of duty after a poor showing at the battle of Chickamauga and sent to command the defenses of Washington. Late in the war he would be removed to the backwater of Arkansas. However, he was still a career soldier—he remained in the U.S. Army until his retirement in 1895, and passed away in Dayton, Ohio in 1903.

2nd (McCook's) Division at Shiloh

The division had its genesis at Camp Nevin, established by Brig. Gen. Rousseau in October 1861 to block the southern approach to Louisville where the Louisville & Nashville Railroad crossed the Nolin River in Kentucky. By mid-October 1861, there were 10,000 men at Camp Nevin, divided into three brigades. They were: 1st Brigade, Brig. Gen. Lovell H. Rousseau; 2nd Brigade, Brig. Gen. Thomas J. Wood; and 3rd Brigade, Brig. Gen. Richard W. Johnson.

With the addition of a 4th Brigade from Pittsburgh, Pennsylvania, under Brig. Gen. James Negley, on October 23, 1861, McCook's division was 14,000 strong. When Major General Don Carlos Buell replaced Sherman in command of the Department of the Cumberland on November 9, he redesignated the above four brigades as the 4th, 5th, 6th, and 7th Brigades of the Army of the Ohio, and McCook's division formally became the 2nd Division.

In November, the division advanced farther south along the Louisville & Nashville to Bacon Creek. In December, Buell ordered the division to advance farther along the railroad to Munfordville on the Green River, 75 miles south of Louisville. During this period, McCook's 2nd Division had the distinction of being in the vanguard of the Army of the Ohio, closest to the enemy at Bowling Green.

That changed in early February 1862, when General-in-Chief McClellan ordered General Buell to advance to Nashville. Buell asked McCook how quickly he could move, and McCook estimated eight to ten days. Buell also asked General

Mitchel of the 3rd Division and Mitchel answered, "Tomorrow morning." Mitchel got the job. McCook's division suffered the humiliation of watching Mitchel and his division march through their lines at Munfordville, cross the bridge over the Green River that McCook's men had rebuilt, and take the lead in the march to Nashville.

The 2nd Division crossed the Cumberland River and occupied Nashville on February 27. There the division spent three weeks in camp while Buell reorganized the Army of the Ohio, and on March 16 started southward overland with the rest of the army to join Grant's army at Savannah, Tennessee. On the march to Shiloh, Buell detached Negley's 7th Brigade to garrison Columbia, Tennessee.

Although it arrived third at Pittsburg Landing, McCook's was by far Buell's largest division at Shiloh, bringing 7,552 men onto the field in Brig. Gen. Lovell Rousseau's 4th Brigade, Col. Edward N Kirk's 5th Brigade, and Col. William H. Gibson's 6th Brigade. General Rousseau was a talented leader with combat experience in the Mexican War. The two colonels, Kirk and Gibson, were inexperienced. Gibson was substituting that day for ailing Brig. Gen. Richard W. Johnson.

The 2nd Division was able to get a battery, Terrill's, across the Tennessee River in time for the battle. However, it took a wrong turn on its approach to the fighting line and served with Nelson's 4th Division during the fighting on Monday.

McCook's 2nd Division went into action much later than Nelson's and Crittenden's, due to its late arrival from Savannah. The van of McCook's division, Rousseau's brigade, took its place in line of battle on Crittenden's right about 8:00 a.m. Kirk's brigade formed in rear of Rousseau. The division advanced along the Corinth Road to Water Oaks Pond, fighting Trabue's Kentuckians from 9:00 to 11:00 a.m. Rousseau's and Kirk's brigades were joined by Gibson's brigade about noon, and McCook sent Gibson into the fight about 1:30 or 2:00 p.m. McCook's last engagement was near Shiloh Church, from which point the Confederates retired from the field.

McCook's was the tardiest of Buell's divisions to reach the battlefield, but in his Memoirs Grant wrote, "Out of justice to General McCook and his command, I must say that they left a point 22 miles east of Savannah on the morning of the 6th. From the heavy rains of a few days previous and the passage of trains and artillery, the roads were necessarily deep in mud, which made marching slow. The division had not only marched through this mud the day before, but it had been in the rain all night without rest."

McCook did well enough in his first battle, advancing when he could and shuttling his reserves back and forth to repel counterattacks against both flanks. However, he displayed a bad habit of giving orders directly to individual regiments instead of operating though their brigade commanders, a practice that inevitably resulted in confusion.

At Shiloh, McCook's 2nd Division lost 88 killed, 823 wounded, and 7 missing, for a total of 918 out of 7,552 engaged—12% casualties, identical to the rate of loss in Crittenden's division.

4th Brigade
Brigadier General Lovell H. Rousseau

After a hard, short childhood, everything seemed to come easily to this gifted Kentuckian. The 43-year-old Kentucky native grew up on a hardscrabble farm in central Kentucky. Upon the death of his father, Rousseau became, at the age of 15, the breadwinner of the family. Determined to rise, he went to Louisville to study law, and in 1841 passed the Indiana bar and began practicing law with his brother and a senior partner from Indiana, whose daughters, Mary and Maria, both Rousseau brothers subsequently married.

The ambitious Lovell Rousseau rose from his law practice to a seat in the Indiana House of Representatives as a successful Whig candidate in 1844, but left the chamber the next year when he was commissioned captain in the Mexican War. At Buena Vista he got his first experience in combat leading his company of volunteers.

Returning from the war to a hero's welcome, Rousseau was elected to the Indiana Senate. He then moved back to Kentucky, where he resumed his law practice and became a leader of the local militia. He repeated his earlier political success, this time in Kentucky, and was elected to the state senate in 1860. There, as the Civil War approached, he took a bold stand against secession. When the war began he resigned his seat and, while Kentucky remained officially neutral, Rousseau covertly raised two regiments of

Unionist Kentuckians at his own expense at Camp Joe Holt in Indiana, across the Ohio River from Louisville. This unit became known as the Louisville Legion. When Louisville was threatened during the Confederate invasion of Kentucky in September of 1861, Rousseau led his Legion south, along with a battalion of Unionists in the Louisville Home Guard, and his show of strength saved Louisville from capture. That month, he was made colonel of the new 5th Kentucky Volunteer Regiment.

Promoted to brigadier general on October 1, Rousseau, at the head of a loosely organized force of a dozen regiments and batteries from Louisville, moved further south to the Nolin River, and there established a forward base which blocked the southern approach to Louisville, which he called Camp Nevin. The brigades that subsequently concentrated there would become the 2nd Division of the Army of the Ohio. However, Rousseau became ill, and General Sherman, who was head of the Department of the Cumberland, named Brig. Gen. Alexander McCook, a West Point graduate and Regular Army veteran, to the command of the troops at Camp Nevin. When he returned, Rousseau was given command the 1st Brigade of the division, redesignated the 4th Brigade when General Buell organized the Army of Ohio in November 1861.

The gruff, bourbon-drinking Rousseau had none of the credentials of the Regular Army man, McCook. Except for his Mexican War company, Rousseau had no military experience. However, he was a natural leader such as McCook could never be. As one admiring officer wrote, "When he showed himself on the battle-field, with his hat raised on the point of his sword, encouraging or urging them into the fight, his influence over them was unbounded. He was their Murat, their Ajax, and at all times, in season and out of season, they recognized him with cheers.... His fine physique, noble bearing, his thoroughbred horse and gorgeous trappings caught their eyes and aroused their enthusiasm. With all this splendor he was without ostentation, and he was easily approached."

Rousseau was dismissive of military training. This same observer acknowledged, "[even] if by reading the tactics and army regulations once over he could have been assured that ever afterward he would have known their contents, it is very doubtful whether he would have taken so much pains. But the men thought he knew it all." Rousseau came to be praised as one of the most conspicuous lights of the war and was eventually promoted to major general.

Before he sent his troops forward in his first battle, at Shiloh, Rousseau made a ringing speech that, according to one, drew three cheers and "cheered us up amazingly." "I tell you we w'ld have faced anything after that," wrote another.

Rousseau drew hurrahs when he passed among the men, even in divisions not his own.

Rousseau performed well and bravely at Shiloh and later at Perryville and Stones River. After missing Chickamauga, however, he was relegated to garrison duty by enemies in the War Department. He ran successfully for Congress in 1864, and after serving two tumultuous terms returned to the army where he was assigned first to Alaska, then as commander of the Department of Louisiana. He died in New Orleans in 1869 at age 50.

4th (Rousseau's) Brigade at Shiloh

Rousseau's 4th Brigade numbered 3,207 men in three volunteer infantry regiments—the 6th Indiana, 5th Kentucky, and 1st Ohio; plus three battalions of Regular Army infantry—the 1st Battalions of the 15th, 16th, and 19th U.S.

The three state regiments were formed early, of good material, but were still untested in battle. The 6th Indiana was the first regiment organized in Indiana for the war. The 5th Kentucky, the "Louisville Legion," was formed in 1836 and had fought in the Mexican War. The 1st Ohio was formed from old militia companies in the war's first week; its ranks were largely filled by young men from some of the wealthiest families of southwest Ohio. At Shiloh, original colonels still led all three regiments.

The three battalions of regulars were indistinguishable from volunteer troops, having been organized for the war. Like the state regiments, they were unfought. Their advantage lay in their commander, a 25-year veteran of the Regular Army.

The 4th Brigade was created in reaction to the Confederate advance into Kentucky and occupation of Bowling Green on September 18. Brig. Gen. William Sherman immediately ordered Rousseau to advance the Union regiments around Louisville about 50 miles south along the Louisville & Nashville Railroad to a bluff above the Nolin River.

The brigade's history between its creation in October 1861 and its appearance on the Shiloh battlefield on April 7, 1862 are sketched in the army and division histories above.

On Monday morning, Rousseau's brigade formed in line of battle on Crittenden's right at 8:00 a.m., in the order: 6th Indiana on the left, 1st Ohio in the center, the single battalions of the 19th, 15th, and 16th United Stated Infantry on the right, and the 5th Kentucky in reserve. The 15th Michigan was attached temporarily to this brigade and served with it all day.

At 9:00 a.m., Rousseau cleared his throat. "They had a little ball game yesterday and we'll have another today," he shouted gaily, "but we'll fix 'em! Shoot low, don't hurt 'em much. Shoot 'em in the shins!" With that, the brigade advanced across Tilghman Branch on the west side of the Corinth Road and engaged Trabue's brigade.

Here, Lt. Col. Manning F. Force's narrative of the battle, written from the point of view of the 3rd Division of Grant's army on McCook's right flank, gives some idea of the back-and-forth quality of the combat: "When Rousseau's Brigade was formed, his right was in the air. McCook, however, held it in place till Kirk's Brigade arrived, when Rousseau moved forward across a ravine to a rising ground a few hundred yards in advance. A company of regulars was sent into the woods in its front as skirmishers. In less than an hour the skirmishers were driven back, followed by the Fourth Kentucky Regiment and the Fourth Alabama Battalion, belonging to Trabue's Brigade. After a fierce attack for 20 minutes the assailants fell back before the rapid and well-directed fire of Rousseau's men, and retired out of sight in the timber. Trabue's regiments rallied and quickly returned to the assault with greater vigor than before. The steady fire of Rousseau's men again drove them to retreat. Rousseau then advanced into the timber and passed through it to an open field, when Trabue once more charged furiously upon Rousseau with his entire brigade. After a desperate struggle Trabue gave way leaving two guns in Rousseau's possession."

About 11:00 a.m., when Trabue retired, Rousseau advanced to Woolf Field, where he found the enemy on its west side. His ammunition being exhausted, Rousseau retired and Kirk's brigade took his place in the first line. As soon as ammunition was supplied, Rousseau's brigade again took its position in the front line and engaged S.A.M. Wood's brigade until it retired from the field.

At Shiloh, Rousseau's brigade lost 28 killed, 280 wounded, and 3 missing, for a total of 311 out of 3,207 engaged—11% casualties.

5th Brigade
Colonel Edward N. Kirk

Edward Kirk, age 44, started out as an Ohio Quaker school teacher. He subsequently studied law and established a practice in Baltimore. In the spring of 1854, he moved west to Sterling, Illinois, where in 1857 the prospering attorney built a large Italianate mansion that is still a showpiece today.

During the war's early days Kirk recruited and organized the 34th Illinois and served as its first colonel.

The 34th Illinois's regimental historian wrote of Kirk's "gallant and deliberate bravery" in a crisis at Shiloh. Kirk's habit of being in the front with his men resulted in wounds in both battles he participated in. Severely wounded in the shoulder at Shiloh and sent home, Kirk was returned to brigade command after his wound healed and was promoted to brigadier general on November 29, 1862. However, he showed poor preparation of his position at his next battle, Stones River. There, he was mortally wounded in the hip in a Confederate attack.

5th (Kirk's) Brigade at Shiloh

The 5th Brigade numbered 2,721 men in four regiments: the 34th Illinois, 29th Indiana, 30th Indiana, and the 77th Pennsylvania.

What would be Kirk's brigade at Shiloh was taken from the 2nd and 3rd Brigades at Camp Nevin. On December 2, 1861, Buell, the new commander of the Department of the Cumberland, redesignated these brigades as the 5th and 6th Brigades.

On January 9, 1862, Col. Edward N. Kirk's 34th Illinois was moved to the 5th Brigade and Kirk was placed in command of that brigade as senior colonel.

The brigade's history between January and its appearance on the Shiloh battlefield on April 7, 1862 are sketched in the army and division histories above.

At Shiloh, the 34th Illinois was commanded by its major and the 29th Indiana by its lieutenant colonel. The 30th Indiana and 77th Pennsylvania were led by full colonels.

The account by the 34th Illinois's regimental historian describes Kirk's brigade's approach to combat: "The men, weary from their march of 27 miles on Sunday, slept on boats which landed at sunrise on Monday morning. They immediately went ashore and marched toward the scene of conflict. General Rousseau's brigade was in advance of [Kirk's] brigade and drove the enemy some distance, while our brigade followed as their support until about 11:00 a.m., when, Rousseau's ammunition being exhausted, he sent word to Col. Kirk asking to be relieved. [Kirk's] brigade moved forward steadily and arrived at the edge of a narrow open field about a hundred yards to the rear of Gen. Rousseau's lines. They halted there until Gen. Rousseau retired. This consumed so much time that the enemy had an opportunity to re-form their lines and was ready for the brigade before they reached the position vacated by Gen. Rousseau."

Kirk's brigade then formed in the front line, behind the Water Oaks Pond, in the following order: 34th Illinois on the left, 30th Indiana in the center, and the

29th Indiana on the right. The 34th Illinois, in the first advance, passed directly through Water Oaks Pond. The 77th Pennsylvania was detached to the left.

The 34th's historian again takes up the narrative: "No sooner had they begun to advance than the swish of canister and the droning of musket balls began to give the men a new experience, and by the time they had gained the position lately occupied by Rousseau, 'music by the full band was turned on.' There was a slight elevation of ground covered with some underbrush just in front of the two right companies of the regiment, but the remainder of the regiment and the 77th Pennsylvania on their left were in the open and in full view of the enemy.

"Colonel Willich of the 32nd Indiana marched his regiment forward and asked leave of Col. Kirk to move his regiment to the front and make a charge. They moved forward, but upon reaching the slightly elevated ground they received staggering fire from directly in front, which checked them and caused them to retreat. The withdrawal of the 32nd caused some confusion in the 34th, which also received the effects of fire directed at the 32nd in addition to the fire it was already receiving from another battery.

"The fierceness of the attack staggered the regiment, and it wavered and might have been thrown into a panic except for the gallantry and deliberate bravery of Col. Kirk, who, with the only unwounded member of the color guard, advanced the flag and called on the regiment to rally to the color line, which it did with coolness and deliberation, and maintained the position, pouring a deadly fire into the enemy with great effect. At about 4:00 p.m. the enemy withdrew."

The fighting here was the last effort of the Confederates to hold their line, and closed the fighting for the day.

At Shiloh, Kirk's brigade lost 34 killed, 310 wounded, and 2 missing, for a total of 346 out of 2,721 present for duty—13% casualties, the highest rate in the division, though only by a slight amount. Individual regimental losses indicate that the fighting was heaviest on Kirk's left.

6th Brigade
Colonel William H. Gibson

At Shiloh, the 6th Brigade's commander, Brig. Gen. Richard W. Johnson, was sick, so command of the brigade fell to the senior colonel, the 49th Ohio's Col. William Gibson.

Known to everyone as "Bill," Gibson was a debater by training, but a warrior at heart. He was born in eastern Ohio in 1821, when Senecas and Mohawks still lived and hunted there. He went to school in a one-room log schoolhouse. With a

Puritan pedigree on his mother's side, he was raised to value hard work, plain dress, and temperance; to champion the unfortunate; and to oppose slavery and aristocracy. The Gibson family also emphasized good oratory and held regular family debates. Bill Gibson entered Ashland Academy in 1841, and there honed his oratory, learned the carpentry trade, and studied law.

Gibson was admitted to the Ohio bar, and entered politics in the 1840s as an anti-slavery Whig. When that party disappeared in the early 1850s, he helped organize the Republican Party in Ohio. With his flair for oratory, Gibson was a spectacular stump speaker. He was the first Republican elected Ohio State Treasurer in 1856, but in 1857 he was dismissed by Governor Salmon Chase for a discrepancy of nearly three-quarters of a million dollars, which had disappeared under Gibson's predecessor (and relative), but which Gibson covered up in order not to embarrass him. It was while Gibson was under this cloud that he answered Lincoln's Call for Troops in 1861—he saw the war as a chance to remove the stigma with manly action.

Gibson turned out to be a natural combat leader. One of his men enthusiastically wrote his hometown newspaper that "men will fight for Bill until there is nothing left to fight for," adding that Gibson was "endowed with Roman firmness."

After his excellent showing at Shiloh, Gibson frequently commanded a brigade, and briefly commanded a division in 1863. However, he could never rise to the rank of brigadier general because his promotion was blocked by Salmon Chase, his Ohio political nemesis, now a powerful member of Lincoln's cabinet in Washington.

After the war Gibson remained involved in Republican politics and also became a Methodist preacher before dying in Ohio in 1894.

6th (Gibson's) Brigade at Shiloh

Gibson's 6th Brigade numbered 3,074 men in four regiments: the 32nd and 39th Indiana and the 15th and 49th Ohio. The men of the 32nd Indiana were the standouts, crack German troops who had single-handedly fought and won the battle of Rowlett's Station the previous December.

By the battle of Shiloh, these four Indiana and Ohio regiments had spent almost six months together. At Shiloh, the two Indiana regiments were commanded by their full colonels. Command of the 15th Ohio had fallen to its major, and the 49th Ohio to its lieutenant colonel.

Gibson's brigade arrived on the field about noon, and advanced along the Corinth Road, stopping in the woods in the rear of Rousseau's brigade at Woolf Field. Rousseau's men were hard pressed and were nearly out of ammunition. The brigade moved forward to take Rousseau's place in line, with Kirk's brigade on its right. Gibson had three regiments, deployed from left to right: the 49th Ohio, 39th Indiana, and 15th Ohio. They opened their ranks to allow Rousseau's men to fall back, and then advanced across Review Field through shot and shell.

The first casualties were all wounded in the legs, showing that the Confederates had the training and discipline to fire low. A Confederate battery got the range of the 15th Ohio early in the action. As the brigade reached its positions, the order was given to lie down and open fire. Colonel Gibson described the action in his report: "The enemy's infantry...opened a terrific fire on our whole line simultaneously. The fire of the enemy's infantry was promptly responded to along our whole line. Our volleys were delivered with rapidity, regularity and effect." Both sides held steady, and the Confederates attempted to turn the left of Gibson's line, held by the 49th Ohio. Gibson changed front and repulsed the effort, only to have the Southerners re-form and try again, this time with a much larger force. As they launched their second attack, Captain Bouton, with two guns from his Chicago Battery (Battery I, 1st Illinois Light Artillery), arrived and quickly silenced the enemy's guns. Gibson was then able to straighten his line as the Confederate assault ground to a halt. With this threat removed, Captain Bouton took his guns to the left of the 15th Ohio's line, which was suffering much from the enemy battery that had been hammering them since they arrived. There, Bouton put the enemy guns out of commission.

General McCook personally detached Willich's 32nd Indiana from Gibson's brigade for a charge on the brigade's right, but Gibson controlled the rest of the brigade competently despite McCook's meddling. Gibson was complimented by Buell, McCook, and Rousseau after the battle.

At Shiloh, Gibson's brigade lost 25 killed, 220 wounded, and 2 missing, totaling 247 out of 3,170 engaged—8% casualties, the lowest rate in the division as a result of being the last engaged.

4th Division

Brigadier General William Nelson

Profane, headstrong, rude, weighing 300 pounds and standing six-foot four-inches, Nelson was a wrecking ball of a man—the most dynamic and the most disruptive of all of Buell's generals.

The son of a doctor, he had led a privileged childhood in Maysville, Kentucky. He was enrolled at Norwich University, a military school in Vermont, at the age of 13, but his classroom education was interrupted when a Kentucky congressman secured a commission for him as a midshipman in the U.S. Navy at the age of 16, and he spent the 21 years before the Civil War in various naval posts.

When the Civil War began, Nelson was a very visible presence at the Washington Navy Yard. In the early summer of 1861, President Lincoln charged him with overseeing the distribution of 10,000 arms to the loyal militia units of his home state of Kentucky. In August, at a time when Kentucky's neutrality policy was ending, recruits from those units were marched into Camp Dick Robinson, established in the rich Bluegrass region at the head of the Wilderness Road that led south to the strategic Cumberland Gap. In September 1861, General George H. Thomas was given command at Camp Dick Robinson, and Nelson, who was made brigadier general on September 16, organized a new brigade at Camp Kenton outside his hometown of Maysville, on the Ohio River in northeastern Kentucky.

During September and October Nelson mounted the Big Sandy Expedition in eastern Kentucky, succeeding in pushing most of the Rebels out of the region. After those operations Nelson returned to Louisville in November 1861, when Brig. Gen. Don Carlos Buell took command of the Department of the Cumberland and created the Army of the Ohio, effective December 2, 1861.

Buell shared Lincoln's admiration for the way Nelson got things done. When Buell established the 4th Division in early December, Nelson's headquarters were still at Maysville, making his the easternmost division, guarding the army's left flank. But Buell ordered the 4th Division immediately to Camp Wickliffe, south of Louisville and directly between the headquarters of the 1st and 2nd Divisions, ready in case either of those main posts should be attacked. Nelson's 4th Division numbered about 8,000 men in January 1862.

Nelson could be overbearing, inconsiderate, tyrannical, and foul-mouthed with his fellow officers. Admitting that he was a disruptive figure, General Buell nevertheless admired the "high tone" that he brought to his division.

Of Nelson, Buell said, "You can hardly say too much in commendation of him as a soldier. He was watchful about the well-being and efficient condition of his troops, exacting about the duty of his inferiors, habitually alert to the extreme of prudence, and yet bold and impetuous in action. He never hesitated about obeying orders, and he threw into his obedience the force of a conspicuously strong physical and mental organization. In view of his known character for energy and zeal, the attempt that has been made in certain quarters to impute tardiness to him on the march from Savannah to Pittsburg Landing ... is as puerile as it is groundless. ... [W]ith a complement of officers such as he proved himself to be, it would be difficult to limit the achievements of an army short of the utmost bounds of possibility. While holding up for deserved admiration his high qualities as a soldier, and his fine general attainments, you will not be able to acquit him of a sometimes harsh and imperious temper in command,—a blemish that unfortunately is not rare in the composition of a strong character."

Although he offended other commanders by what Buell called Nelson's "blemish" of temper, Nelson was generally well-liked by his men, and was always in the thick of the fighting. After Shiloh, a soldier in the 6th Ohio wrote, "Old Nelson is a gay fellow he was cool as a cucumber during the whole fight."

Nelson would not be killed by enemy fire, but murdered by another Union general. In September 1862, during the buildup of Union troops in Louisville to meet the approach of the Confederate army that would culminate in the battle of Perryville, Union general Jefferson C. Davis, angered by Nelson's characteristic brusque behavior, shot Nelson dead in a hotel lobby. Davis was never tried for the crime.

4th (Nelson's) Division at Shiloh

William "Bull" Nelson's 4th Division numbered 4,541 men in three brigades and attached cavalry. Nelson's brigadiers' quality was uneven: he had two West Pointers in Ammen and Hazen, and a horse breeder in Bruce.

The 4th Division made winter camp in mid-December 1861 at Camp Wickliffe, 30 miles south of Louisville, drilling daily for two months until mid-February 1862. During this time, Col. Hazen's 19th Brigade was organized on January 7, 1862, and Col. Bruce's 22nd Brigade was assigned to the division on

February 11. Nelson's division was unique in that he ordered the regiments of the 4th Division to engage in daily skirmish drill and specified that "particular attention will be paid to the instruction of the Officers in the bugle calls," which were necessary to give orders to skirmishers at great distances.

On February 14 the division marched to Louisville and there, on February 16, boarded steamboats with orders to move to Fort Donelson to reinforce Grant's embattled army. Before Nelson's arrival, however, the fort surrendered, so Nelson and his men remained on their transports and steamed up the Cumberland River to Nashville, arriving there on February 24, 1862. They were the first division of the Army of the Ohio to arrive at the Tennessee capital, and had the honor of capturing and occupying it. The other divisions of Buell's army followed after an overland march from central Kentucky, all arriving in Nashville by March 8.

The 4th Division spent three weeks in camp with the army at Nashville. During this time, Col. Milo Hascall's 15th Brigade was transferred to Brig. Gen. Wood's 6th Division. On March 16, Nelson's division started marching toward Savannah, Tennessee, with the main body of the Army of the Ohio.

On March 17, the army reached the Duck River at Columbia. The bridge over the river having been burned by Rebel cavalry and the river being very high, the army was delayed for two weeks repairing the bridge. Before this was finished, the river fell, and Nelson ordered the 4th Division to ford the river. It waded across on March 29 while the other divisions awaited the completion of the span, and Nelson's men hurried on to Savannah, which they reached on April 5, ahead of the rest of the army.

Savannah was on the eastern bank of the Tennessee River, eight miles north of Grant's army at Pittsburg Landing on the western bank. On April 6, while the battle raged at Shiloh Church, there were no transports available to carry Nelson's 4th Division to the Landing, and thick swamps discouraged a march toward the battle.

On the afternoon of the battle, however, a local pro-Union resident was found to guide the 4th Division through the swamps, and the advance finally started: Ammen's brigade first, then Bruce's, then Hazen's. At 5:00 p.m. the lead elements arrived at the crossing point on the east bank of the river. Desperate to begin moving his men across the river, Nelson commandeered any floating craft he could and pressed them into service shuttling men of the 4th Division to the west bank. Despite his best efforts, however, by the time the Confederates launched their final attacks around 6:00 p.m., only about 500 men of the division—the 36th Indiana of Ammen's 10th Brigade—had made it across. The rest of the division was over the river by 9:00 p.m.

The 4th Division brought no artillery to Pittsburg Landing. Brigadier General Nelson had been forced to leave it at Savannah.

On Monday morning at 7:00 a.m. the 4th Division formed on the north side of Dill Branch, on the far left of the combined Union armies. There, General Nelson awaited the completion of the line, with Ammen's brigade on the left, Bruce's in the center, and Hazen's brigade on the right, connecting with Crittenden's division. At 8:00 a.m. the 4th Division advanced, aided by General Beauregard's neglect to post the Confederate army where it could contest Nelson's crossing of Dill Branch. Nelson's brigades crossed the ravine unopposed and attacked the Confederates in the Peach Orchard. Mendenhall's Battery fought with Nelson's right and Terrill's Battery with his left. The division gained the south side of the Peach Orchard by 2:00 p.m., when the Confederates retired. This closed the battle on the army's left. The fighting appears to have been heaviest on the division's right; Hazen's brigade took the lion's share of the casualties, Ammen's brigade was least hurt.

The division remained in line until night and bivouacked with its left in David Stuart's camps, its right near Prentiss's former headquarters.

At Shiloh, Nelson's division lost 93 killed, 603 wounded, 20 missing, for a total of 716 out of 4,541 engaged—16% casualties, the heaviest rate in the Army of the Ohio.

10th Brigade
Colonel Jacob Ammen

At 56, "Old Jakey" (as his men enjoyed calling him) was Buell's oldest brigade commander. He was West Point-trained, but he had been out of the service for 24 years when the war began and was more of a teacher than a soldier. Still, he was a stickler for rigid discipline and strict adherence to Army Regulations.

Ammen was born in 1806 in Virginia, but early in life moved with his family to Brown County, Ohio, near Cincinnati. He graduated from West Point 12th out of 33 in the Class of 1831, then remained at the academy as an assistant professor of mathematics and instructor in infantry tactics, and later was an assistant professor of philosophy. After living the army life at garrisons in Connecticut and South Carolina, he resigned from the army in 1837.

For the next 12 years Ammen was an itinerant professor of mathematics, teaching at four different colleges in Indiana, Kentucky, and Mississippi. He then returned to Brown County and was the superintendent of its public schools from 1855 to 1861.

Even though he was in his mid-fifties at the outbreak of the Civil War, Ammen volunteered as a private. Within less than a month, however, he was lieutenant colonel of the 12th Ohio Infantry, and in June 1861, he was appointed colonel of the 24th Ohio, which he led in the skirmishes at Cheat Mountain and Greenbrier River in western Virginia.

When the 10th Brigade was organized at Camp Wickliffe in November 1861, Ammen, as senior colonel, became its brigadier.

Ammen was an aggressive leader. In a meeting with Nelson and Grant on Sunday morning, Ammen lobbied to push ahead to Pittsburg Landing in the hours before the battle of Shiloh, and he made sure his brigade would be the first of the Army of Ohio to arrive on the battlefield. Nelson had high praise for his handling of the brigade after the battle.

Ammen was promoted to brigadier general after Shiloh, but, perhaps because of his age, spent the rest of the war in backwater administration posts. After the war he became an engineer and surveyor, participating in preparation for the Panama Canal, before his death at age 87 in 1894 in Ohio.

10th (Ammen's) Brigade at Shiloh

Ammen's 10th Brigade numbered 1,876 men in three regiments: the 36th Indiana, the 6th Ohio, and the 24th Ohio.

The 10th Brigade was organized on December 2, 1861, at Camp Wickliffe, near New Haven, Kentucky, 30 miles south of Louisville. Jacob Ammen of the 24th Ohio, as senior colonel, was named commander.

At Shiloh, the 36th Indiana was the only regiment in the brigade under the command of its colonel. The Ohio regiments were led by lieutenant colonels.

Ammen's 10th Brigade crossed the Tennessee River at 5:30 p.m. on Sunday. Eight companies of the 36th Indiana and four companies of the 6th Ohio were formed a quarter of a mile in front of the crest of the bluff at Pittsburg Landing, in support of Stone's Battery. These companies participated in the final repulse of the Confederates Sunday evening.

On Monday, Ammen's 10th Brigade formed line of battle with the 36th Indiana on the left, the 6th Ohio on the right, and the 24th Ohio in reserve. After the brigade crossed Dill Branch, at 8:00 a.m. Ammen's men became engaged on the extreme left of the Union line, near the Tennessee River. At about 11:00 a.m. Ammen's advance was checked by an attempt by Confederates to turn his left. Reinforced by the 2nd Iowa, he repulsed the attack. He reached Stuart's camp at about 1:00 p.m., but retreated in the face of a Confederate counterattack, leaving Terrill's Battery to fend for itself. At 2:00 p.m. the brigade advanced again, and the Confederates retired from that part of the field.

After the battle, division commander Nelson praised Ammen, noting, "The style in which Col. Ammen handled his brigade excited my admiration." Later, he again called attention to Ammen, saying, "The cool, wary, and vigorous method in which he fought his brigade, protecting all the while the left flank of the army, gave me a profitable lesson in the science of battle."

At Shiloh, Ammen's brigade lost 16 killed, 106 wounded, and 8 missing, for a total of 130 out of 1,876 present for duty—7% casualties, the lowest rate in the division.

19th Brigade
Colonel William B. Hazen

William Babcock Hazen, 31, was exacting, aggressive, and quarrelsome. He made many enemies in the army by his contentious nature, but made many admirers by his abilities.

Hazen grew up on a farm in northeast Ohio. He graduated from West Point in 1855 and in the years before the Civil War served in posts in California, Oregon, Washington, and Texas, where he learned soldiering by fighting Indians. After recovering from a wound dealt him by Comanches in 1859—a bullet went through his right hand and lodged between his ribs—he taught tactics at West Point, where the war found him.

A committee of Ohioans petitioned President Lincoln on Hazen's behalf and secured his appointment to the colonelcy of the 41st Ohio Infantry regiment being organized in Cleveland. On October 29, 1861, the 41st was mustered in with Hazen at its head. Hazen was a strict disciplinarian, and posted long lists of rules that regulated every aspect of his men's lives. Letters home were filled with stories of Hazen's demands for strenuous drill, frequent cleanings, and long recitations of drill book routines.

Hazen's contentious nature was soon evident. In November 1861, in the 41st's first assignment up the Ohio River to a post opposite western Virginia, Hazen immediately became embroiled in an argument about jurisdiction with General William Rosecrans, the western Virginia department commander.

Later in November, Hazen and the 41st were ordered back down the Ohio to Louisville to join Nelson's 4th Division in the growing Army of the Ohio under General Buell. Hazen was given command of the 19th Brigade on January 3, 1862.

Hazen's excellence shone from early in the war, when division commander Nelson judged Hazen's 41st Ohio to be "the best reg't under my command, and the best commanded." At Shiloh, although Hazen had not fought a battle since his Indian-fighting days, he lost only one man missing in the confused fighting on the Union left on Monday. Young and vigorous, he personally led the 6th Kentucky in a bayonet charge. He had a habit of riding up and down his line, gesturing with his rattan horsewhip. One of his officers said later, "I remember distinctly that the sight of that switch steadied me."

He was a hero of the battle of Stones River at year's end, and a Union mainstay at 1863's Chickamauga. By the war's conclusion, Hazen was leading an entire corps as a major general.

After the war, Hazen continued his military career as an Indian fighter and Chief Signal Officer of the U.S. Army, continually squabbling with notable men, including George Custer, William T. Sherman, and Robert Todd Lincoln. He died in 1887 at age 56 in Washington, D.C., after taking ill at an affair hosted by President Grover Cleveland.

19th (Hazen's) Brigade at Shiloh

Hazen's 19th Brigade numbered 1,761 men in three regiments: the 9th Indiana, 6th Kentucky, and 41st Ohio Infantry. At Shiloh, the first two of these were under full colonels. Only Hazen's own 41st Ohio had fallen to a lieutenant colonel unused to command.

On January 7, 1862, the brigade was organized at the headquarters of General Nelson's 4th Division at Camp Wickliffe, near New Haven, Kentucky, about 30 miles south of Louisville, and at that time it consisted of Hazen's 41st Ohio, the 6th Kentucky, and the 46th and 57th Indiana.

In mid-February, the brigade was put on steamers to join Grant at Fort Donelson, but when it arrived at Paducah, Sherman detached both Indiana regiments from Hazen's brigade, and as Hazen wrote later, "I never saw them again." They were soon transferred to Pope's Army of the Mississippi, operating in Missouri.

At Nashville, the 9th Indiana, just returned from western Virginia, was assigned to the brigade. It was the brigade's most veteran regiment, coming to Buell's army after marching and fighting in difficult terrain. However, Col. Hazen was not impressed, writing, "I naturally expected more of it in the way of accurate soldiership than from the other regiments. On the contrary, it was not only far behind the others, but seemed fixed in many vicious habits, acquired while in the three months' service in Western Virginia."

Hazen's brigade reached the Shiloh battlefield at 9:00 p.m. on Sunday evening and bivouacked on the right of the division, behind Grant's siege gun battery, in the order: 9th Indiana on the left, 6th Kentucky on the right, and the 41st Ohio in reserve.

On Monday morning, the brigade advanced and was unopposed until about 8:00 a.m., when, as the brigade approached Wicker Field, Confederate infantry and artillery opened up. Hazen ordered a bayonet charge, and the brigade surged to the Davis Wheat Field, where the 41st Ohio captured a Rebel battery and spiked its guns. The brigade only held this advanced position a few minutes; it soon fell back, somewhat disorganized, to Wicker Field. Later, Hazen led a second bayonet charge to the Davis Wheat Field, where the brigade was shattered in an inclusive fight. It was here that Hazen, uncharacteristically, became lost in the woods. The brigade was not again engaged, and bivouacked there Monday night.

After the battle, division commander Nelson praised Hazen for his gallantry and wrote that the brigade "maintained itself gloriously."

At Shiloh, Hazen's brigade lost 48 killed, 357 wounded, and 1 missing, for a total of 406 out of 1,761 engaged—23% casualties, by far the highest rate in the Army of the Ohio.

22nd Brigade
Colonel Sanders D. Bruce

A lieutenant on General Nelson's staff derided Bruce as "a real Kentucky-Colonel type [who] kept a barrel of whisky on tap." He was no doubt voicing Nelson's own view. General Nelson had put Bruce under arrest during the winter, and the two men despised each other. (Bruce, it is fair to point out, was not the only officer to despise Nelson.)

Perhaps General Nelson thought Col. Bruce was a dilettante. The colonel, after all, was a country gentleman—a graduate of Transylvania University, a merchant, and a horse-breeder. Perhaps, too, what prejudiced Nelson against Bruce were his associations: Bruce was brother-in-law of Confederate cavalry raider John Hunt Morgan, and he had served in the pre-war Kentucky militia under Confederate general Simon Buckner.

Bruce's militia association with Buckner had been as captain of the Lexington Chasseurs militia cavalry. Once the Civil War began, these same militiamen combined with other groups to form the loyal 20th Kentucky regiment at Smithland, which was mustered into Federal service with Bruce as colonel on January 6, 1862. When the 1st and 2nd Kentucky regiments came back to Kentucky from western Virginia that month, they were brigaded with Bruce's regiment at Bardstown. Since the more veteran 1st and 2nd Kentucky regiments had recently had changes in command, the green-as-grass Col. Bruce found himself the senior officer, and was named commander of the 22nd Brigade on January 18, 1862.

Division commander Nelson was so contemptuous of Bruce's ability that, according to a staff officer, Bruce was "repeatedly in arrest and the brigade was practically in command of Col. Sedgewick" of the 2nd Kentucky. Nelson's report of the battle of Shiloh, while it praised brigadiers Ammen and Hazen, was conspicuously silent about Bruce. Further, Nelson's refusal to communicate directly with him evidently hamstrung Bruce's already meager ability to control his brigade: none of Bruce's subordinates mentioned Bruce in their reports, either.

There is no way of determining Bruce's ability once he was out from under Nelson, because he suffered a stroke less than two months after the battle which unfitted him for further field command. He moved to New York City after the war and became involved with horse racing and breeding before his death in 1902.

22nd (Bruce's) Brigade at Shiloh

The 22nd Brigade numbered 1,898 men in three infantry regiments: the 1st, 2nd and 20th Kentucky.

The 1st and 2nd Kentucky contained hundreds of Cincinnatians who had enlisted in Kentucky regiments at the beginning of the war, after Ohio had filled its quota of recruits. These two regiments were schooled in campaigning by five months' experience in the Kanawha Valley, in western Virginia.

On February 11, Bruce's new 22nd Brigade was assigned to Nelson's 4th Division, but remained in its camps while the other two brigades of the division were floated to Fort Donelson to reinforce Grant's army.

After the fall of Fort Donelson, Bruce's 22nd Brigade marched south in late February with the 1st, 2nd, and 3rd Divisions and rendezvoused with Nelson and the rest of the 4th Division in Nashville.

At Shiloh, the 1st and 2nd Kentucky were commanded by newly named colonels. The 20th Kentucky was commanded by a lieutenant colonel.

Bruce's 22nd Brigade held the center of Nelson's 4th Division all day, with Ammen's brigade on its left and Hazen's brigade on its right. Its regiments were arranged, from left to right: 2nd Kentucky, 1st Kentucky, 20th Kentucky. Advancing through the Wicker Field, the brigade was shelled by a masked battery near the Peach Orchard. The 2nd Kentucky was then ambushed by two regiments of Confederate infantry hidden in the underbrush near the battery, and fighting raged near the north end of the Sarah Bell Field. Bruce's men were engaged in a charge across the Peach Orchard, in which an enemy battery was captured, then lost again. At 2:00 p.m. the enemy retired and Bruce's brigade took position on the south side of Peach Orchard, where it bivouacked Monday night.

At Shiloh, Bruce's brigade lost 29 killed, 138 wounded, and 11 missing, for a total of 178 out of 1,898 engaged—9% casualties. The disparity between Bruce's brigade and Hazen's brigade to its right indicates that Bruce's brigade was held out of the hard fighting.

5th Division

Brigadier General Thomas L. Crittenden

The hard-living and hard-drinking Crittenden wore a felt hat folded up at the sides and was known as "Tom" to his friends. But he was high-born, the son of the Kentucky senator famous for the Crittenden Compromise in the Secession Winter of 1860. His family had then been ripped apart by the war: his brother was a Confederate general.

Crittenden, 41 years old at Shiloh, was admitted to the Kentucky bar as a young man, but volunteered as an aide to Zachary Taylor in the Mexican War and served as lieutenant colonel of the 3rd Kentucky Volunteer Infantry. After that war, he went to Liverpool to serve as U.S. consul.

Returning to Kentucky, Crittenden considered going into the family business by running for Congress, but thought being in Washington would worsen his bad habits. As it was, he was dismissed by one journalist as "a country lawyer." He stayed active in local military circles, however, and by 1860 was a major general in the Kentucky militia.

At the beginning of the Civil War, he helped recruit the 1st and 2nd Kentucky regiments and stayed in the rear to continue recruiting for the Union. He was appointed brigadier general on September 27, 1861, assigned to the command of troops organizing in Owensboro and Henderson. Despite the esteem that went with his name and high rank, however, Crittenden was undistinguished. When department commander William T. Sherman interviewed him before he went to Henderson to organize the troops there in early October, Sherman only muttered afterward, "He'll do." When Buell organized the Army of the Ohio on December 3 and designated the Owensboro troops as the 5th Division, Crittenden was still shadowed by doubt. "I don't know what to think of [Crittenden]," an officer confided to his wife on December 10. "He is a very fine man in his manners, easy and makes you at home at once; he possesses a great deal of pluck and courage I have no doubt, but whether he is the man for the place is the question—that is the question."

In his first battle, at Shiloh, Crittenden was the least effective of the Union division leaders. His command decisions were widely considered to have been suggested by those around him. The erratic pace of his division caused vulnerable gaps to develop between it and Buell's two other divisions. Crittenden delayed Nelson's men in the morning, and another hesitation around noon forced McCook to commit reserve units to protect his own left flank at the Review Field. Later in the day, he made the opposite mistake after he had driven the enemy from a position in his front—he pulled back to align his division with Nelson to his left. The enemy reoccupied the position, and Crittenden's men, especially Smith's brigade on his left, suffered needless casualties taking the position a second time. By the end of the battle, Crittenden had allowed his command to become so shamefully scattered that it drew Buell's attention.

After further disasters at Stones River and Chickamauga in 1863, Crittenden was discredited. He served for a time in the IX Corps in the East and then resigned. He remained active in veterans groups after the war before his death in 1893.

5th (Crittenden's) Division at Shiloh

The 5th Division was the smallest of Buell's three full divisions at Shiloh, numbering 3,825 men in two brigades and two batteries: Brigadier General Jeremiah T. Boyle's 11th Brigade, Col. William Sooy Smith's 14th Brigade, Capt. Joseph Bartlett's Battery B, 1st Ohio Light Artillery, and Capt. John Mendenhall's Battery H and M, 4th U.S. Artillery. Mendenhall's battery was Regular Army, and had returned in January 1862 from service against the Indians in the West. Crittenden's two brigade leaders were of wildly uneven quality: Smith, though only a colonel, was a West Pointer who was destined for division command in the Civil War, while Boyle was "political general," a highly visible Kentucky lawyer with no military experience.

On December 3, 1861, the troops organized at Henderson and Owensboro on the Ohio River in western Kentucky were designated the 5th Division in Don Carlos Buell's Army of the Ohio. These two posts straddled the mouth of the Green River, and the troops there were intended to guard the army's right flank in Kentucky. The 5th Division at that time consisted of two brigades: Col. Charles Cruft's 13th Brigade and Col. William Sooy Smith's 14th Brigade.

In January 1862 Brig. Gen. Thomas L. Crittenden marched the 5th Division, now grown to 5,000 men, south to Calhoun on the Green River, 50 miles from its confluence with the Ohio, to protect navigation on the river, and then he returned to Owensboro.

Early in February, in response to a request by Halleck in St. Louis, Buell sent Cruft's brigade of Crittenden's Division to Fort Henry to join Grant for his assault on Fort Donelson. Cruft's brigade remained with Grant thereafter, never returning to the Army of the Ohio.

On February 15, Buell ordered Crittenden to embark the remainder of his division at Owensboro and follow Nelson's 4th Division up the Cumberland River to Nashville. Crittenden's division arrived at the Tennessee capital after Nelson's men but before the rest of the army, which traveled overland from Bowling Green. The Army of the Ohio camped around Nashville until mid-March. On March 9, Brig. Gen. Jeremiah T. Boyle's 11th Brigade was transferred from George H. Thomas's 1st Division to the 5th Division, to replace the loss of Cruft's 13th Brigade.

The 5th Division departed Nashville with the rest of Buell's army on March 16–17, 1862, and was blocked at the destroyed bridge over the Duck River until March 30, when they forded the river the day after Nelson's 4th Division demonstrated that it could be done. The 5th Division then followed the leading 4th Division on the road to Savannah, 75 miles away on the Tennessee River. On Sunday evening, April 6, Crittenden's two brigades and two batteries steamed upriver from Savannah, arriving at Pittsburg Landing between 9:00 and 11:00 p.m., and bivouacked along the Corinth Road in the rear of Nelson's division.

On Monday morning the 5th Division lined up on Nelson's right at Cloud Field, at about 8:00 a.m., with Smith's brigade on the left and Boyle's brigade on the right. The division used the Eastern Corinth Road as its line of advance.

Bartlett's Battery, on the right near the fork of the Eastern Corinth Road, was engaged until noon, when it retired to Pittsburg Landing for ammunition. Mendenhall's Battery went to the left and was loaned to Nelson, supporting his right until after noon, when it took position in the rear of the 5th Division and was there engaged until the close of the action.

The two brigades of infantry were engaged along the Sunken Road and east of Duncan Field—the scene of the Hornets' Nest on Sunday—for about four hours, during which both brigades were repeatedly engaged. The 5th Division advanced, capturing some guns, then was repulsed and driven back to the road several times. At about 2:00 p.m., coincident with the Rebel withdrawal, it gained and held the Hamburg-Purdy road, which ended the fighting on that part of the line. At Shiloh,

Crittenden's division lost 60 killed, 377 wounded, and 28 missing, totaling 465 out of 3,825 present for duty—12% casualties, identical to the loss-rate in McCook's division.

11th Brigade
Brigadier General
Jeremiah T. Boyle

Boyle knew nothing of war, but he was one of the first prominent Kentuckians to help organize loyal troops in the state. On October 6, 1861, Bluegrass lawyer Jeremiah T. Boyle announced that he would put a hand to raising a brigade of four Kentucky regiments. Since the Lincoln administration was convinced that Boyle's deep Kentucky roots would be valuable in keeping Kentucky in the Union, he was minted a brigadier general.

Boyle, 43 years old at Shiloh, was raised in the rich region near Lexington, born to privilege as the son of a Kentucky Chief Justice. He studied at eastern universities, then returned to the Bluegrass to study law at Transylvania University in Lexington, and practiced in nearby Harrodsburg and Danville. In addition to his law practice, he was engaged in business with his brother-in-law, a former United States Congressman. Although a slave-owning Whig politically, he argued for a gradual emancipation of slaves. Boyle supported middle-of-the-road candidate John Bell for president in 1860, the leading vote-getter in Kentucky.

Boyle was the quintessential "political general." In the first winter of the Civil War, he raised a brigade of infantry for service in the Union Army. President Lincoln, anxious to win hearts and minds in Kentucky, saw men like Boyle as catalysts for Union feeling in the state, and General Sherman, as one of his last acts as head of the Department of the Cumberland, appointed Boyle a brigadier general, despite Boyle's total lack of military experience. On November 5, 1861, Boyle wrote his acceptance, adding, "I confess my want of military knowledge."

Having gone from private citizen to brigadier general with the stroke of a pen, Boyle was given command of the 11th Brigade of Buell's Army of the Ohio in November 1861.

It is perhaps a comment on Boyle's performance that, after Shiloh, Abraham Lincoln removed him from combat command and appointed him Military Governor of Kentucky, an administrative post.

Boyle spent most of his tenure as Military Governor responding to threats from Confederate guerrillas and raiders. In June, Boyle began implementing counterinsurgency tactics, particularly arresting Southern sympathizers and forcing them to pay for damages done by guerrillas. Kentuckians, both loyal and not, criticized these policies and wrote to Lincoln complaining about the situation in the state. They also charged that Boyle had used the military to influence state elections, particularly the 1863 gubernatorial election. That same year, when the Union began plans to enlist black soldiers in Kentucky, Boyle resisted and soon fell out of favor with Federal officials. On January 2, 1864, having lost support in both Kentucky and Washington, Boyle was removed from command.

In July 1864 Boyle resigned his commission. He returned to a business career and became involved in land speculation and the railroad industry. He died in Louisville in 1871.

5th Division, 11th (Boyle's) Brigade at Shiloh

On November 9, 1861, Boyle's 11th Brigade was among the original brigades created when Don Carlos Buell assumed command of the Department of the Ohio.

Nearly a month later, on December 5, the brigade, stationed in Columbia, Kentucky, was assigned to George H. Thomas's 1st Division in the Bluegrass region, on the left flank of the Buell's Army of the Ohio. At the time it included Boyle's own creation, the 9th Kentucky, and two Ohio regiments, the 19th and the 59th, the latter arriving in Columbia on December 11. Boyle's 11th Brigade marched to Bowling Green with the 1st Division in mid-February, where it was joined by the 13th Kentucky. It moved south to Nashville at the end of the month when the Army of the Ohio concentrated there.

In the days following the army's occupation of Nashville, the 11th Brigade was transferred to Crittenden's 5th Division, which had been recently depleted by the transfer of Cruft's brigade to Grant's army at Fort Donelson.

The four regiments of the 11th Brigade were all commanded by colonels at Shiloh. It was a talented group: three would rise to brigade commands, and two—the 13th Kentucky's Col. Edward H. Hobson and the 19th Ohio's Samuel Beatty—would be promoted to brigadier general.

On Monday morning, at 8:00 a.m., Boyle's 11th Brigade formed in rear of Smith's 14th Brigade in the order from left to right: 9th Kentucky, 13th Kentucky, and 19th Ohio, with the 59th Ohio in reserve. At about 10:00 a.m. it became engaged on the east side of Duncan Field, the 19th Ohio in front of Bartlett's Battery. Boyle's brigade relieved the 14th Brigade and was engaged on the front line in two or three engagements. It finally took position on the right of the 14th Brigade and held it until night.

At noon, the 19th Ohio was sent to the support of Nelson's 5th Division and was engaged in the Peach Orchard.

After the battle, Crittenden gave Boyle a boilerplate commendation, writing, "General J. T. Boyle behaved with conspicuous gallantry, sharing every danger of his command, inspiring his troops with a confidence and courage like his own."

At Shiloh, Boyle's 11th Brigade lost 33 killed, 212 wounded, and 18 missing, totaling 263 out of 2,145 present for duty—12% casualties, a lower rate than Smith's, but on par with the rest of the Army of the Ohio.

14th Brigade
Colonel William Sooy Smith

Smith, 31, was a civil engineer from a military family—his grandfather fought in the Revolution, and his father in the War of 1812. He grew up near Columbus, Ohio, and graduated from Ohio University in 1849 with an engineering degree before attending West Point, where he graduated sixth in the class of 1853. He quit

the army after one year to start his engineering career, first taking a position with the Illinois Central Railroad. In 1857 he was made chief engineer of the Trenton Locomotive Works, specializing in iron bridge building.

At the start of the Civil War, Smith returned to Ohio and trained recruits at Camp Dennison near Cincinnati. On June 26, 1861, he was appointed colonel of the 13th Ohio Infantry. His regiment marched and fought in the western Virginia campaign during the summer and fall, where he was mentioned for gallantry in the battle of Carnifax Ferry.

The 13th Ohio was moved to Louisville, Kentucky, in November, and Smith was elevated to brigade command—14th Brigade, 5th Division, Army of the Ohio—when Buell organized his army on December 2, 1861. Smith was one of the few brigade commanders in Buell's army with a West Point education.

When the 14th Brigade marched from Nashville to join Grant at Pittsburg Landing, Smith stayed in Nashville to take charge of repairs to the railroads there, and was reunited with his brigade on its march to Savannah, only one or two days before the battle of Shiloh.

Smith the engineer, able as he was, was apparently not charismatic, inspiring few remarks about his leadership. A week after the battle, however, William Sooy Smith was promoted to brigadier general. He later commanded divisions in the Army of the Ohio and the Army of the Tennessee, though is currently best remembered for his humiliation at the hands of Nathan Bedford Forrest at Okolana, Mississippi in 1864. He continued to excel in civil engineering after the war and lived until 1916, when he died at the age of 85.

5th Division, 14th (Smith's) Brigade at Shiloh

General Buell organized Col. Sooy Smith's 14th Brigade in early December, 1861. He organized Charles Cruft's 13th Brigade at the same time, and the two brigades comprised Crittenden's new 5th Division, guarding the right of the Army of the Ohio, stationed near Owensboro, Kentucky. In February 1862, when Buell's army started the advance southward that would end at Shiloh, Cruft's brigade was sent to Grant's army, and Smith's 14th Brigade embarked on steamboats to Nashville for the army's concentration there before the final long march to Savannah, Tennessee to join Grant.

At Nashville, the 13th Ohio regiment, which had been brigaded with McCook's 2nd Division since its return from western Virginia, was reunited with Smith (who had been its original colonel) and his 14th Brigade at Nashville. The 13th Ohio's men were the brigade's only veterans.

At Shiloh, the 14th Brigade numbered about 1,400 men in three regiments: the 11th Kentucky, 26th Kentucky, and 13th Ohio. Only the 11th Kentucky was led by its colonel; lieutenant colonels led the other two regiments during the battle.

On Monday, the second day of Shiloh, the 14th Wisconsin, which had just arrived at Pittsburg Landing to join Grant's army, was attached to Smith's 14th Brigade in time for its attack. That morning, Smith's brigade formed for battle at 8:00 a.m. between the Hamburg-Savannah Road and the junction of the Corinth Road and the Eastern Corinth Road. The regiments faced southwest, and were in the order, from left to right: 26th Kentucky, 13th Ohio, 14th Wisconsin. The 11th Kentucky was held 200 yards to the rear in reserve.

The brigade advanced, with its right on the Eastern Corinth Road, and became engaged along the Sunken Road. The first attack by Smith's brigade was completely disordered by crowding, and was probably not much more than an assault by a huge mob. The same ground was fought over three times. The brigade crowded through the thick brush, became entangled, and was forced to retire.

A second assault succeeded in capturing an enemy gun; however, disorganized after its charge, the brigade was again thrown back. In the final action about 2:00 p.m., the brigade finally succeeded in pushing as far forward as the Hamburg-Purdy Road, where Confederate resistance ended for the day. Here Smith's brigade captured some guns of Harper's Battery, which were successfully held as trophies. Many prisoners were also captured, among them Col. Battle of Tennessee.

At Shiloh, Smith's 14th Brigade lost 25 killed, 157 wounded, and 10 missing, for a total of 192 out of about 1,170 present for duty—16% casualties, a higher rate than Boyle's.

6th Division

Brigadier General Thomas J. Wood

Thomas J. Wood, 38 years old at Shiloh, was a career soldier, born in Munfordville, Kentucky, to a military family. He was the son of an army officer and Elizabeth Helm, who was a blueblood Kentuckian. Through the Helms, Wood was the cousin of Confederate general Benjamin H. Helm. (In turn, Benjamin Helm was an in-law, through Mary Todd, of Abraham Lincoln.) Wood was an 1845 graduate of West Point, finishing 5th of 41 cadets, and was commissioned as a second lieutenant in the United States Army Corps of Engineers.

In 1846, when the Mexican War erupted, Wood joined General Zachary Taylor's staff. However, he soon requested a transfer to a fighting unit. He joined the U. S. 2nd Dragoons and was cited for valor at Buena Vista. After that war, he served in a succession of cavalry posts on the frontier. On leave of absence from the army after 1859, Wood traveled in Europe until the start of the Civil War.

During the early days of the war, Wood helped organize several volunteer regiments in Indiana while still serving as an officer in the U.S. cavalry. In October 1861, he was promoted to brigadier general and given command of the 5th Brigade in McCook's 2nd Division at its creation in November 1861. On February 11, he was made commander of Buell's new 6th Division, in time for its advance to Nashville, Savannah, and Pittsburg Landing.

Later in the war, he became most renowned for obeying an order, at the battle of Chickamauga in 1863, to move his division to fill a gap which he knew did not exist. His division's departure left a division-sized hole in the line which Longstreet's wing of the Confederate army struck, winning the battle.

Wood's career not only survived the Chickamauga incident, esteem for his ability as a military leader was demonstrated by his promotion to major general in

January 1865. After the war, he retired due to disability from his wounds in 1868, and died at the age of 83 in Dayton, Ohio, in 1906.

6th (Wood's) Division at Shiloh

The 6th Division was a new creation. Buell organized it on February 11, 1862, while the Army of the Ohio was briefly in its camps around Nashville, before it undertook the march across Tennessee to join Grant's army. The division numbered about 2,000 men in two new brigades, the 20th under Brig. Gen. James Garfield and the 21st Brigade under Col. George D. Wagner.

At mid-day on Sunday, when Wood's vanguard was still 18 miles from Savannah, he received an order to push forward with his command. A second order followed which suggested that the enemy had made only a "forced reconnaissance," but that he should "press forward as rapidly as possible." He was hindered in this by the trains of the preceding divisions, so that "it was impossible to advance more than a mile an hour."

Wood, with Wagner's brigade, reached Savannah on Monday morning and Wagner's men boarded transports for Pittsburg Landing, followed by Garfield's brigade at noon.

Wood, with Wagner's brigade, did not arrive at the fighting front until about 2:00 p.m. He was ordered into line on Crittenden's right, but when Wagner got into position, the battle was almost over, and only one regiment of the brigade became engaged, and only for a few minutes—the 57th Indiana's casualties amounted to four men wounded.

20th Brigade
Brigadier General
James A. Garfield

It is no accident that Horatio Alger, writer of American rags-to-riches stories, chose James Garfield as the subject of one of his first books, *From Canal Boy to President, or the Boyhood and Manhood of James A. Garfield.* Garfield was the model of the successful American striver of the nineteenth century.

Born in 1831 in a log cabin just south of Cleveland, Garfield was raised from age two by his mother. He was physically clumsy— spectacularly at odds with axes as a youth, and a failure at his first career, at 16, as a canal boy on the Erie lakefront—but disciplined, ambitious, and a voracious reader. Once he settled on entering school, at the advanced age of 17, he excelled, graduating from Geauga Seminary in 1850; from Western Reserve Eclectic Institute in nearby Hiram, a one-building frontier college, three years later, in 1851; and from Williams College, in Massachusetts, in 1856, where he delivered the commencement address as a respected scholar in subjects from literature to metaphysics.

The restless Garfield soon turned from a career as a professor to politics. Returning to Ohio, he accepted an eager nomination by local Republicans and won a state senate seat, which he surrendered in 1861 at the outbreak of the Civil War. He had no military training, but read treatises on Napoleon and Wellington, alive to the promise of high political office that was awarded to successful generals. He offered his services to Ohio's governor, who in August 1861 named him as colonel of the 42nd Ohio regiment, whose muster rolls he helped to fill with his neighbors and former students.

On December 14, 1861, General Buell ordered Garfield and his 42nd Ohio from Camp Chase, near Columbus, where it was training, to Catlettsburg, Kentucky, on the border with western Virginia, at the mouth of the Big Sandy River, where 2,000 Confederates had recently invaded. General Buell gave Garfield a brigade and the task of driving the Big Sandy Rebels out of Kentucky. At a skirmish called the Battle of Middle Creek, on January 9, 1862, Garfield forced the retreat of the Rebel invaders. Although there were less than 50 total casualties, Garfield's "battle," along with the battle at Mill Springs little more than a week later, solidified Union control of east Kentucky for the next year.

The North was starved for good news from the front at the beginning of 1862, and Garfield gained national celebrity with the modest affair on the Big Sandy, which he pumped up, McClellan-style, with a proclamation to the Sandy River Kentuckians: "I have come among you to restore the honor of the Union, and to bring back the old banner which you once loved, but which, by the machinations of evil men, and by mutual misunderstanding has been dishonored." Garfield's Ohio supporters dunned the governor for a battlefield promotion for their favorite son, and in March 1862, Garfield received a promotion to brigadier general.

On April 1, Garfield and his command steamed to Louisville, where an order arrived from General Buell for Garfield report to the Army of the Ohio on its march toward the rendezvous with Grant's army at Savannah, Tennessee. Garfield left his 42nd Ohio and caught up with Buell's army about halfway between Nashville and Savannah. There, he was put in command of Buell's new 20th Brigade.

He would never lead it in battle, however. On April 7, Garfield's brigade reached the Shiloh battlefield in the early afternoon, and by the time he had rushed it to the front, the battle was over. That summer Garfield's health deteriorated and he returned to Ohio, where, during his convalescence, he was elected to Congress.

Before he took his seat, however, he returned to the field and became chief of staff to Major General William S. Rosecrans. Old Rosy gave him much responsibility in planning for the upcoming strategically significant Tullahoma Campaign in 1863. After being surprised and defeated at the battle of Chickamauga that September, Rosecrans was discredited and Garfield was considered as a replacement. Even though he was promoted to major general, the post went to General George H. Thomas instead.

Garfield left the field and took his seat in Congress. His political rise continued, and he was ultimately elected president in 1881, only to be assassinated by a disgruntled office-seeker 100 days after his inauguration.

21st Brigade
Colonel George D. Wagner

Thirty-one-year-old George Wagner was a farmer from Warren County in rural west central Indiana. In 1856, at the age of 25, he parlayed his prosperity as a farmer into a successful bid for a state legislature seat, riding the Republican surge in Indiana in that presidential election year. Two years later, he was elected to the state senate, and made president of the Indiana State Agricultural Society.

In the first summer of the Civil War, the 15th Indiana regiment was raised in nearby Lafayette, Indiana, and Wagner, the prominent farmer-politician, was installed as colonel. The regiment was immediately put on trains for western Virginia, and Wagner and his regiment joined General George B. McClellan's tiny Union army on July 11, during the battle of Rich Mountain, the battle which propelled McClellan to celebrity. Eleven days later, McClellan was invited to Washington to be the savior of the country, and the 15th Indiana served under General William Rosecrans, staying long enough to fight in the inconclusive skirmish at Greenbrier River in October before departing on November 19. Wagner's regiment reported to General Buell at Louisville at the end of November.

Buell put Wagner's regiment in Nelson's 4th Division, where it stayed in its mid-Kentucky camps for the winter months of December, January 1862, and the first part of February. The army started its march to Nashville in the aftermath of the capture of Ft. Donelson on February 10, and on February 11 Buell put Wagner at the head of the newly formed 21st Brigade, which was assigned to the new 6th Division under Brig.Gen. Thomas J. Wood when it reached Nashville. He would lead his 21st brigade as a colonel at the battle of Shiloh—what little combat experience he had in western Virginia was more than most brigadiers in Buell's army.

After Shiloh, Wagner led his 21st Brigade at the battles of Perryville—where it was the only brigade engaged in the entire 2nd Corps—and Stones River in 1862, and he was promoted to brigadier general in April 1863, one year after Shiloh. His brigade served through the Tullahoma campaign, at Chattanooga, and through the Atlanta campaign. He rose to command of the division when General Thomas stalked Hood's army back through Tennessee

Wagner suffered a reversal of fortune at the battle of Franklin on November 30, 1864, where he disobeyed orders with near-disastrous consequences for the Union army. In the face of the criticism that followed, he resigned, giving the reason that he had to return home to be with his dying wife.

After the war, he started a legal practice in Indiana, but the stress of the war had been too much for him. He died in 1869 of an overdose of the medication his doctor had prescribed to alleviate his nervous suffering.

21st (Wagner's) Brigade at Shiloh

Boats floated Wagner's men from Savannah downriver to Pittsburg Landing on Monday morning, April 7. It was almost noon before they reached the battlefield. Grant ordered the brigade to reinforce the left of the army, which, according to Wagner, was being "hotly pressed by the enemy."

The 57th Indiana regiment was first engaged, coming in on the left of General McCook. Here, the prose of Wagner's report turns purple, with the regiment "advancing upon the enemy under a heavy fire with the coolness of veterans until the enemy was driven from the field." According to Wagner, he brought up the rest of the brigade, and again advanced, "driving the enemy before us, until ordered to halt." At that point, "the enemy attacked us with infantry, cavalry, and artillery. The cavalry were soon dispersed by a few volleys from our advanced line with considerable loss to themselves."

Wagner reports capturing 40 prisoners. Division commander Wood was not present, being occupied with bringing up his other brigade—James Garfield's 20th, which did not reach the front in time to take part in the fighting. Wood, however, commended Wagner's men after the battle for "driving the enemy from his last strong stand, and compelling him, by a vigorous pursuit, into a rapid retreat."

In the fighting Wagner's command lost four men wounded, all in the 57th Indiana regiment.

Army of the Mississippi

General Albert S. Johnston

President Jefferson Davis had a military background. He himself had graduated from West Point, fought in the Mexican War, and served as Secretary of War under President Franklin Pierce. It is significant, then, that Davis considered Albert Sidney Johnston the greatest soldier in the country, an unmatched military genius.

At 59, Johnston was a magnificent-looking man standing taller than six feet, broad-shouldered and deep-chested, his features strong and handsome. He was dignified and eloquent, with a commanding presence to which other military men naturally deferred. His military reputation was unsurpassed. After graduating as a medical student from Transylvania University in his native Kentucky at age 15, he entered West Point, where he befriended Davis—who said that Johnston treated him like a younger brother. He fought in the Black Hawk War with Davis, then moved to Texas. He went from the rank of private to general in the Texas Revolution, and served afterward as the Secretary of War for the Republic of Texas. After Texas became a state, Johnston served in the U.S. Army in the Mexican War and was commended for bravery at the battle of Monterrey, where he again fought side-by-side with Jefferson Davis. He was by now a leading light in the U.S. Army—he was chosen to lead the Army's expedition in 1857 against the Mormons in Utah; fought against Native Americans in northern Texas; and when the Civil War broke out, he was commander of the U.S. Army's Department of the Pacific.

When word reached him of the secession of his home state of Texas, Johnston left his residence in San Francisco and rode overland across the entire continent to report in person to President Davis in Richmond, a five-month trek that seized the imagination of the entire South. When he arrived at the beginning of September 1861 to an ecstatic greeting at the Confederate White House, Davis immediately commissioned Johnston a full general—ranking him above all other active generals—and placed him in command of the Western theater, officially called "Confederate Department No. 2," a huge territory stretching from the Appalachian Mountains in the east through the Indian Territory in the west. Years later, U.S. Grant would say, "His contemporaries at West Point, and officers generally who came to know him personally later and who remained on our side, expected him to prove the most formidable man to meet that the Confederacy could produce."

His first act, a September advance into Kentucky on a broad front, was a successful bluff. For about five months, it deceived Union commanders, especially those in Louisville and Cincinnati, into thinking Johnston's force was stronger than it actually was. Obliged by lack of numbers to remain on defense in his department, his defensive line by October stretched thinly across the length of Kentucky.

There was no Union movement until the new year. The first battle, a Confederate defeat at Mill Springs in late January 1862, on the eastern end of Johnston's Kentucky line, was a setback for Johnston, but eastern Kentucky's vast wilderness presented as many problems as opportunities for a Federal advance in that direction. It was the disastrous surrender to Grant in western Kentucky, at Forts Henry and Donelson in February, that brought Johnston's bluff to an end and collapsed his defensive line. It also collapsed Johnston's reputation. To begin with, the miserable condition of those important forts was a result of months of neglect by Johnston, who had been preoccupied with the defenses of his immediate surroundings at Bowling Green, and had left the preparation of the forts to subordinates.

Even so, timely reinforcements by either Johnston from Bowling Green or his subordinate, Leonidas Polk, from Columbus on the Mississippi River, could have prevented the disaster at the forts, ended Grant's high-stakes gamble, and crushed Grant's army. But on February 3, when Brig. Gen. Tilghman at Fort Henry had wired Polk to send more men and guns, Polk refused, thinking that the attack was a feint, meant to draw strength away from Columbus, and that it presaged a major assault on his own "Gibraltar of the West" there. The responsibility for Polk's poor judgment ultimately lay with Johnston, whose control over his subordinates was everywhere loose and ineffective. He failed to order Polk to reinforce Tilghman.

Johnston himself duplicated Polk's failure of nerve. After the capture of Fort Henry, when the wires from the river forts told that Grant's army was turning toward Fort Donelson, Johnston held a council of war with subordinates General P. G. T. Beauregard and Major General William J. Hardee. They conceived a bold plan to transport Johnston's Central Army of Kentucky at Bowling Green by rail to Fort Donelson and crush Grant's isolated force, then return quickly before Buell, who had been inert for months, could capture Bowling Green. Johnston, however, decided on a cautious course. Convinced that Fort Donelson would soon fall to Grant's awesome gunboats, he decided to retreat Hardee's 16,000 men at Bowling Green to Nashville. Judging that he needed extra time for Hardee to safely cross the Cumberland River at Nashville, he ordered Generals Gideon Pillow and John Floyd to take command of the 9,000 central Kentucky troops closest to Fort Donelson, march there and keep Grant's army at bay as long as possible, then retire and join him for the defense of Nashville.

Here was another failure of judgment: Pillow and Floyd were weak reeds on whom to lean for the defense of forts that were the keys to Kentucky and Tennessee. Pillow was a spectacularly inept commander who had just resigned as second-in-command to Polk at Columbus. Floyd was a lawyer who had never seen a battle and who derived his lofty rank from the fact that he had been President James Buchanan's Secretary of War.

With Johnston, then, lies the responsibility for the catastrophe at the subsequent battle for Fort Donelson, where Grant's army succeeded in sealing off the escape of all but 2,400 of Pillow's army of 15,000. More than 12,000 Confederates—nearly half of Johnston's strength in central Kentucky—were captured and taken to prison camps in the Northwest, men who would be unavailable to Johnston in the weeks ahead.

Johnston evacuated his army from Bowling Green and reached his fallback position at Nashville, the center of the Confederate effort in the West, which was protected on its northern side by the Cumberland River. Here again was evidence of Johnston's lack of attention to critical details: when his troops reached the city, they were amazed to find that there were no fortifications built around Nashville, nor any other preparation for the defense of this crucial strategic prize. He retreated Hardee's men again, to Murfreesboro 35 miles to the southeast.

With the Tennessee and Cumberland rivers now flowing unvexed from deep within the Confederacy to the Ohio River, Johnston's forward defensive line was shattered from the Appalachians to the Mississippi. Richmond had sent General P. G. T. Beauregard to command Polk's large army in Columbus, but Johnston's and Beauregard's wings of the Western army were now separated by Grant's army at Fort Donelson, and, just as important, the Union troops' communications were swift and secure along the inland rivers. With those advantages, the Union armies of Grant and Buell could combine and crush each of the Rebel armies—Johnston's at Murfreesboro and Beauregard's at Columbus—in turn. It was obvious that Johnston and Beauregard must unite and, if possible, defeat any isolated Union forces that offered themselves as targets of opportunity as they advanced.

The point where the two armies would unite was the great question. It followed from an even greater question: which area of the West was more critical to the success of the Confederacy—the Mississippi Valley or central Tennessee? Strategically, the correct answer was central Tennessee. Nashville was to the West what Richmond was to the East: a capital of the region, a depot of supplies, a center of manufacture for ordnance and army supplies, and a rendezvous for civilian refugees as well as new recruits. From Nashville to Chattanooga and on to Atlanta ran a railroad that acted as an artery of supply for the region. The greatest strategic advantage of the region, however, was its distance from the Union-controlled waterways. Only here, in these inland fastnesses, could a Confederate army operate freely, safe from constant flanking by Union water-borne armies.

But Johnston here again surrendered the initiative, this time to his new second-in-command, Beauregard, who named Corinth, Mississippi—the key to the defense of the Mississippi Valley—as the place for the armies' concentration. The considerations that prevailed in Beauregard's mind were not strategic but political. The Southern aristocrats, concentrated in the cotton empire of the Mississippi Valley, with its "capital" at Memphis, would never consent to being sacrificed, even for the survival of the Confederacy. It would be the Mississippi Valley, then, that would be defended, even though with the water routes in Union hands, that defense must ultimately fail.

In this period after the debacle at the river forts and Johnston's subsequent retreat, the rise of Beauregard's influence was due to the ruin of Johnston's popularity in a Southern population that, like the Northern generals, thought Johnston's army was stronger than it really was. A false rumor spread that Johnston had been drunk when Donelson surrendered. The Tennessee Legislature sent delegates to Richmond demanding Johnston's removal "because he is no general." The troops, too, were disheartened and lost faith in their leader.

Much of the blame for the collapse in Johnston's Western Department, in fact, lies with the Richmond government. The general's appeals for reinforcements in late 1861 had fallen on deaf ears—rather than the needed troops, Richmond sent Beauregard. Now Johnston deferred to Beauregard, not only in the choice of the concentration point for the armies, but also in the planning of the attack on Shiloh.

When Johnston, at the head of his army, reached Corinth after a month-long withdrawal across Tennessee, eyebrows were raised when he offered command of the combined army to his subordinate, Beauregard. Johnston's son later explained why Johnston thought the gesture only proper: "General Johnston felt constrained to make this offer, because he had brought with him the smaller fraction of the united forces, and he was on a field that he had set apart for Beauregard's control. That officer had been for some time on the ground, and [Johnston] was unwilling that a subordinate should suffer by his arrival." The younger Johnston immediately adds, "it was in no wise his intention to abdicate the supreme command, or the superintendence of affairs in the management of the department or the movements of the army." Beauregard was too sick for the rigors of full command, and he refused Johnston's proposal, but the result of Johnston's over-generous offer was the dangerous one of confirming Beauregard's belief in his own *carte blanche* in the decisions of the next few days.

In most cases, when Johnston appeared to be merely an onlooker it was because his subordinate needed no correction. In one important particular, however, the army suffered because Johnston failed to insist on his own way. In an April 3 dispatch to President Davis, Johnston outlined his own, superior plan of attack, where the corps would attack side by side—Polk on the left, Hardee in the center, and Bragg on the right, with Breckinridge in reserve. Before the battle, however, Beauregard substituted his own flawed plan, in which the corps lined up one behind another. Johnston discovered the change when the army was marching toward Shiloh, but he considered it too late to reverse the order. Here, Johnston, ever the gentleman, was responsible for accepting an attack formation that ensured that the Confederate lines would become tangled once the fighting began, resulting in confusion and delay.

During the last hours before the attack, it was Johnston's resolve and good judgment that steadied the army on its course when Beauregard, his nerve failing, despaired that surprise had been lost and wanted to call off the attack and return to Corinth.

Johnston committed one final failure of judgment, however, and it was fatal to him. In the battle, Johnston insisted on taking a place at the front with the men, more like a brigade or division commander, leaving Beauregard to take the army leader's customary position at the rear, directing the movement of reserves and supplies. Johnston's decision would alter the future of the Confederacy. He was hit behind the knee by a bullet about mid-afternoon. The bullet severed an artery, and Johnston, who a few minutes earlier had detached his personal surgeon to care for a group of injured soldiers, quickly bled to death. He would be the highest-

ranking soldier to die in battle on either side during the war. After the war, Davis wrote, "When Sidney Johnston fell, it was the turning point of our fate; for we had no other hand to take up his work in the West."

General P. G. T. Beauregard

In the first year of the war prior to the battle of Shiloh, the idol of the Confederacy was not Robert E. Lee, nor even Jefferson Davis. It was General Pierre Gustave Toutant Beauregard.

In April 1861, he was "The Hero of Sumter," extravagantly and often praised for demanding the surrender of the Charleston fort, then pummeling it into submission.

Summoned to Richmond as a savior, his train was stopped at every station by jubilant, adoring crowds. In Virginia, with Northern newspapers shouting, "On to Richmond!" he was given the task of planning for the impending first battle with Union troops. In that battle, Beauregard's green Confederate army routed the equally green Union army. "The Hero of Sumter" became "The Hero of Manassas," and his fame and popularity rose to new heights.

Not only was he hailed as the hero of the first two victories of the South in its war for independence, he was the most colorful general in the Confederacy. He was an exotic in the overwhelmingly Anglo-Saxon Southern army, born in Creole Louisiana to French-speaking sugar cane plantation owners with pedigrees from *Ancien Regime* France. He did not even speak English until he was sent to boarding school in New York City when he was 12 years old. His image, carefully burnished (a slave waxed his short mustache every morning), conjured a chivalric, romantic, Old World vision. He was stern and proud, with the arrogance of a man born and bred to command. People called him "The Young Napoleon."

He had the unfortunate habit, however, of angering high-ranking men around him. In the months following the victory at Manassas, he angered Jefferson Davis himself, criticizing the president in his public report of the battle. Davis was well known to be thin-skinned, and in January 1862 he responded to Beauregard's slight by removing the Creole general to the Western Theater of the war.

Beauregard was now second-in-command to the leader in that theater, General Albert Sidney Johnston, ordered to report to his new post in command of Major General Leonidas Polk's army at Columbus, Kentucky, the "Gibraltar of the West" on the Mississippi River.

Beauregard welcomed the change of scene. He was bored with the military stalemate in the East that had prevailed after Manassas, chafing as second-in-command to General Joseph E. Johnston of the Virginia army, and anxious to escape the political labyrinth in Richmond. Beauregard had never been a good second-in-command to anybody, which was why he was being ordered out of Virginia. Vain and headstrong, he was a man of fantastic schemes. He believed the West would be the proper theater for the grand scope of his plans, which now were to unite Major General Earl Van Dorn's Arkansas force with Polk's at Columbus and march triumphantly into the Union stronghold at Cairo. In early February 1862, cheering multitudes crowded railroad stations along his route from Richmond to Nashville, where he was presented to the state legislature.

Beauregard went from Nashville to Bowling Green to confer with General Johnston and Major General William J. Hardee. What he learned stunned him. Things in the West were much worse than he had been led to believe. He found that "present for duty" figures for the Western army that he had been shown before he left Virginia had been vastly inflated. There would be no crushing offensives from Columbus.

And there was a new reason that Confederates could mount no offensives in the area dominated by major rivers. In January 1862, Union ironclad gunboats steamed into view for the first time.

Grant's attack on the Confederate line at Fort Henry was launched on February 6, during Beauregard's visit to Bowling Green. After Fort Henry was captured, Beauregard, on the train ride to his new command in Columbus, became bedridden in Jackson, Tennessee, by a relapse of a painful recurring throat condition. From his sickbed, however, Beauregard's dominant personality asserted itself. While Johnston was retreating his Bowling Green force into Tennessee, Beauregard, through a flurry of communications with western Confederate governors, other military leaders, and the administration in Richmond, succeeded in combining Polk's western Tennessee army with Major General Braxton Bragg's Gulf army and regiments sent north from Louisiana under the banner of what Beauregard now called his "Army of the Mississippi." He also adopted a superior tone in his dispatches to Johnston, suggesting that Johnston join him at the vital rail hub of Corinth, Mississippi.

Once Johnston's Bowling Green force united with Beauregard's army at Corinth in the last week of March 1862, Johnston remained passive while Beauregard advanced his plan for the corps organization of the new army, and dictated the Confederate movement toward Grant's army camped at Pittsburg Landing. To the men in the ranks, it was the popular "little Napoleon" who was doing the lion's share of the planning. It was Beauregard who seemed the prime mover as the surprise attack on Grant's Army of the Tennessee was set in motion.

Beauregard's sense of *carte blanche* in the organization of the attack resulted in his insistence on a flawed plan in which the corps lined up, one behind the other, in miles-long lines. This had the inevitable result of causing the commands to be inextricably mixed and scattered once the Rebel lines came crashing into the enemy camps. Beauregard's influence was damaging, too, in its concentration of strength on the left of the assault, rather than on the right, where Johnston intended it to accomplish his plan to pry Grant's army away from its river lifeline at Pittsburg Landing and destroy it by driving it inland against the impassable swamps of Owl Creek. Beauregard would be criticized for stopping the Shiloh attack late in the afternoon, but it was in fact his initial organizational mistakes that doomed Confederate success on the first day of the battle.

Beauregard's great failing on the second day of the battle was, again, before its outset rather than at any point during the actual fighting. Relying on a mistaken report that Grant's relief, Buell's Army of the Ohio, was in northern Alabama and would not arrive, Beauregard was overconfident, convinced that the second day would only be a mopping-up of Grant's defeated army. The Young Napoleon neglected to reorganize or resupply his own scattered units, which he allowed to bivouac wherever was convenient the evening before. He thus allowed his Army of the Mississippi to go into battle unprepared against an army that had been reinforced by 24,000 men.

Despite his ongoing feud with Jefferson Davis, Beauregard continued to play major roles in the war and also afterward among veteran groups, upon returning to New Orleans. He died peacefully in 1893 at the age of 74.

Army of the Mississippi at Shiloh

The Army of the Mississippi began as the creation of Tennessee's Governor Isham Harris. Harris rebuffed Lincoln's Call for Troops on April 15, 1861, with a bugle blast: "Tennessee will not furnish a single man for coercion, but fifty thousand if necessary for the defense of our rights or those of our Southern brothers." He then set to work in earnest, building the army he needed to defend

Tennessee's rights as he saw them. When Harris transferred his Provisional Army to Confederate service three months later, it would boast 24 regiments and 10 artillery batteries, with an Engineer Corps, Quartermaster and Ordnance departments, and an Ordnance bureau.

It was no accident that the Tennessee Provisional Army's command was headquartered at Memphis, which after New Orleans was the biggest Southern city on the Mississippi River. When the Mississippi became closed to all but Confederate traffic below its confluence with the Ohio, the outcry in the Northwest had been bitter and vehement, and it was sure that the dispossessed Union states would try to regain control of the river, which was the longest, widest highway for the movement of commodities in America. Besides its strategic importance, the fertile land fronting the Mississippi River was the obsession of the most influential group in Tennessee, the cotton planters in the Mississippi Delta, whose unofficial capital was Memphis. After Tennessee joined the Confederacy on June 10, 1861, Memphis was an armed camp for months.

For these reasons, Governor Harris, who was charged with recruiting and organizing an army for the defense of the whole of Tennessee, concentrated almost exclusively on defending his state's bank of the Mississippi River against invaders that were sure to float down from all the northern states in the Mississippi and Ohio river valleys. He ignored the defense of the northern border of Tennessee, trusting the neutrality of Kentucky to protect that 350-mile expanse. He ignored also the Tennessee and Cumberland rivers, two highways into the Confederacy with hardly less strategic importance than the Mississippi, but without wealthy interest groups to agitate for their defense. Fort Henry and Fort Donelson, the lone defenses against invasion on the Tennessee and Cumberland, respectively, remained unfinished throughout the first summer of the war. Harris was busy constructing forts on the Mississippi, and concentrated 15,000 men in those strongpoints, leaving fewer than 4,000 to guard Nashville and all of middle Tennessee, and only one post, at Knoxville, in eastern Tennessee.

When Leonidas Polk, who had been Bishop of Louisiana for the previous 20 years, came to Tennessee in the first weeks of the war to oversee progress on his University of the South, Governor Harris, knowing that Polk was an old West Point friend of Jefferson Davis, met with him and asked him to go to Richmond as an envoy to plead for more men and supplies for Tennessee. Polk agreed. He met with President Davis, and on July 4, Davis created a new department in the West, "Department No. 2," and sent Polk, who had left the army after his graduation from West Point in 1827, back to Tennessee as the major general in command.

Department No. 2 was considered the most important area in the Confederacy, excepting only Northern Virginia. It included western Tennessee between the Mississippi and Tennessee rivers, where the cotton interests ruled. It also included the counties adjacent to the Mississippi River, on both sides, all the way down to the Red River in Louisiana. Not only did the inexperienced Polk have the same urgency as Governor Harris for men and defenses along the Mississippi River, but the same unconcern for everything east of it.

Upon arriving in Tennessee, Polk soon became anxious about the Mississippi riverfront in Kentucky, which, he was convinced, was about to be invaded by Union troops. He conceived the high bluffs at Columbus, just south of where the Mississippi and Ohio rivers met, to be the indispensable anchor to the defense of everything on the Mississippi downriver. So on September 3, 1861, consulting neither Tennessee Governor Harris in Nashville, nor Kentucky Governor Magoffin in Frankfort, nor Confederate President Davis in Richmond, he sent a column under Brig. Gen. Gideon Pillow to invade Kentucky and seize the city. Kentuckians along the whole length of the state were shocked by Polk's dash for Columbus, and the Kentucky state government swooned into the arms of the Union.

Polk's invasion is generally considered to be one of the biggest strategic blunders of the Civil War. It prompted Ulysses S. Grant in Cairo to move into Kentucky to seize Paducah at the mouth of the Tennessee River on the Ohio; and Smithland at the mouth of the Cumberland, ten miles east of Paducah. Most destructive was the fact that, in one stroke, Polk's invasion uncovered the 350-mile stretch of the northern border of Tennessee that the neutrality of Kentucky had until then protected.

Polk had long thought that the command of the West properly belonged to his West Point classmate General Albert Sidney Johnston, who since the beginning of the war had been unavailable, while crossing the continent on horseback from his post in California. Johnston arrived in the Confederate capital just as Polk was precipitating the uproar in Kentucky by his move to Columbus. On September 10, Davis gave Johnston command of Polk's Department No. 2, now enlarged to include Arkansas, Missouri, Kentucky, all of Tennessee, and the western half of Mississippi.

Johnston's department, now called the "Western Department," contained 27,000 troops when he took over in September 1861. The lion's share, about 21,000 men, were Polk's. Of these, almost 20,000 were manning forts along the Mississippi River, from Columbus to Memphis. Polk had assigned only 1,400 men to guard the 100 miles between the Mississippi and Tennessee rivers. Only 6,000 troops were scattered throughout the rest of Tennessee. Forts Henry and Donelson remained in pitiful condition.

Johnston's first anxiety was for Tennessee's northern border. He ordered Brig. Gen. Felix Zollicoffer at Knoxville to occupy Cumberland Gap in Kentucky to anchor his line on its eastern end. Thus, when Johnston reached Nashville and took command of his department on September 14, 1861, his left and right flanks—Polk in Columbus and Zollicoffer at Cumberland Gap—were forward of his center, at Nashville. The Tennessee capital was the strongest defensive position for his center, secure behind the barrier of the Cumberland River, but Johnston judged that to move his center forward would relieve the threat to his advanced flanks, guard the fertile grain fields north of Nashville, and disguise the weakness of his center with a bold move. Brigadier General Simon Bolivar Buckner, an able general who had been at the head of the pro-secession "State Guard" militias in Kentucky during its neutrality, had recently resigned in Kentucky and had sped to Nashville to join Johnston.

Johnston put Buckner at the head of 4,000 volunteers hastily assembled at Nashville. They boarded railroad cars and rolled northward 70 miles, arriving on September 18 at Bowling Green, behind the Big Barren River, where they blocked any enemy advance toward Nashville along the Louisville & Nashville Railroad. In keeping with Northern generals' chronic habit of overestimating Rebel forces, the Union department heads in Louisville—Brig. Gen. Robert Anderson in September, then Brig. Gen. William T. Sherman in October—vastly overrated Buckner's force and panicked at the threat to Louisville. Buckner's numbers at Bowling Green were inferior to the Union army in Louisville, but the Union leadership would remain too timid to approach the modest Confederate outpost for the next several months.

While the Union army in Kentucky spent the rest of 1861 organizing instead of advancing, Johnston ordered every available reinforcement, including Hardee's 3,600-man Arkansas army, to Bowling Green. Most importantly, Johnston himself joined the troops assembled there in mid-October, where he personally oversaw this small army, which he called the "Central Army of Kentucky."

Johnston succumbed to the common delusion of generals that the enemy will surely attack where they themselves are, and he became convinced that the Union army's advance in the West would be by Major General Don Carlos Buell's Army of the Ohio, based in Louisville, to capture Nashville by way of the Louisville & Nashville Railroad, through Bowling Green. In doing so, Johnston ignored the other enemy armies: Major General Henry Halleck's in Missouri and Illinois, and Brig. Gen. George H. Thomas's huge division in eastern Kentucky.

Polk shared Johnston's delusion: he expected a momentary attack on his own position in Columbus, and he also was too preoccupied with his own post on the Mississippi to mind the river defenses at Forts Henry and Fort Donelson. Polk placed Brig. Gen. Lloyd Tilghman in command at Fort Henry in December, but both he and Johnston ignored Tilghman's warnings that "instant and powerful steps must be taken" to improve the works at both Fort Henry and Fort Donelson, and that "I shall require a stronger infantry force also on these points."

Winter slowed movement in the West on both sides until mid-December, when Buell cautiously advanced McCook's division south along the Louisville & Nashville Railroad line to Munfordville on the Green River. This forward movement, hesitant as it was, halting 40 miles away from Bowling Green, had the effect of confirming Johnston in his belief that the main Union thrust would be aimed at Bowling Green. On December 24 he ordered the transfer of Bowen's Division of two brigades from Polk's force around Columbus to Bowling Green.

By the end of 1861, Johnston's defensive line had stabilized. The number of troops present was as follows, from left to right:

At Fort Smith, Arkansas, under Major General Earl Van Dorn, were 5,600 men.

In the forts along the Mississippi under Major General Leonidas Polk—after his transfer of Bowen's Division to Bowling Green—were 21,800 men.

At Forts Henry and Donelson, Tilghman reported 4,000 men at Ft. Henry and 3,500 at Ft. Donelson.

At Hopkinsville, about midway between Forts Henry and Donelson and Bowling Green, under Brig. Gen. Charles Clark, were 2,300 men.

At Bowling Green, in the Central Army of Kentucky under Major General William J. Hardee, were 20,000 men.

In what Johnston called the "Eastern Tennessee Army," Major General George B. Crittenden was newly in charge of Zollicoffer's force of 6,300 men.

In the rear, there were 6,000 volunteers in camp in Tennessee.

On the Confederate right, Zollicoffer had, from the beginning, been charged with covering the longest section of the line with the smallest force and with the fewest adequate weapons. It was also the region barest of supplies, with the roughest terrain, the worst roads, and the most hostile local population. In January 1862, General Crittenden, finding Zollicoffer's poorly trained, flintlock-armed force exposed north of the rain-swollen Cumberland River, ordered him to strike the 10,000-strong force under George H. Thomas before Thomas could combine with another nearby Union force and crush Zollicoffer. On January 19, 1862, at the battle of Mill Springs, in rough terrain and in a driving rainstorm, a confused Zollicoffer rode toward the Union lines in his white raincoat and was killed, and his troops broke and ran. Crittenden succeeded in getting the survivors to safety across the Cumberland River, but his army had to leave all its artillery and supplies on the north bank. During the crushing defeat and the following 80-mile retreat to Carthage, Tennessee, much of Crittenden's army melted away. The right flank of Johnston's defense of the West had collapsed.

In the same week, General P. G. T. Beauregard in Virginia accepted the offer from the War Department to take command of Polk's wing of the Western army at Columbus and act as second-in-command to General Albert S. Johnston in the West.

News of Beauregard's arrival in the Western theater sped to the Union generals, who, guessing (wrongly) that he must be bringing a powerful Eastern contingent with him, hurried up Grant's plan for a strike on the middle of the Confederate line, at Fort Henry. On February 6, 1862, during Beauregard's first meeting with General Johnston at Bowling Green, there came news of the surrender of Fort Henry to an amphibious attack—the new, terrible ironclad gunboats' 65 guns had quickly silenced the 12 guns at Fort Henry and captured the fort without help from the infantry. The fall of Fort Donelson, and with it, the capture of 12,000 Confederate troops inside, followed ten days later.

On February 15, at the conclusion of his meeting with Johnston at Bowling Green, Beauregard took the train to Columbus to meet his new command, but was afflicted with the recurrence of a chronic throat illness which prevented him from traveling any further than Jackson, Tennessee. From his sickbed, Beauregard took the initiative in preparing for the next crucial battle in the West.

Johnston's and Beauregard's wings of the Western army, now separated by Grant's army at Fort Donelson, were now each in danger of being defeated in detail, and must unite. There were two great railroads that were available to bring Beauregard's and Johnston's armies together. The two railroads resembled the hands of a clock reading 11:15. The Mobile & Ohio Railroad was the short hand that ran roughly south from Polk's army at Columbus. The Memphis & Charleston Railroad was the long hand that ran east-and-west just below Tennessee's southern border, and could transport Johnston's army west to meet Beauregard. The two railroads met at the middle of the dial, at Corinth, Mississippi, a crossroads town adjacent to the Tennessee River. Once it was decided that the Mississippi Valley must be saved at the expense of central Tennessee, it followed that Corinth could not be lost, and Johnston agreed with Beauregard's suggestion that here was the proper place to combine.

On February 25, Beauregard ordered Polk to withdraw his force from Columbus and move south along the Mobile & Ohio Railroad. At the same time

Beauregard wired all the Confederate governors in the West and made an urgent plea for reinforcements. His most important telegram, however, was the one to Richmond asking Inspector General Samuel Cooper to send him Major General Braxton Bragg from Pensacola. "When well, I will serve under him, rather than not have him here," wrote Beauregard.

His uncharacteristically submissive tone struck just the right note with Bragg. When Cooper telegraphed Bragg to recommend the move, Bragg immediately began the removal of 10,000 men from his Pensacola and Mobile garrisons to Corinth. He went ahead to meet personally with the ailing Beauregard, and in early March received Beauregard's permission to organize the new army and issue orders in his name. Bragg, appalled at the lack of discipline and drill among Polk's troops, organized the reinforcements coming into Corinth and exercised his soldierly influence on the assembling army in the month before Shiloh.

One salutary effect of the disaster at Forts Henry and Donelson was that it got the attention of Richmond. New Secretary of War Judah Benjamin wrote Johnston, "The condition of your department, in consequence of the largely superior forces of the enemy, has filled us with solicitude, and we have used every possible exertion to organize some means for your relief."

Besides the telegram to summon Bragg's Pensacola and Mobile troops, Secretary Benjamin shifted eight regiments from Virginia to eastern Tennessee to allow Crittenden's army stationed there to join Beauregard, Johnston, and Bragg in Corinth.

In addition, Benjamin ordered Major General Mansfield Lovell, defending New Orleans, to withdraw "five or six regiments of his best troops" and send them to Corinth. Those regiments, 5,000 strong, would soon arrive under the command of Brig. Gen. Daniel Ruggles.

Because the Confederacy was so extravagantly dedicated to the sovereignty of the individual states, the sacrifice of the Gulf States in sending troops to defend the Mississippi Valley deserves keen appreciation. Senators and congressmen from those states were every day pressing demands in the Confederate capital that their troops be kept home for their states' protection. Now, a year into the war, they were sending their men to the defense, not of their own states, but of the Mississippi Valley.

Johnston's own Kentucky army would be the last to arrive in Corinth. When he abandoned Nashville, Johnston moved the army southeast to Murfreesboro. This served two purposes. First, it provided a rendezvous point for Hardee's Central Army of Kentucky, the debris of Fort Donelson, and Crittenden's 15 regiments from east Tennessee. At the same time, it disguised Johnston's intent to unite with Beauregard in the Mississippi Valley. After reaching Murfreesboro on February 23, Johnston organized his army, now numbering 17,000, in three divisions under Hardee, Crittenden, and Pillow, with a reserve, the "Kentucky Brigade," under Breckinridge.

To save meager railcar space for munitions and provisions, Johnston in Murfreesboro undertook to march his army across the muddy width of Tennessee so his powder and pork could go by train. At sunrise on February 28, Johnston's army took up its march, prescribed at 12 to 15 miles a day, and moved south through Shelbyville and Fayette, striking the Memphis & Charleston Railroad at Decatur, Alabama. Making the soldiers march overland was fraught with some hazard, since any delay in getting to Corinth risked interruption by a Union force sent up the Tennessee River to block the Memphis & Charleston. (Indeed, as Sherman saw it, the purpose of Grant's Tennessee River invasion was to "move forward in force, make a lodgment on the Memphis & Charleston road, and thus repeat the grand tactics of Fort Donelson, by separating the rebels in the interior from those at Memphis and on the Mississippi."

Fortunately for Johnston, Henry Halleck, in the weeks following the capture of Donelson, did not direct his Union armies with the urgency necessary to make real the threat of separating the Confederate armies. After Johnston's army's slow, soggy march south to Decatur, they boarded westbound trains on the Memphis & Charleston for Corinth. Almost a month after it started out from Murfreesboro, Johnston's vanguard arrived in Corinth on March 22, 1862, and the Confederate Western army was concentrated for the first time in the war.

On March 16, before Johnston's army arrived in Corinth, Beauregard was presented with an opportunity to fall on what was, for the moment, a smaller Union force just starting to assemble on the Shiloh plateau near Pittsburgh Landing. However, in the month before the battle, Beauregard was hampered by an incomplete knowledge of where the Union army was. Any attack was therefore deferred until Johnston's wing of the Confederate army arrived. When Johnston arrived at the head of his column, he and Beauregard agreed on the necessity to attack Grant's army gathering at Pittsburg Landing before Grant was joined by Buell's army, which was reported to be at Columbia, Tennessee, 75 miles distant.

The tail of Johnston's column arrived at Corinth by March 27, and over the next few days, the combined army—which kept Beauregard's name, the Army of the Mississippi—was organized, albeit in a crude way: each of the major generals would head a corps, and it did not matter how many men were in it. The main disadvantage of Beauregard's *ad hoc* organization resulted from the differences in the sizes of the corps. Bragg's Second Corps was unwieldy, more than twice the size of Hardee's, and would be difficult to maneuver in the coming battle, in the confined space of the Shiloh plateau.

In the first few days of April there were two last-minute changes:

Brig. Gen. A. P. Stewart brought two regiments with him from Island No. 10 and took command of a brigade in Polk's First Corps.

General Crittenden and one of his brigadiers, Brig. Gen. William H. Carroll, were charged with drunkenness, relieved of command, and dismissed from the army. Crittenden was replaced with John C. Breckinridge, an inexperienced political general who had been the previous Vice President of the United States and the pro-slavery Democratic candidate in the 1860 presidential election. Carroll's brigade was scattered for garrison duty in the surrounding area.

Johnston and Beauregard delayed in attacking Grant at Pittsburg Landing to await the arrival of the Army of the West, the 20,000-strong Arkansas army under Major General Earl Van Dorn, which was making its way to Corinth to add heft to the assault. However, when a reconnaissance by Cheatham's division at Bethel on the Confederate left bumped into Lew Wallace's 3rd Division's outpost at Adamsville on the Union right, Wallace sent his whole division to the front and put it into line of battle. Hearing of the aggressive-seeming Union move on the morning of April 3, the generals in Corinth decided that now must be the time to strike, especially with Buell's army approaching and expected in a week.

Beauregard framed the plans for the advance, once more taking the initiative from Johnston and leaving that general commanding in name only. For three days the corps stumbled forward in the confusing terrain, and they reached their positions for attack a day late, on April 5. The delay would be fatal to their plan of destroying Grant before Buell arrived.

The Army of the Mississippi bivouacked that Saturday night with Hardee's corps in the front line across the Corinth Road. Bragg's corps was 800 yards to the rear of Hardee. Polk's corps was in column of brigades to the rear of Bragg's line. Breckinridge's corps was one mile to Polk's rear.

The forward movement to the attack commenced at about sunrise Sunday morning, April 6. General Johnston accompanied the right—Gladden's and Shaver's brigades—in person until the first camp was attacked. He then rode to the left, where Cleburne's brigade was advancing to the attack, and from there conducted Stewart's brigade to the right. Johnston then directed the movements of Chalmers's and Jackson's brigades to the army's right, while Hardee directed Shaver, Wood, and Stewart to the army's left. General Johnston then ordered Breckinridge's Reserve Corps forward, and at 12:30 placed these troops in position south of the Peach Orchard. For over and hour, Johnston and his staff occupied a position due south of the Peach Orchard, on the army's left center.

From this point Johnston went forward behind Bowen's Brigade in an attack, and was killed near the southeast corner of the Peach Orchard at 2:30 p.m., a direct result of his style of commanding from the front.

It was Beauregard who acted as the army commander, setting up a field headquarters in the rear on Sunday morning at the intersection of the Corinth Road and Bark Road. From there he directed the deployment of the reserves, with his staff coursing over the field and bringing back reports. At 10:00 a.m. Sunday morning, Beauregard and his staff moved forward to within a half-mile of the Union camps. About noon he moved up to the Rhea House, and at 2:00 p.m. he moved forward to the main crossroads of the Corinth Road and Hamburg-Purdy Road. Here he received information of the death of General Johnston and assumed command of the army.

Besides the inexperience of the troops and the difficulty of the terrain, the biggest contributor to the sluggishness of the Confederate assault was its high command's random supervision, which was a result of Beauregard's long Confederate battle lines. Senior commanders had to move back and forth along a miles-long front to try to direct the assault. The Confederate left, where two-thirds of the army was concentrated, and where Beauregard had intended to deliver the brunt of the attack, suffered especially. Hardee, who had been in charge on the army's left in the morning, was satisfied with Hindman's progress and departed for the right. But Hindman was soon wounded, and the attack stalled.

When Bragg approached the front with the second line, he quickly concluded that the attack on the left was going badly, and, rather than reinforce what he saw as failure there, he too rode away to the army's right. The corps commanders subsequently agreed to each oversee a sector of the front, and put Polk in charge of the left. When Polk arrived there, however, the long absence of a guiding hand, plus the noon counterattack against the left by Sherman and McClernand, had caused the Confederate attack there to stall; Polk concluded that the troops on the left were fought out, and the focus of the battle passed to the Hornets' Nest in the center.

With the Confederate confusion about not only where Grant's army was deployed in the early afternoon but also where their own army was deployed, the wisdom of making frontal attacks on the Hornet's Nest salient went unquestioned. The encirclement and capture of the Union contingent in the Hornets' Nest was finally accomplished in the late afternoon only after hours of costly attacks that pushed back the Union forces on either side.

Beauregard's most controversial act at Shiloh was his decision to suspend the army's attack at about 6:00 p.m. on the first day, before the final attack on the last

Union line in front of Pittsburg Landing. Beauregard's reasons for halting, however, were solid. His brigadiers were reporting that their men were too exhausted and too scattered to make another concerted attack after 13 hours of fighting. There was nothing left undone that could not be done the next morning, when the men were rested and collected. Unsurprisingly, it was Bragg who started the backbiting about the stoppage, writing in his report on April 30 that another attack had "every chance of success." Bragg's own reserve of two brigades, however, had tried to force Grant's last line and failed. Confederate units were already retiring without orders from weariness. Beauregard, too, could not have known that Buell's army would arrive during the night. All his corps commanders, when they gathered in Beauregard's headquarters that night—in Sherman's tent near Shiloh Church—were confident of success in the morning.

During the chaos of that rain-soaked night, however, amid thousands of casualties and scattered commands—with Union gunboats blindly hurling shells into the mix—both officers and men found it difficult to reassemble, even if they still had the energy to do so.

The Confederates on the second day of the battle were strategically surprised by the fresh troops of Buell's Army of the Ohio, formed opposite the Confederate right at Pittsburg Landing, and Grant's fresh 3rd Division, under Lew Wallace, arrived opposite the Confederate left at the Owl Creek bridge. When the Union attack began at sunrise, many of Beauregard's units were still asleep in their bivouacs of the night before, miles from the front. The Confederate line, which only numbered about 20,000 troops, was not fully formed until Buell's and Grant's combined forces had reclaimed the battlefield up to the Sunken Road at the Hornets' Nest of the day before.

When they were finally in place, the segments of the Confederate line were commanded by, from left to right: Bragg, Polk, Breckinridge, and Hardee. The Confederates still managed to offer a spirited resistance, counterattacking continually, but in this back-and-forth fighting of the second day the Rebel army was outnumbered by about two-to-one, and as the day progressed the men grew increasingly dispirited by their reversal of fortune. In the early afternoon, the Union numbers and the Confederate fatigue became telling. Beauregard's men had retreated to their third line of the day. Finally, about 2:30 p.m., Beauregard sent orders to the corps commanders to retire, and the Confederates left the field in good order. Beauregard stayed to personally place a brigade and several pieces of artillery in position on the first ridge south of Shiloh Branch. He also placed a battery at Wood's house, and Breckinridge's corps, as rearguard, on the high ground near the Bark Road, and then, with his staff, retired to Corinth via Monterey.

At Shiloh, the Army of the Mississippi lost 1,728 killed, 8,012 wounded and 959 missing, for a total of 10,699 out of 44,699 present for duty—24% casualties (compared to the Union Army of the Tennessee's 22% and the Union Army of the Ohio's 12%).

The losses to enemy fire (the killed and wounded) were 22% of the total, compared to the Army of the Tennessee's 17% and the Army of the Ohio's 11%.

First Corps

Major General Leonidas Polk

Leonidas Polk was famous as the "Bishop General," who had resigned from the U.S. Army only months after graduating West Point in the Class of 1827 and entered the Episcopal ministry. By the time of the Civil War, he had been Bishop of the Episcopal Diocese of Louisiana for 20 years.

Even while the armies started to gather in the late spring of 1861, Polk was still wearing his cleric's gown, and his most active interest was in his work as the founder of the University of the South at Sewanee, in south central Tennessee. When Polk travelled to Sewanee on business in May 1861, Governor Isham Harris met with Polk and asked him to go to Richmond as an envoy for Tennessee to ask for war supplies from Polk's West Point classmate and friend, Jefferson Davis.

Polk was an exponent of the cotton-growing, slave-rich Mississippi Valley interest group centered in Memphis. After his meeting with President Davis, he returned from Richmond a major general, with his headquarters in Memphis and with command over the Mississippi Valley defenses. His construction of the defenses on the Mississippi was accomplished with energy and skill, but he neglected the defense of the rest of western Tennessee, the area that stretched 100 miles to the Tennessee River.

Polk had his greatest impact on the course of the war when, on September 3, 1861, he invaded politically neutral Kentucky to seize Columbus, a town on a high bluff on the Mississippi River, which Polk thought indispensable to the river's defense. After Polk's rash act—ordered without consultation with the governors of Kentucky or Tennessee or the high command in Richmond—Kentucky immediately aligned with the North, threatening Nashville and the entire 350-mile length of northern Tennessee, which had previously been protected by the buffer of neutral Kentucky.

Polk moved his department headquarters to Columbus, which was only 15 miles from the Union stronghold at Cairo, Illinois. At Columbus, he was content to stay on the defensive, restrained by his own lack of competence to conduct any large-scale assault, and intimidated by the timberclad Union gunboats that regularly drifted down the river to scout the Rebel emplacements.

Polk's one experience with combat came in November 1861 as a result of an attack on Belmont, across the river from Columbus, by his Union counterpart at Cairo, Ulysses S. Grant. In that small battle, Polk demonstrated poor judgment in sending his incompetent second-in-command, Brig. Gen. Gideon Pillow, across the river to meet the emergency. Paralyzed by his belief that the Belmont attack was a feint and that Columbus was the ultimate target of Grant's attack, Polk held back reinforcements for his troops on the opposite bank. With four steamboats at Columbus and plenty of strength on hand to crush Grant, or at least cut off Grant from his transports and capture the whole force, Polk hesitated and lost the opportunity.

Three months later, during the crisis of the Forts Henry and Donelson in February 1862, Polk could have sent enough men from Columbus to crush Grant again, but he declined again, preferring to defend his "Gibraltar of the West" at Columbus, Kentucky, rather than save Tennessee.

Polk was popular with his men. Tall and commanding, he made a majestic appearance, and cultivated the persona of the humble, pious bishop who buckled his sword over his robes out of a sense of duty to the South. However, when General Albert Sidney Johnston arrived to take command of the Western Department in September, a sinister side to Polk's personality came to the fore. With his 20 years at the head of the Episcopal Church in the Southwest, Polk had learned to lead but not to follow. He frequently demonstrated his insubordination, following orders only when it suited him. This trait, combined with his lack of military experience, made him a liability to the Army of the Mississippi. Jefferson Davis, by commissioning Polk as major general in June 1861 in a moment of bonhomie, set in train a calamity for the military fortunes of the western Confederacy. Braxton Bragg, with his clearer military eye, had no faith in Polk's ability; in his estimation, Polk was "an old woman, utterly worthless."

In June 1864 during the Atlanta Campaign, Polk, accompanied by other officers, was scanning Union positions from atop Pine Mountain near Marietta when a Federal cannonball tore through his body. When he heard the news, Sherman informed Secretary War of Edwin Stanton, ending his telegram update by saying, "We killed Bishop Polk yesterday."

First (Polk's) Corps at Shiloh

The provenance of most of the regiments in the First Corps could be traced back to Governor Harris's Provisional Army of Tennessee, and those regiments had seen only garrison duty on the Mississippi River. They had not maneuvered together except on the march to Corinth. A few had fought at Belmont. Soldiers from the other corps, upon encountering Polk's contingent, commented on their lack of discipline.

Arriving in July 1861 to take charge of what would become the First Corps at Shiloh, Major General Leonidas Polk soon moved his center of operations from Memphis, Tennessee, to Columbus, Kentucky, on September 3, 1861, to occupy a strongpoint—what Polk would call "The Gibraltar of the West"—on a bluff above the Mississippi River at Columbus. Polk's army would huddle in and around the Columbus fortress until six weeks before the battle of Shiloh.

During its entire independent existence in the nine months before Shiloh, the esprit of Polk's command suffered from a lack of any sense of urgency. Polk never seriously considered an offensive against the nearest Union concentration at Cairo, Illinois, under Ulysses S. Grant, especially after the appearance of timberclad gunboats on the Mississippi in October signaled Union superiority on the rivers. Thus, given the impossibility of an amphibious Confederate operation anywhere north of Columbus, and with the difficulty of coordination with other commands in Missouri due to Polk's lack of authority in that state, Polk's strategy for the Mississippi Valley became that of the hedgehog, entirely defensive. Besides his lack of aggressiveness, Polk was not a hard taskmaster, and drill and discipline remained lax in his command. The battle of Belmont on November 7, 1861, forced on Polk by the more pugnacious Grant, was the only battle experience Polk's men had, and it was limited to just seven of the sixteen regiments Polk would bring to Shiloh.

Among the leaders in action at Belmont, Frank Cheatham shone brightest, both in energy and leadership. Robert Russell, who would later lead a brigade at Shiloh, acted as a brigade commander at Belmont, but he was wasted in a battle that was fought regiment by regiment and even company by company.

When General P.G.T. Beauregard organized the Army of the Mississippi in March 1862, he named Polk's command the First Grand Division of that army. Major General Braxton Bragg with his Gulf States army arrived that same month, and Bragg was not secret about his poor opinion of Polk's men, calling them a "mob" and "undisciplined volunteers."

After General Beauregard's Army of the Mississippi merged with General A.S. Johnston's Central Army of the Kentucky on March 29, Polk's First Grand Division was redesignated the First Corps, Army of the Mississippi.

At Shiloh, Polk's First Corps, with 9,404 men in two divisions of two brigades each, formed Saturday night in column of brigades with its center on the Corinth Road. The 1st Corps formed the third wave of Confederate infantry, behind Hardee's Third Corps and Bragg's Second Corps. In its approach to battle on Sunday morning, the spearhead of Polk's corps, Stewart's brigade, passed Beauregard's headquarters at the fork of the Bark Road and Corinth Road at 7:00 a.m.

Polk's two divisions, under Ben Cheatham and Charles Clark, splintered before reaching the first camps of the enemy and did not fight in the battle as divisions.

At the opening of the battle, Stewart's brigade of Clark's division was detached to the right. Russell's brigade of Clark's division, next in line, was led directly to the front and became engaged under the personal direction of Clark and Polk. General Clark was soon wounded and left the field. General A. P. Stewart succeeded to the command of the 1st Division, but did not bring the division under his immediate control.

General Cheatham, commanding Polk's 2nd Division, sent Bushrod Johnson's brigade directly to the front, where it was engaged under Polk's orders. Cheatham then took personal direction of Stephens's brigade, conducting it first to the left, and then, at 10:30 a.m., to the right, where Cheatham joined General Breckinridge, who was engaged at the Peach Orchard.

General Polk himself followed the line of the Corinth Road. He assumed personal direction of the battle at Rhea Field, and when the line was finally carried he pushed his command forward without waiting to reorganize it.

By noon, he was the only corps commander present on the army's left, and his brigades bore the brunt of Sherman's and McClernand's counterattack. In his report, he stated that his three brigades—Stewart's, Russell's, and Johnson's—with occasionally a regiment from some other corps, fought over the same ground three times. Later in the afternoon, after regaining the ground lost on the left, Polk moved his men to the right, to the fighting at the Hornets' Nest. There he was present at the surrender of Prentiss, and directed some of the troops toward Pittsburg Landing. In the evening, when Beauregard ordered the army to withdraw, Polk retired all the way to his bivouac of Saturday night.

On Monday Polk commanded the left center again and fought over the same ground as on Sunday.

At Shiloh, Polk's First Corps lost 385 killed, 1,953 wounded, and 19 missing, for a total of 2,357 out of 9,404 present for duty—25% casualties, the second lowest rate of the four Confederate corps.

The losses to enemy fire (killed and wounded) were also 25% of the total, due to Polk's corps' low number of men reported missing after the battle.

First Corps, 1st Division

Brigadier General Charles Clark

A descendant of a Mayflower colonist, the 51-year-old Clark was an aristocrat planter turned politician. His politics were like his travel through life, going further Deep South as he went along. He was born in Cincinnati and graduated from Augusta College in Kentucky, after which he emigrated to Natchez, Mississippi, then to Benton, Mississippi, where he taught school while he studied for the bar. After starting his law practice, he became active in politics, serving as a Whig candidate for the Mississippi legislature. He entered the Mexican War as a captain in the 2nd Mississippi infantry, and was elected its colonel when his predecessor resigned. The 2nd Mississippi, however, saw no combat.

Initially a Unionist, Clark's politics changed in the 1850s, when he moved to Mississippi's Bolivar County and became a successful planter. Defeated for Congress as a Whig, he became a secessionist Democrat. After Mississippi seceded, he was appointed a brigadier general of state troops and was subsequently promoted to major general. When the Mississippi troops were accepted into Confederate service, he was appointed brigadier general in the Confederate Army on May 22, 1861.

After less than a month in Virginia commanding Longstreet's old brigade in the fall of 1861, Clark was transferred to General Albert Sidney Johnston's Central Army of Kentucky and given command of an independent brigade stationed in Hopkinsville, halfway between the river forts Henry and Donelson and Hardee's main body at

Bowling Green. During the crisis at Fort Donelson, his brigade was sent there as part of Brig. Gen. Pillow's reinforcements. Clark, however, refused to recognize Pillow's authority, and when Johnston sided with Pillow as commander, Clark resigned in protest. Thus, when Clark's brigade was captured and subtracted from Johnston's army after the surrender at Fort Donelson, Clark was not captured with them.

Less than a month later, on March 12, Clark replaced Pillow at the head of the 1st Division of Polk's corps for the upcoming attack on Grant's army at Pittsburg Landing.

Clark was a mediocre leader of fighting men. Career soldier A. P. Stewart called him "vigilant, prudent, and capable," but this lukewarm commendation notwithstanding, it may be a reflection on Clark's abilities that at Shiloh his two brigades were ordered in different directions by higher-ups at the start of the battle. He was leading only two regiments—half of Russell's Brigade—into action when he was severely wounded in the right shoulder.

Clark's long-term effectiveness would remain unproven, since he was wounded twice in succession—first at Shiloh, then at Baton Rouge the following August, where he was captured. Returning to Mississippi on crutches, he was elected governor in October 1863, until being removed by Federal authorities after the war. He died in 1877 at age 66.

First Corps, 1st (Clark's) Division at Shiloh

Clark's 1st Division totaled 4,988 men in two brigades. The first was a veteran brigade under Col. Robert M. Russell, who was himself unproven. The second was a newly assembled brigade under Brig. Gen. A. P. Stewart, who was able and reliable. Both brigades were accompanied by a battery of six guns—a common practice in the early days of the war but an organizational mistake, since placing batteries with brigades hindered the massing of artillery fire.

This had been Pillow's division until Pillow's recent dismissal by President Davis in the aftermath of the debacle at Fort Donelson. Although Clark was new to Polk's corps, the brigadiers and regiments of the division were familiar with each other, having been together under Polk since their beginnings in Confederate service.

Clark's division did not fight as a division at Shiloh. Its two brigades were separated at the start of the fighting at Seay Field when Johnston ordered Polk to detach Stewart's brigade to the Confederate right. Clark himself accompanied Russell's brigade going straight ahead.

At Shiloh, Clark's 1st Division lost 190 killed, 933 wounded, and 3 missing, for a total of 1,126 out of 4,988 present for duty—23% casualties.

1st Brigade
Colonel Robert M. Russell

Russell, a native Tennessean, was West Point, Class of 1848, but spent just two years in the infantry in the Regular Army, resigning in 1850. He spent the next three years as a miner in California before moving to Austin, Texas, to farm.

When the war started, he was appointed colonel of the 12th Tennessee, organized at Jackson in western Tennessee. In November 1861, Russell led an informal brigade at the battle of Belmont, but was undistinguished, making a disappointing showing for a former professional soldier—"The chap that run so in the battle of Belmont," was how one of his Louisiana soldiers remembered him.

Russell's regiments fought largely on their own hook at Belmont, and they did so again at Shiloh. Only 7 of the 20 companies of the 11th Louisiana and 22nd Tennessee, led personally by Russell in the opening attack on Rhea Field, made it through the thick underbrush to their objective: the camp of the 53rd Ohio. Both regiments were repulsed, and ran in panic. For most of the battle, Russell led only his own 12th Tennessee.

The next month his regiment refused to reelect him colonel, and he passed out of the army until he became a colonel of cavalry later in the war, afterward disappearing from history.

1st Division, 1st (Russell's) Brigade at Shiloh

At Shiloh, Russell's Brigade numbered approximately 2,700 men, and consisted of the 11th Louisiana and the 12th, 13th, and 22nd Tennessee Infantry Regiments, supported by Bankhead's Battery. Composed entirely of regiments that had fought at the battle of Belmont, it was the most veteran brigade in the Army of the Mississippi, even though it boasted experience in only one battle.

The 11th Louisiana, recruited largely in New Orleans, was the first of the four Louisiana regiments recruited in the summer of 1861 to defend the Mississippi River Valley. Sent to Polk's army at Columbus, Kentucky, it was considered among the most poorly trained and least respected regiments. For their part, the cosmopolitan men of the 11th Louisiana disliked being brigaded with the rowdy Tennesseans—"lashed on to the tail of a Tennessee rabble," was how one Louisiana recruit put it.

The 12th and 13th Tennessee were inseparable. From September 1861 at Columbus, they fought in the same brigade, almost without interruption, until the end of the war.

All the regiments were led by colonels except Russell's own 12th Tennessee, which was led by the very able Lt. Col. Tyree Bell in his absence. A month after Shiloh, Col. Russell and Col. Freeman of the 22nd Tennessee would fail to be reelected by their regiments, and Col. Vaughn of the 13th Tennessee would take command of the brigade.

On Saturday night, Russell's brigade bivouacked in the order, from left to right: 11th Louisiana, 22nd Tennessee, 13th Tennessee, and 12th Tennessee, with Bankhead's Battery in the rear. In the advance on Sunday morning, Russell's brigade followed the Corinth Road to near the ravine of Shiloh Branch. Having no orders, it moved to where the fighting was heaviest. It became engaged on the right of the road—the 11th Louisiana on the left joined the 17th Louisiana of Anderson's brigade and the 6th Mississippi of Cleburne's brigade in their attack on the camp of Sherman's 53rd Ohio regiment. (The fact that three regiments from three different brigades mingled in this first attack signaled the command chaos that would mark the entire day on the Confederate side.) In this attack the 11th Louisiana was disorganized. Bragg was watching, and remarked, "To my dismay, I found Mark's [sic] Louisiana regiment disgraced.—They belonged to Polk's mob." A part of the 11th afterwards joined Stewart's brigade and a part continued under Russell.

After the opening attack by the 11th Louisiana, the brigade was divided into two wings, the rallied remnants of the 11th Louisiana with the 22nd Tennessee on the left commanded by Col. Russell, and the 12th and 13th Tennessee on the right commanded by division commander General Clark. The 11th Louisiana and 22nd Tennessee under Russell engaged first, and they broke and ran (the 11th Louisiana for the second time) under a vicious fire.

The 12th Tennessee passed to the right of the 53rd Ohio's camp into the 4th Illinois Cavalry's camp, where it joined Stewart's brigade and supported the 4th Tennessee in a charge upon McAllister's Battery. Afterwards it supported Bankhead's Battery on the ground abandoned by McAllister.

The 13th Tennessee also passed to the right of the 53rd Ohio's camp, then wheeled to the left and charged Waterhouse's Battery in the flank, capturing two guns. It then moved directly past Shiloh Church, and from there along the Corinth Road to Duncan Field, where it supported Stanford's Battery in Ruggles's artillery line in the afternoon.

The 22nd Tennessee, the only one of Russell's regiments remaining under Russell's command, moved through the Union camp and over the Waterhouse Battery position to near the central crossroads of the Corinth Road and the Hamburg-Purdy Road, where the 5th Tennessee of Cleburne's brigade attached itself to Russell. Russell then joined Trabue's left in front of Marsh's brigade camp. Then, with the 22nd Tennessee, Russell moved into the valley of Tilghman Branch and advanced up that creek to the place where Prentiss surrendered. Russell says that Prentiss surrendered to men of the 22nd Tennessee. The 12th and 13th Tennessee joined Russell here, but no part of the brigade advanced further.

Bankhead's Battery was in action against the 53rd Ohio camp at 9:00 a.m. in the morning. At 11:00 a.m., it was moved forward to the northwest corner of Review Field. At 4:00 p.m., the battery shelled the Hornets' Nest as part of Ruggles's massed artillery line.

On Monday Col. Marks and 60 men of the 11th Louisiana were engaged on the army's right. The remnant of the three Tennessee regiments, a very small force, was engaged on the left, next to Pond's brigade, where they met Rousseau's troops along the northern edge of Review Field. In this fight, both Russell's flanks were turned, and, in the 20 minutes that followed, the Federal crossfire caused Russell's men to withdraw to avoid annihilation.

At Shiloh, Russell's brigade lost 97 killed and 512 wounded, for a total of 609 out of about 2,700 present for duty—22 % casualties, the same as Stewart's, the other brigade in the division.

2nd Brigade
Brigadier General Alexander P. Stewart

A. P. Stewart—"Old Straight" to his men, out of respect for his "by the book" style—was an aggressive, hard-hitting, no-nonsense soldier. At Shiloh, he would be leading troops into battle for the first time, but he was a trained military man.

Born in the eastern hills of Rogersville, Tennessee, Stewart was a voracious reader from early childhood. His high grades earned him an appointment to West Point, where he graduated 12th out of 52 graduates in the Class of 1842. His field service as an artilleryman lasted only a year, at Ft. Macon in North Carolina. He returned to West Point to teach mathematics from 1843 to 1845 and then resigned.

The classroom agreed with Stewart. After a stint as professor of Mathematics and Experimental Philosophy at Cumberland University, a Presbyterian school in

Lebanon, Tennessee, he put down roots in the town, developed a deep Presbyterian faith, and became renowned as a great scholar in the state.

As a Whig, he voted for the middle-of-the-road Bell ticket in the 1860 presidential election. When Tennessee seceded from the Union after Fort Sumter, he worked on the state's military board, making contracts and organizing training camps. Although offered the colonelcy of an infantry regiment, he felt he could make himself more useful in the artillery, and was appointed major in the Provisional Army of Tennessee's artillery corps, in command of the state's heavy artillery battalion, the big guns used for river defense.

On August 15, 1861, Stewart and his battalion were accepted into Confederate service and stationed by department commander Polk at Island No. 10, a defensive post on the Mississippi River. In September, Stewart and his guns went to Columbus, Kentucky, after Polk occupied that city.

On November 7, 1861, Stewart's guns lobbed shells on Grant's men during their raid on Belmont, Missouri, across the river from Columbus. At new department commander Albert Sidney Johnston's request, Stewart was made a brigadier general effective November 8, and within the month he had his own independent brigade of mixed infantry and artillery at Columbus.

On March 1, 1862, Stewart and his brigade moved to New Madrid as part of the evacuation of Columbus, but on the night of March 13–14, Stewart and his brigade abandoned the post in the face of an overwhelming Union force under John Pope. Although the abandonment of such an important post was humiliating, an observer remarked that Stewart's coolness and self-possession were an inspiration to his men. From New Madrid, Stewart and his brigade moved south to Fort Pillow, then to Corinth for the concentration prior to the battle of Shiloh.

In the two days of battle, Stewart never commanded all the regiments of his brigade. All his many ad hoc commands, however, responded to his lead. Stewart himself received orders from Bragg, Polk, Breckinridge, Johnston, Beauregard, and a full litany of staff officers, and it is no wonder that he lost control of his command.

Stewart's superiors showed the sincerity of their faith in his ability by consistently promoting him, finally raising him to Confederate corps command at the rank of major general. Stewart would remain with the army until its final surrender, and after a successful postwar career died in Mississippi in 1908, age 86.

1st Division, 2nd (Stewart's) Brigade at Shiloh

Stewart's brigade was one of the most recently organized in the army, assembled at Corinth in late March 1862, mere days before the battle of Shiloh. It numbered approximately 2,300 men in four regiments—the 13th Arkansas and 4th, 5th, and 33rd Tennessee—and Stanford's Mississippi Battery, built around troops Stewart had recently evacuated from Island No. 10.

Lt. Colonel Venable's 5th Tennessee Regiment had come with Stewart from Fort Pillow. Colonel Neely's 4th Tennessee was from Island No. 10, and approached Corinth by way of Memphis. Also joining Stewart at Corinth were Col. Tappan's 13th Arkansas (without Col. Tappan, who was furloughed sick) and Col. Campbell's 33rd Tennessee.

The regiments had been garrison troops on the Mississippi for their entire existence, either at Columbus or New Madrid or Fort Pillow. The three Tennessean regiments were from west Tennessee. They were motivated by the defense of their nearby homes, but they were poorly armed with flintlocks, hunting rifles, and shotguns. Only the 13th Arkansas had "seen the elephant"—at Belmont, where it lost 80 men.

Stewart's brigade formed the advance of Polk's corps and bivouacked on Saturday night across the Corinth Road in the order from left to right: 5th Tennessee, 33rd Tennessee, 13th Arkansas, and 4th Tennessee, with Stanford's Battery in the rear.

The brigade moved forward at 7:00 a.m. Sunday morning and its left regiment, the 5th Tennessee, came into Fraley Field, where it received a shot from a Union battery that killed one man and cut the flagstaff. General Johnston directed the brigade to the right. General Stewart moved his brigade by the right flank due east, from the north side of Seay Field until his right reached the Eastern Corinth Road. His brigade was now in front of Peabody's abandoned camp. Here, losing sight of General Johnston, Stewart moved his men through the camp and beyond it.

From there, Stewart cooperated with the movement of Wood and Shaver to the left, moving by the left flank along the rear of Peabody's camp, behind Gibson's brigade. Stewart led his three left regiments north across a small stream and ordered them to lie down while he looked for the 4th Tennessee, which had gotten lost. Stewart found the 4th and brought it forward to his brigade's position, but found that his other three regiments had moved forward under the temporary command of General Hardee.

Here Stewart received orders to charge McAllister's Battery at the northwest corner of Review Field. He passed to the right behind Wood's brigade and, joining Shaver's left, charged the battery and captured one gun at 11:00 a.m.

General Hindman proposed to Stewart that his brigade join Shaver's attack on the Hornets' Nest. While arranging for this movement, General Hindman was disabled, and General Stewart took command of Hindman's force. Placing the 4th Tennessee on the left of Shaver's brigade, he moved through the woods to Duncan Field and briefly engaged the Union force that occupied the east side of that field until Shaver reported his troops out of ammunition. At about noon, Stewart reattached the 4th Tennessee to the 12th Tennessee in support of Bankhead's Battery, which was being closely pressed by Union troops. The 4th Tennessee then retired for ammunition.

In the meantime, General Hardee had ordered the 5th and 33rd Tennessee and the 13th Arkansas forward from the ravine where Stewart left them, and they became engaged under Preston Smith's command near the crossroads of the Eastern Corinth Road and the Hamburg-Purdy Road.

Later the 5th Tennessee was attached to Russell's command farther to the left. It attacked the right flank of the Union men at the Hornets' Nest and then retired to a camp for the night.

The 33rd Tennessee joined General Stewart again to the right of Ruggles's massed artillery batteries and moved by the left flank along the road, where it remained until night and then retired to a camp near the crossroads of the Eastern Corinth Road and the Hamburg-Purdy Road.

After its engagement at the crossroads of the Eastern Corinth Road and the Hamburg-Purdy Road, the 13th Arkansas was in support of Smith's Battery, where its Lt. Col. Grayson was mortally wounded. It then retired to Beauregard's headquarters, and bivouacked for the night.

The 4th Tennessee, after its separation from General Stewart, joined Preston Smith's command in Marsh's brigade camp and was engaged from about 1:00 to 2:00 p.m. It bivouacked Sunday night near where it captured McAllister's gun that morning.

General Stewart, after the regiments of his own brigade had passed from his command one by one, organized a command consisting of Walker's 2nd Tennessee, part of the 11th Louisiana, and another regiment of Cleburne's command, and made a second attack at Duncan Field. Falling back, he was joined by the 33rd Tennessee and moved along the Corinth Road and into the Hornets' Nest at the time of the Union surrender.

On Monday Stewart had the 2nd Tennessee and the 13th Arkansas under his command on the Confederate right.

Colonel Strahl reported that the 4th Tennessee was engaged on Monday on the Confederate right, supporting the Washington Artillery. On Monday the 5th Tennessee was with Chalmers on the extreme right, while the 33rd Tennessee was on the left with General Cheatham.

On Monday, Stanford and his gunners confronted Rousseau's troops on the east end of the Review Field about 1:00 p.m. There, they lost four of their six guns while holding off one of the last desperate Federal charges at canister range. When the enemy closed within 75 yards, Stanford gave the order to withdraw, but too many horses had been killed, and those still living were tangled in their traces. The battery was overrun. By his action in sacrificing his battery, Stanford bought time for the infantry to rally and form a new line in the rear. The guns were recaptured a short time later, but Stanford did not have enough surviving horses to get them off.

At Shiloh, Stewart's brigade lost 92 killed, 421 wounded, and 3 missing, for a total of 516 out of about 2,300 present for duty—about 22% casualties, the same as Russell's, the other brigade in the division.

First Corps, 2nd Division

Major General Benjamin F. Cheatham

Rough-hewn, hard-swearing, heavy-drinking, tobacco-chewing Frank Cheatham, 41 years old, was the darling of the rough-and-ready Tennessean rank and file and a favorite of General Polk, but he was despised by the stolid, soldierly Braxton Bragg.

Cheatham was born into privilege in the planter aristocracy of Nashville. His family plantation, "Westover," consisted of 3,000 acres. His mother was a descendant of the founder of Nashville, and the Cheathams had been pillars of middle Tennessee for generations, as plantation owners, lawyers, doctors, and mayors.

When he was still in his twenties, Cheatham served as an officer in two Tennessee regiments during the Mexican War. After that conflict, he went to California in 1849 for the Gold Rush, but returned to his Tennessee plantation in 1853 and served as a general in the Tennessee Militia.

When the Civil War began, Cheatham was one of the Provisional Army of Tennessee's senior officers during the period before it was accepted into the Confederate army. He became a brigade commander, then a division commander under Major General Leonidas Polk, and first led men in combat at the battle of Belmont on November 7, 1861, where he seized the initiative and threatened to cut Grant's entire force off from its transports. He brought order out of chaos and turned the tide of the battle. In December, Cheatham and his division received the Thanks of Congress "for the skill and gallantry by which they converted what at first threatened so much disaster, into a triumphant victory."

Cheatham was promoted to major general on March 10, 1862, and was appointed commander of the 2nd Division, First Corps, Army of the Mississippi.

Cheatham would continue to do solid work, evidenced by his rise to the command of a corps by war's end. His nemesis was the bottle: he would be staggering drunk at the height of the battle of Stones River, nine months after Shiloh, and he has frequently been suspected of a liquid oblivion when Schofield's army squeezed out of Hood's carefully laid trap at Spring Hill in November 1864.

Cheatham stayed with the colors till the end, surrendering along with Joe Johnston in North Carolina the following April. After the war he married and had five children before dying in Nashville in 1886.

First Corps, 2nd (Cheatham's) Division at Shiloh

Cheatham's Division totaled 3,032 men in two brigades under Brig. Gen. Bushrod R. Johnson and Col. William H. Stephens. Each brigade was accompanied by a battery with six guns.

In the weeks before the battle of Shiloh, Cheatham's Division at Bethel, Tennessee, held the left flank of the Army of the Mississippi, which was centered at Corinth. There, it protected the Mobile & Ohio Railroad against the threat of the Union 3rd Division, newly arrived at Crump's Landing.

On April 3, Cheatham precipitated the battle of Shiloh when he alerted General Beauregard that there was a sudden forward concentration by 3rd Division troops at nearby Adamsville. Combined with the news that Buell's army was approaching, this fed Beauregard's fear that the Union army was about to attack. Anxious to strike first, Beauregard responded by putting into motion the climax of the campaign: the attack by the Army of the Mississippi on the main body of Grant's Army of the Tennessee at Shiloh.

Beauregard ordered Cheatham's Division to join Polk's corps at Mickey's, a farm on the road to the corps' final approach to the battlefield. Cheatham's division did not fight as a division at Shiloh, but as two separate brigades. Cheatham himself was detached with Stephens's Brigade and acted as a brigadier, putting Stephens's men in position personally. Johnson's Brigade was not under his control. For the movements of those brigades on Sunday, see the separate brigade accounts below.

Half the division's regiments remained separated overnight, and on Monday they fought in pieces on the army's right. At noon, Cheatham led a remainder—the 154th (Senior) Tennessee, 6th Tennessee, six companies of the 9th Tennessee, a portion of the 15th Tennessee, and 100 men of (Walker's) 2nd Tennessee—in an assault on what remained of Sherman's and McClernand's Union divisions, who were then advancing against the Confederate left around Water Oaks Pond. At the same time, Col. Maney led a Confederate attack a half mile to the east, at Review Field. Both Cheatham and Maney achieved only momentary gains, then withdrew.

At Shiloh, Cheatham's Division lost 195 killed, 1,020 wounded, and 16 missing, for a total of 1,231 out of 3,032 present for duty—34% casualties.

1st Brigade
Brigadier General
Bushrod R. Johnson

Bushrod Johnson, 44 years old, was a rare bird: a lifetime military man who was raised in a pacifist sect, and a Confederate officer who was raised in the North. Born in eastern Ohio adjacent to Virginia, he was brought up a Quaker and even worked with his uncle on the Underground Railroad. Despite his family's peace-loving beliefs, Johnson entered West Point, and thereafter his life was devoted to the military. Posted to the infantry, he fought Seminoles in Florida and afterward served on frontier duty in the West until the Mexican War, where he saw action at Palo Alto, Resaca-de-la-Palma, and Monterey.

His downfall came at Vera Cruz, where he had been detached from his combat role and appointed instead to the commissary. While in that role he approached his commanding officer in New Orleans with a profiteering scheme. The officer turned him in, and after a government inquiry, Johnson was allowed to resign without prosecution. His Regular Army career was over.

Johnson responded to the end of his career as a soldier by becoming a college professor and sometime superintendent at the Western Military Institute, first in Kentucky and then as an adjunct to the University of Nashville (where his fellow Shiloh brigadier, A.P. Stewart, taught mathematics). Johnson taught Natural Philosophy (the precursor of physics), Chemistry, Mathematics, and Engineering. He was active in the militias of Kentucky, where he was lieutenant colonel, and Tennessee, where he rose to colonel by the time the Civil War broke out.

With the advent of the war, Governor Harris appointed Johnson colonel and Chief Engineer of the Provisional Army of Tennessee. In January 1862 he was promoted to brigadier general, and on February 7, after the fall of Fort Henry, he was installed as the commander at Fort Donelson, but was superseded by General Pillow, who arrived a few hours later. Johnson was given a brigade at Donelson, and his men helped throw back the Union right flank on February 15, opening the way for the fort's garrison to escape, but Pillow did not follow up the opening, and 12,000 men of the garrison were surrendered the next day. A few days after the surrender, Johnson walked calmly through the Federal lines and escaped. He then violated his parole by riding to Nashville and rejoining the Confederate army there.

On March 10, Johnson was ordered to Jackson, Tennessee, to join Beauregard's Army of the Mississippi. There, he was given command of Col. Preston Smith's Brigade of Cheatham's Division.

Johnson was wounded by the concussion of a shell early in Sunday's fighting at Shiloh, but returned to lead the brigade at Perryville. Despite his heavy drinking habits, he would remain in command of brigades and divisions for the rest of the war. He commanded a division at Chickamauga, was promoted to major general, and led a division in the Siege of Petersburg. However, he drew the anger of Lee, who dismissed Johnson from the service the day before he surrendered at Appomattox.

Johnson returned to teaching at the University of Nashville after the war, and then retired to a farm in Illinois, where he died in 1880.

First Corps. 1st (Johnson's) Brigade at Shiloh

Johnson's Brigade numbered 2,052 men in four regiments and one battery, Polk's Tennessee Artillery. It was a rarity in the Confederate army at that time: a veteran brigade. All of its four regiments—the 2nd, 15th, 154th (Senior) Tennessee, and Blythe's 1st Mississippi Battalion—had seen combat on a brigade scale at Belmont, where the regiments had crossed the Mississippi with General Cheatham in mid-day to reinforce the embattled Belmont garrison.

All the regiments were led at Shiloh by their longtime colonels or, in the case of the 15th Tennessee, its lieutenant colonel.

Blythe's Mississippians disliked being brigaded with Tennesseans. Colonel Blythe begged fellow Mississipian Brig. Gen. Charles Clark, who commanded Polk's other division, to "prize us out, and we will deem it one of those favors never to be forgotten."

The 2nd Tennessee, Irish dock workers from Memphis, were recruited and outfitted by their colonel, J. Knox Walker, who was the nephew of former president James Knox Polk. The 154th (Senior) Tennessee was so called because it was the oldest militia regiment in the state, dating back 20 years. The brigade had until recently been commanded by the 154th's Col. Preston Smith. The battery captain, Marshall T. Polk, was West Point and Regular Army before the war.

Johnson's Brigade was prevented from fighting as a unit at Shiloh due to the detachment of Johnson's regiments by higher-ups Bragg and Polk. Johnson complained about it in his report: "I have to regret that, from orders apparently given to the subordinates of my command, I was prevented from bringing the whole brigade together handsomely into action. To this object all my efforts had been most zealously and carefully directed. Had I accomplished my purpose, I am convinced I would now have to report much more satisfactory results."

Johnson's brigade moved forward Sunday morning along the Corinth Road, third in the division's column of brigades. Crossing Fraley Field at 8:30 a.m., it came under fire from artillery. Here division commander Cheatham was detached with Stephens's brigade, and Brig. Gen. Johnson led his own brigade, first obliquely to the left, then by the right flank until it centered again on the road, its regiments in order from left to right: 2nd (Walker's) Tennessee, 15th Tennessee, Blythe's Mississippi, 154th (Senior) Tennessee, with Polk's Battery in the rear. Where the road crossed Shiloh Branch, Johnson came up to the fighting front with the brigades of Cleburne, Anderson, and Russell, which had mingled and were making ineffectual attempts to force the Union lines. General Polk at once assumed direction, and, without waiting to reorganize the shattered brigades, ordered the whole force forward without regard for corps, division, brigade, or even regimental organization.

Bragg redirected the right two regiments—Blythe's Mississippi and the 154th (Senior) Tennessee—to the right to attack Waterhouse's Battery. Blythe's Mississippi, with the 17th Louisiana, attacked the battery on its right flank. In this action Col. Blythe was killed, and his regiment halted in a ravine between the battery and Shiloh Church. The 154th (Senior) Tennessee, with other troops, attacked Waterhouse's Battery in front just as the 13th Tennessee reached its left flank. Both regiments claimed the two guns captured there. (Polk awarded them to the 13th Tennessee.) The 154th pressed forward toward Woolf Field, capturing another gun of Waterhouse's Battery and one gun of Schwartz's Battery near the crossroads of the Corinth Road and the Hamburg-Purdy Road. Here the 154th was joined by the three left regiments of Stewart's brigade and took position in Woolf Field, where their mixed force was engaged and finally driven back.

Brigadier General Johnson was engaged with his left regiments in the attack upon Barrett's Battery and Buckland's brigade of Sherman's division. They carried the position, after several repulses, in conjunction with other commands, but Johnson was knocked to the ground by the explosion of a shell in the final assault near Shiloh Church at 11:00 a.m., and had to be carried off the field. The command of the brigade then passed to Col. Preston Smith of the 154th, but it took time for Smith to be found.

During this conflict the brigade's attached battery, Capt. Polk's, was stationed near the Rhea House, where Polk was severely wounded and his battery disabled, so that only one gun went forward to the Corinth and Hamburg-Purdy crossroads, where it was captured.

At the crossroads Col. Smith learned of Brig. Gen. Johnson's wounding and took command of the brigade, which was now greatly reduced, the 15th Tennessee having only 150 men, Blythe's Mississippi only 200. Smith formed the remainder of the brigade just beyond the crossroads. He had scarcely formed his line when the enemy advanced upon him through the woods from the north and made a fierce attack, which was sustained for more than an hour, during which Smith brought up the 4th and 33rd Tennessee to reinforce his line. He finally succeeded, at about 2:00 p.m., in driving back the Federals. Smith then moved along the Corinth Road to Duncan Field. There, the 154th (Senior) Tennessee supported Swett's Battery in Ruggles's artillery line, and (Walker's) 2nd Tennessee supported the 38th Tennessee. The 15th Tennessee and Blythe's Mississippi were sent for ammunition and did not return. None of the brigade's regiments advanced beyond the place of Prentiss's subsequent surrender.

That night, the brigade remained splintered. Part of (Walker's) 2nd Tennessee bivouacked at the crossroads, Blythe's regiment bivouacked near Shiloh Church, and the other regiments, with Col. Smith, returned to their Saturday night bivouacs to the south.

On Monday the 154th (Senior) Tennessee, a portion of Blythe's Mississippi, and one company of (Walker's) 2nd Tennessee, under Col. Smith, joined Chalmers on the Confederate right and retired with him in the afternoon. The 15th Tennessee was engaged under Col. Maney on the Confederate right.

At Shiloh, Johnson's brigade lost 120 killed, 607 wounded, and 13 missing, for a total of 740 out of 2,052 present for duty—36% casualties.

2nd Brigade
Colonel William H. Stephens

Stephens, 46 years old, was one of twin brothers who were born in Maryland and who migrated to Jackson, Tennessee, where they taught school and subsequently studied law. A licensed lawyer at age 22, Stephens was appointed clerk of the Supreme Court of Tennessee in Jackson in May 1840, and held the office until June 1857, when he resigned to run unsuccessfully for Congress as a nominee of the Whig Party. In February 1861 Stephens was one of the 12 delegates elected by the legislature of Tennessee to attend the Peace Conference in Washington.

In April 1861 Stephens assisted in raising a company of Tennessee troops and was elected its captain, then unanimously elected colonel of the 6th Tennessee Infantry Regiment, whose service kept him near his home in western Kentucky and Tennessee in the months preceding the battle of Shiloh. The regiment's historian states that in these early months, the unit became "the crack regiment" of its brigade, and commends Stephens thus: "Colonel William H. Stephens deserves great credit for the skill displayed in bringing the regiment to such a high degree of efficiency. He possessed the genius of command in an eminent degree, and succeeded in infusing his spirit of discipline and pride into the regiment. It is due to truth to say here that the brilliant subsequent career of this superb regiment was largely due to the energy, skill, and spirit of its first Colonel, who impressed upon it the habit of discipline, made it highly proficient in drill, and infused into it the spirit of generous emulation."

Stephens, as senior colonel, was raised to command of his brigade in the organization of the Army of the Mississippi at Corinth. In the approach to the battle of Shiloh, however, he had to rise from his sickbed in Corinth to lead his brigade in the march to the battle. At Shiloh, division commander Cheatham directed Stephens to remain as brigade commander only until Col. Maney arrived on the field. Cheatham personally positioned Stephens's brigade during the brief time when Stephens was still upright in the saddle. Shortly before his brigade's first charge on the Hornets' Nest, Stephens's horse was wounded and threw him, but Stephens accompanied his brigade in its charge and its subsequent retreat. He then fell from exhaustion and took no further part in the action.

After the battle, the 6th did not reelect Stephens colonel, probably because of his poor health. His term of service ended May 15, 1862, and he returned to Jackson to take his place as a circuit judge. He moved to Memphis at the close of the war and then to Los Angeles, California, in 1875, and to a farm in San Gabriel in 1877, where he died ten years later.

First Corps, 2nd (Stephens's) Brigade at Shiloh

Stephens's 2nd Brigade numbered 1,620 men in four regiments—the 7th Kentucky, a battalion of the 1st Tennessee, and the 6th and 9th Tennessee—supported by Smith's Mississippi Battery of six guns.

As early as August 1861, in New Madrid, Missouri, Col. Stephens commanded a brigade in Cheatham's division which included his own 6th Tennessee regiment and the 9th Tennessee. These two regiments would be brigaded together for the entire war.

As recently as March 1862, the month before the battle of Shiloh, the brigade was enlarged by the addition of the 7th Kentucky, 21st Tennessee, and Smith's Mississippi Battery.

Stephens's Brigade formed the rear of Polk's corps and bivouacked Saturday night across the Corinth Road in the order from left to right: 7th Kentucky, 9th Tennessee, 6th Tennessee, 1st Tennessee Battalion, with Smith's Mississippi Battery in the rear.

Before the forward movement began on Sunday, the brigade's temporary commander during Stephens's illness, Col. George Maney, with his 1st Tennessee Battalion and the 19th Tennessee from Breckinridge's Reserve Corps, was ordered to the army's right to guard a ford of Lick Creek. In his absence Col. Stephens, accompanied by General Cheatham, commanded the brigade. The brigade moved forward on the Corinth Road one mile when, at about 8.30 a.m., it was shifted to the left to support Bragg's line.

After half an hour Beauregard ordered the brigade to the right, and at 10:00 a.m. it reached a position in front of the Hornets' Nest, where it formed line of battle. Here, the 7th Kentucky was on the left with its flank extended into Duncan Field, the 9th Tennessee was in the center, and the 6th Tennessee was on the right in the Wheat Field. Smith's Battery was placed in position on Duncan Field and engaged the enemy for about an hour. Starting at 11:20 a.m., General Cheatham led the brigade in an assault on the Hornets' Nest, where it was mauled and repulsed.

Falling back to the Hamburg-Purdy Road, the brigade moved to the right at noon, and joined General Breckinridge's force south of the Peach Orchard. Here Col. Maney rejoined the brigade and assumed command.

At 2:30 p.m. Maney led the 1st, 9th, and 19th Tennessee in a charge across the Peach Orchard that broke the Union line. General Cheatham brought up the 6th Tennessee and 7th Kentucky, and the brigade took position in a small ravine east of the Hamburg-Purdy Road and awaited a supply of ammunition. It was not further engaged on Sunday.

The 1st Tennessee and four companies of the 9th Tennessee, under the command of Col. Maney, bivouacked Sunday night on the field, and on Monday were joined by the 15th Tennessee and were engaged on the right of the Confederate line under General Withers.

The 6th Tennessee and six companies of the 9th Tennessee retired Sunday night with General Cheatham to Saturday night's bivouac. On Monday at noon, Cheatham led those men, along with other remnants of the division, into a firefight on the Confederate left, near Water Oaks Pond. There they blunted the counterattack by what remained of Sherman's and McClernand's Union divisions. This lasted until 2:30 p.m., when they were ordered to retire.

There is no record of where the 7th Kentucky camped Sunday night. On Monday it served under General Breckinridge on the army's right.

Smith's Battery was first engaged for an hour in front of the Hornets' Nest on Sunday. Two of its guns were engaged with General Cheatham on Monday.

At Shiloh, Stephens's Brigade lost 75 killed, 413 wounded, and 3 missing, for a total of 491 out of 1,620 present for duty—30% casualties.

Second Corps

Major General Braxton Bragg

Braxton Bragg, 45 years old, was entirely devoted to the Confederate cause, a tireless worker, an expert at administration, and a master at instilling military discipline, with unassailable credentials as a professional soldier. Unfortunately, Bragg was also an irritable, impatient, and quarrelsome faultfinder who alienated his officers, publicly embarrassed them, and sought scapegoats among them for his own mistakes. So bad was his temper that, in the Mexican War, his own troops made two attempts to assassinate him. He was blighted by chronic headaches and dyspepsia, which contributed to his irascibility and left him thin and stooped, with a sickly, cadaverous appearance. British Col. Arthur Fremantle, who toured the Southern military fields in 1863, called him "the least prepossessing of the Confederate generals." Eventually, despite his military gifts, the combination of his petulance and poor health would result in the collapse of his ability to lead men.

At the time of Shiloh, however, Bragg's military record still shone brightly. He was West Point, Class of 1837, and a veteran of the Seminole Wars and Mexican War, where he won three brevet promotions for gallant and distinguished conduct in the battles of Monterey and Buena Vista, and the defense of Fort Brown, Texas.

Bragg continued in frontier duty until 1856, when he retired to Louisiana to become a sugar planter. There, too, he rose to a high administrative post, appointed Commissioner of the Board of Public Works of the State of Louisiana from 1859 until the opening of the Civil War. In the early months of 1861, he was appointed major general in the Louisiana Militia.

In March 1861 Bragg was appointed brigadier general in the Confederate army and soon was charged with defending the Gulf States. He started with the command of the Army of Pensacola, was promoted to major general in October of 1861, and his command was expanded to include Alabama and a second small army, the Army of Mobile.

In March 1862, Richmond summoned Bragg to Corinth, Mississippi, to bolster Beauregard's Army of the Mississippi in its defense of the Mississippi

Valley. With Beauregard barely able to speak and bedridden with a throat ailment, Bragg on March 19 assumed command of all troops at and near Corinth. In the final organization of the Army of the Mississippi, after General Albert Sidney Johnston arrived with his Central Army of Kentucky troops, Bragg commanded the Second Corps, the largest in the army.

In the battle of Shiloh, Bragg wasted his men in futile, costly frontal attacks. His orders to his subordinates to "go where the fight is thickest" contributed to a preoccupation with combat around the salient at the Hornets' Nest that distracted much of the army from the overall Confederate objective, which was to destroy Grant's army. Bragg destroyed the organizational integrity of the army's divisions and brigades by riding around the battlefield detaching, for his own purposes, whatever units were at hand.

In June 1862, two months after the battle of Shiloh, while General Beauregard was on sick leave, Jefferson Davis replaced him with General Bragg as the commander of the Western Department and the Army of the Mississippi, and Bragg directed the Confederate war in the West for the next year. When his relationships with his subordinates had deteriorated to the vanishing point after the battle of Chattanooga, Bragg petulantly offered his resignation in November 1863 and was dismayed when it was accepted by Davis. President Davis thereafter employed Bragg as a personal military advisor.

After the war Bragg proved just as contentious in business as in the military, switching from job to job until his chronic ill health caught up with him. In 1876 he died suddenly in Galveston, Texas, at the age of 59.

Second (Bragg's) Corps at Shiloh

In the Army of the Mississippi at Shiloh, the Second Corps under Bragg was the largest by far, numbering 16,279 in two divisions, each with three brigades. Most of the men had been stationed along the Gulf Coast. Ruggles's Division was comprised of troops sent north from New Orleans. Withers's Division was composed of the men of Bragg's Army of Mobile and Army of Pensacola. These Mobile and Pensacola troops had benefited from strict training under Bragg, but only a handful of men in the whole corps had ever been shot at, in the unsuccessful attack on Santa Rosa Island the previous October. For the Second Corps brigades, Beauregard ordered flags of the same design he had used in the Eastern Theater: 12 white stars on a blue St. Andrew's cross on a field of red—what would come to be recognized as the Confederate battle flag.

Brigadier General Arthur M. Manigault, who arrived in Corinth with his South Carolina brigade after the battle of Shiloh, observed that Bragg's men from Mobile and Pensacola were a cut above the rest of the army in appearance and discipline. His opinion certainly jibed with Bragg's, who boasted that his Alabama and Mississippi troops were "far superior" to Polk's and Hardee's undisciplined frontiersmen. General Bragg's men were well trained as a result of long months of arduous drill in the Gulf cities.

Braxton Bragg had been in command of the Rebel force at Pensacola in the winter and spring of 1861, when its harbor fort, Fort Pickens, was a flash point for Southern fire-eaters' demands, very much like Fort Sumter in Charleston Harbor. When Sumter erupted in cannon fire in April 1861, Confederate regiments began arriving in Pensacola to guard against a Federal invasion there, and five months later, on October 1, 1861, the field return for the garrison at Pensacola counted 6,533 men in two brigades, under Brig. Gen. Daniel Ruggles and Brig. Gen. Richard H. Anderson.

In early October 1861, the abrasive Ruggles was sent to a new command at New Orleans, and Bragg replaced him at Pensacola with one of his own favorites, Brig. Gen. Adley H. Gladden, formerly colonel of the 1st Louisiana regiment.

On October 7, Bragg's command was expanded to include nearby Mobile, Alabama, and the new command was called the Department of Alabama and West Florida, and included the coastal defenses in those states. Brigadier General Withers's troops in Mobile came to about 4,200—"mostly raw, and inefficiently organized, armed, and equipped, and very destitute of military instructors," according to Bragg at the end of October.

On February 18—the same date that Bragg wired Judah P. Benjamin, the Confederate Secretary of War, that he had sent three of his regiments to Knoxville—he received a dispatch from Benjamin ordering him to send all his remaining Pensacola and Mobile troops to Beauregard's "Tennessee line" now being assembled in the awful aftermath of the capture of Forts Henry and Donelson. In the end, Bragg brought from his department ten infantry regiments, four cavalry companies, and three artillery batteries.

At the same time, Major General Mansfield Lovell in New Orleans sent eight regiments and a battery from his Louisiana department to the forces assembling at Corinth. Called "Ruggles's Brigade," these regiments would be brigaded under Colonels Gibson and Pond in Ruggles's 1st Division of Bragg's Second Corps. General Lovell also announced that Louisiana's Governor Moore had sent two more New Orleans infantry units and one battery.

In all, the rickety Confederate railroads hauled to Corinth about 5,000 troops headed north from New Orleans under General Ruggles, and about 10,000 troops headed west under General Withers from Mobile and General Gladden from Pensacola.

The other regiments put under Bragg's command—which he called "the mob we have miscalled soldiers"—were raw recruits, but in the month at Corinth before the march on Pittsburg Landing, they absorbed military discipline as a result of Bragg's hours of drill.

Bragg was given command of the Second Corps at the time of its organization, March 29, 1862. Beauregard, who had a high opinion of Bragg's soldierly abilities, made sure that Bragg would command the lion's share of the army's troops. Bragg's corps was by far the largest in the Army of the Mississippi, approximately twice the size of the other corps. Bragg divided his corps into two divisions of three brigades each.

In addition to commanding his corps, Bragg was obliged by Beauregard's illness to assume the role of chief-of-staff and to direct the organization of the army in the weeks leading up to the Confederate attack.

In the confused and muddy final approach to the battlefield, Bragg's Second Corps lined up second, behind Hardee's Third Corps.

At Shiloh, Bragg's two divisions formed Saturday night, 800 yards in rear of Hardee's first line, placed across, and perpendicular to, the Corinth Road. Gladden's brigade of Withers's division was the exception: it went forward, on loan to Hardee's corps, and fell in on the right of Hardee's first line. In Bragg's second line, Ruggles's three-brigade Louisiana division was on the left, with its right on the Bark Road; Withers's division—now consisting only of Chalmers's and Jackson's brigades—was to the right of the Bark Road.

The corps went forward at about 6:30 a.m. on Sunday. Soon afterward, Bragg's leftmost brigade, Pond's, was detached to the left, and Chalmers's brigade moved forward to the right of Gladden. The advance continued in this order until Hardee's line became engaged, when Bragg, "finding the first line unequal to the work before it," moved his whole corps to its support. In this movement Ruggles's division intermingled with Hardee's first line, and was not separated from it for the rest of the battle.

Withers on the right kept Chalmers's and Jackson's brigades well in hand and, leading them to the extreme right, continued in command of them all day. These brigades, however, did not accomplish the Confederate task of driving the Union left away from Pittsburg Landing and seizing this crucial link with Buell's approaching reinforcements.

General Bragg himself followed his right and was with Gladden's brigade when Prentiss's camp was captured. Generals Johnston, Bragg, Hardee, Withers, Hindman, and several brigade commanders were together at that time. General Bragg remained in this vicinity until 10:30 a.m. when he met General Polk, and by agreement with him went forward and directed several charges at the Hornets' Nest, without success.

Learning that General Johnston had been killed, Bragg went to the right and assumed command of the forces there, which consisted of Breckinridge's two brigades, Withers's two brigades, and Stephens's (now Maney's) brigade of Cheatham's division. With this force he pushed back the Union left along the Hamburg-Savannah Road until he reached the rear of Prentiss and Wallace, pivoted left, and connected his troops with those of the extreme Confederate left. This surrounded and compelled the surrender of Prentiss.

Bragg reformed his commands and was placing his troops in order for another advance when he received Beauregard's order to withdraw his troops. Bragg remained with Beauregard at his headquarters near Shiloh Church Sunday night.

On Monday morning Bragg was sent to the Confederate left, where, from left to right, the troops of Pond, Wood, Cleburne, Cheatham, Gibson, Anderson, and Trabue slowed the Union advance to a crawl all day. Under General Beauregard's orders he began to retire his troops at 2:00 p.m.

At Shiloh, Bragg's Second Corps lost 553 killed, 2,441 wounded, and 634 missing and captured, for a total of 3,608 out of 16,279 present for duty—22% casualties, the lowest rate of the four Confederate corps.

Bragg's losses to enemy fire (the killed and wounded) were 17% of the total, also the lowest rate of the four Confederate corps (and identical to Grant's Army of the Tennessee's 17%). The men of the Second Corps may have been more reticent fighters than those in other corps because of their total lack of combat experience.

1st Division

Brigadier General Daniel Ruggles

Daniel Ruggles was only 52, but he looked like an Old Testament prophet with his straight white beard that jutted all the way to his stomach. He was insufferable: one of his subordinates wrote home, "He is an old brute. Being an old army officer and a New Englander, he had no conscience nor mercy on anyone." Like his superior Braxton Bragg, he combined a bad temper with an insistence on strict military discipline. Whether it was his Yankee ways or his testy personality, his superiors in the Confederate army consistently transferred him away at their first opportunity.

Born and raised in Massachusetts, Ruggles graduated from West Point in 1833 and had remained a soldier ever since, fighting in the Seminole Wars and the Mexican War, where he won two brevets for Gallant and Meritorious Conduct, and on frontier duty in the interwar years. He was on sick leave for the two years prior to the outbreak of the Civil War.

He had married into a wealthy Virginia family, so after Fort Sumter Ruggles resigned from the U.S. Army and was appointed brigadier general in the Virginia State Army, assigned to watch the Rappahannock River line at Fredericksburg in the war's early days. Made a brigadier general in the Confederate Army in August 1861, he was transferred away from the Virginia army and sent to Pensacola to report to Bragg.

In Pensacola, he became embroiled in a seniority dispute with Richard H. Anderson, and after only one month of active duty, in October 1861, he was transferred again, this time to New Orleans. There, poor health prevented him from performing his duties until December. In February, Bragg asked General Mansfield Lovell in New Orleans for troops for the concentration in Corinth, and Lovell dispatched Ruggles, who arrived on February 17 with four regiments—the 16th, 17th, 18th, and 19th Louisiana Infantry, which were soon joined by a half dozen more Louisiana regiments.

In the final organization of the Army of the Mississippi before the attack on Grant at Pittsburg Landing, Ruggles was given command of a division in Bragg's corps, and the Louisiana regiments were scattered among his brigades.

His division command at Shiloh was the only combat command Ruggles held during the Civil War—within a month he was transferred away from the army to assist with the defenses of Port Hudson, but was transferred from there to a minor district post. He never saw another battle.

After the war Ruggles returned to Virginia, where he died in 1897 at the age of 87.

Second Corps, 1st (Ruggles's) Division at Shiloh

Ruggles's division numbered 7,672 men in three brigades, commanded by Col. Randall Gibson, Brig. Gen. J. Patton Anderson, and Col. Preston Pond.

The bulk of the troops were Louisianans. The seven numbered regiments—the 4th, 13th, and 16th through 20th Louisiana—were known as "Ruggles's Brigade," and had been sent to the Army of the Mississippi in answer to the War Department's February order to New Orleans to furnish 5,000 troops to reinforce the Army of the Mississippi in Tennessee. Other units—the Confederate Guards Response Battalion, the Crescent Regiment, and the Orleans Guard Battalion, all guarding New Orleans—followed after General Beauregard's further plea to the governors of Tennessee, Alabama, Mississippi, and Louisiana to furnish troops for the defense of the Mississippi Valley after the fall of Forts Henry and Donelson. Louisiana's Governor Moore was the only governor to respond with a large contingent, probably because Beauregard was a native son from New Orleans. These were joined in Ruggles's division by a few late-arriving units from other Gulf States.

The soldiers of the division had not fought together, nor even maneuvered in groups larger than regiments. They had been in their camps since the beginning of the war, guarding the Louisiana and Mississippi coastline, and had no combat experience.

At the dawn of the battle, Ruggles's division of three brigades made up the left of Bragg's second line. Pond's brigade was on the left, extended to near Owl Creek; Anderson's brigade was in the center; and Gibson's brigade was on the right, extended to the Corinth Road.

Soon after the division started forward on Sunday morning, two regiments from Pond's brigade were detached to guard the left flank of the army, and Gibson's brigade was moved to the right to support Shaver's brigade in Hardee's first line of battle.

Anderson's brigade and the right of Pond's brigade moved directly forward and became engaged in front of the first Union camps, where Anderson's brigade became mixed up with Cleburne's brigade of Hardee's corps, and both brigades became disorganized. A part of each followed the Corinth Road under Ruggles's command until they reached Duncan Field about 3:00 p.m.

There, General Ruggles gave his personal attention to massing the artillery, some 50–60 guns, to enfilade the right flank of Prentiss's division at the Hornets' Nest. The artillery, thus placed, bombarded Prentiss's command, and drove back the reinforcements coming to his assistance, so that within an hour the entire command surrendered to an infantry attack, in which Ruggles's men played an important part.

On Monday, Ruggles, with portions of his division, fought on the Confederate left until the troops were ordered to retire. During the day he shared his men's danger, on one occasion leading a charge of the 17th Louisiana with its regimental flag in his hand. During the Confederate withdrawal, Ruggles took command of the second line of the rear guard.

The battle of Shiloh was the highpoint of Ruggles's war career: it was on his initiative that the Union command at the Hornets' Nest was finally reduced and forced to surrender. However, Ruggles's brigades received orders from half a dozen generals, and his missing were a glaring 18.5% of his casualties, an indication of laxity in control.

At Shiloh, Ruggles's division lost 255 killed, 1,137 wounded, and 318 missing, for a total of 1,710 out of 7,672 present for duty—22% casualties, a slightly lower rate than Withers's division, the other division of Bragg's corps.

1st Brigade
Colonel Randall L. Gibson

Gibson was the flower of Southern society, a Louisiana aristocrat 29 years old, svelte, handsome, immaculately groomed, suave, well-traveled, wealthy and Yale-educated. He had roomed at Yale with General Albert S. Johnston's son, William, who served during the war as one of President Jefferson Davis' aide-de-camps.

Gibson had started the war as a military aide to Louisiana Governor Thomas O. Moore, then was named captain of the 1st Louisiana Artillery. He resigned this post to become colonel of the 13th Louisiana Infantry in September 1861. Since he had no military experience, his family's connections and his own intimacy with Generals Johnston, Polk, Beauregard, and Breckinridge were instrumental in his success in "politicking" to be elected colonel of the 13th Louisiana. He was also familiar with Braxton Bragg, since that general had owned a sugar plantation near the Gibson family's. Unfortunately, that association bred only bad blood between the two rival planters, exacerbated, once the war brought them together in uniform, by Bragg's loathing of "political" officers.

With the 13th Louisiana regiment, Gibson was summoned to join General Polk's army in Columbus, Kentucky, in November. With Polk, Gibson and his regiment evacuated Columbus in February 1862 and concentrated with Bragg's Gulf coast troops at Corinth. In late March, although Polk attempted to keep Gibson under his own command, Gibson and the 13th Louisiana were assigned to the 1st Brigade of Bragg's 1st Division under Ruggles, where Gibson was, as well as anyone could reckon, the senior colonel.

Despite being new to military life, and so new in brigade command that he was little known to his regiments, one of his men reported that "Colonel Gibson, an exceedingly bright man, soon mastered tactics, and was never after at a loss in handling regiment or brigade." At Shiloh, Gibson exerted enough control to attack the Hornets' Nest four times in succession, under the critical eye of corps commander Bragg.

Gibson proved competent enough to alternate in and out of brigade command for the rest of the war, and would later be promoted to brigadier general. After the war, Gibson was elected Congressman from Louisiana for eight years and then Senator for eight more, dying while in office in 1892.

1st Division, 1st (Gibson's) Brigade at Shiloh

Gibson's Brigade numbered 2,560 men in four infantry regiments: the 1st Arkansas and the 4th, 13th, and 19th Louisiana. They were supported by Bain's Mississippi Artillery Battery and two companies of cavalry.

Gibson noted that his brigade had been "recently thrown together & officers & men alike unacquainted with each other & myself. . . . We were all tyros," he said, "all the rawest and greenest recruits." The 1st Arkansas had been to Virginia and back during the first year of the war but had done no fighting. Its colonel was a Mexican War veteran. The Arkansans chafed at the assignment since they wanted to be brigaded with other Arkansans.

The Louisiana regiments were three of the seven regiments of "Ruggles's Brigade," sent north to Corinth by New Orleans's commander, General Lovell. One observer described the 4th Louisiana as "Young sugar planters and slave-owners...wealthy, refined, gentlemanly fellows." The 13th Louisiana were diverse New Orleans workers, mostly laborers and draymen. One ungenerous observer called them "a very low set of men being composed of low Irish and the scum of creation." The core of the regiment was its six companies of Zouaves. The regiment drilled in French because it was the only language everyone understood; indeed, the 13th Louisiana developed an excellent reputation for its disciplined drill and eventually was one of the best in the army. The 19th Louisiana, from the northern part of the state, was particularly hard hit by disease: out of 873 men in the regiment in early December, only 300 were still available for duty as the regiment approached Shiloh.

Brigadier General Lucius Marshall Walker commanded the brigade, but he was absent, sick, and a temporary brigade commander had to be selected from among four colonels. Because of some technical flaws in their commissions that made it impossible to determine their seniority, Col. James Fagan of the 1st Arkansas, Lt. Col. Henry Watkins of the 4th Louisiana, and Col. Benjamin L. Hodge of the 19th Louisiana insisted that Gibson take command.

One man later described the circumstances surrounding Gibson's unexpected leadership role as "a curious illustration of the freshness of life and of the imperfect organization of that host, that four regiments found themselves on picket without even having seen the brigadier [Gibson] assigned to them." What he described as "imperfect organization" was actually symptomatic of the confusion that reigned within the army's entire infrastructure and crippled its ability to fight. As Gibson noted later, most of the troops and officers, even many of the generals, were totally inexperienced, with little in their past lives to prepare them for the grisly task ahead of them.

Gibson's brigade was initially on outpost duty between the two enemy armies, and orders failed to reach him in time for him to take his position in the van of the Confederate column in its approach to Shiloh. When he saw the army coming up, he was surprised. Gibson remembered that "Genl Bragg was vexed because he had failed to have his orders properly communicated to me and because I mentioned the matter to him in the presence of Genl Johnston—who turned to Genl Bragg and asked him how the mistake was made." Gibson had committed a serious breach of military protocol in airing the matter with Bragg in front of Johnston, Bragg's superior. Bragg's ire was compounded with jealousy when General Johnston replied affectionately to Gibson, his son's former college roommate, telling Gibson to move as soon as he could get his troops together.

Gibson's brigade bivouacked Saturday evening on the right of Ruggles's division, which was in the second line, following Hardee's corps. Gibson's right was on the Corinth Road, in order of regiments, from left to right: 4th Louisiana, 13th Louisiana, 1st Arkansas, 19th Louisiana.

On Sunday morning, starting at about 6:30 a.m., when the Confederate army went forward, Bragg pulled Gibson's brigade away from the rest of Ruggles's division and directed it to follow Wood's and Shaver's brigades (from Hardee's corps) to the front of the first enemy camp. There, with its right in the woods and its left in the Rhea Field, Gibson's men came under the fire of Waterhouse's Battery. The 4th Louisiana, being on the left and exposed in Rhea Field, suffered the most from Waterhouse's fire, while the 19th, on the right, suffered only two wounded.

Passing through Peabody's camp, Gibson's brigade came up with Shaver's brigade and fired a few shots from the edge of Barnes Field at retreating Union troops and received a few shells from Munch's Battery in reply. Wood's and Shaver's brigades presently moved off to the left, leaving Gibson's brigade in the front line.

The brigade rested in Barnes Field until noon, when General Bragg found it and ordered it forward to attack Tuttle and Prentiss at the Hornets' Nest. The right of the brigade, the 19th Louisiana, moved half a mile to the right across the Hamburg-Purdy Road and into the Davis Wheat Field and attacked the enemy in dense undergrowth; the left of the brigade, the 4th Louisiana, came into Duncan Field. The brigade was then repulsed by the Union defenders in the Sunken Road. Gibson and his colonels requested artillery support, but there was none to be had—all the batteries were either to the far right or far left. Under orders from Bragg, however, Gibson's brigade charged again and again, until four unsupported frontal attacks had been four times beaten back. After the last repulse the brigade retired to Barnes Field and was not engaged again on Sunday. Bragg, in his official report, would blame Gibson for the repulses.

Gibson's brigade bivouacked near Shiloh Church on Sunday night. The 19th Louisiana became separated from its brigade during the night and on Monday fought on the army's right at the Davis Wheat Field where they had fought the day before.

The other regiments were on the left on Monday, next to Pond's brigade, where they charged the enemy and captured a part of Thurber's Battery on Jones Field, but were unable to hold it. Pond was ordered to the right and Gibson held the extreme left until ordered to retire to the Shiloh Church area.

There they participated in Cheatham's attack at the crossroads of the Corinth Road and Hamburg-Purdy Road against Sherman's and McClernand's troops around noon. By this time the men were exhausted and the regiments were hopelessly mixed. The battle seesawed until about 2:00 p.m., when the Army of the Mississippi began to withdraw from the field.

At Shiloh, Gibson's brigade lost 97 killed, 488 wounded, and 97 missing, for a total of 682 out of 2,560 present for duty—27% casualties. Most were lost in the forlorn attacks on the Hornets' Nest on Sunday.

2nd Brigade
Brigadier General James Patton Anderson

General Bragg was notoriously hard to please, but he had an especially affectionate regard for "Patton" Anderson, who he thought was "as noble and true a soldier as any age can boast." This was especially remarkable because Anderson was a politician and not a West Pointer, a combination that was almost always a black mark with Bragg.

Anderson, 40 years old at Shiloh, was a man with a remarkable number of facets. Born in Tennessee in 1822, he moved to Kentucky at age nine, then to Mississippi at age 16. He attended medical school at Jefferson College in southern Pennsylvania, then returned to Mississippi four years later, where he practiced medicine. He moved to Frankfort, Kentucky, to study law and was admitted to the bar in 1843 at the age of 21. He moved back to Mississippi, just south of Memphis, to practice law and serve as county sheriff.

Patton Anderson entered the Mississippi militia with the rank of captain when the Mexican War started in 1846. He raised a Tennessee regiment for the war, but it arrived too late to do any fighting. Afterward he returned to his law practice in Mississippi and developed a political career, winning election to the Mississippi legislature in 1850, where he befriended Jefferson Davis. His opposition to the Compromise of 1850 prevented him from being re-elected in

1851, but got him noticed in national Democratic Party circles. Two years later, President Franklin Pierce appointed him U.S. Marshal for Washington Territory.

In 1857, his interest in the increasing sectional tension over slavery drew him back to the South, where he managed his aunt's plantation in Florida. By 1860, he had established himself strongly enough in his new state to be elected as a delegate to Florida's secession convention and get appointed to the provisional Confederate Congress, from which he resigned to organize an infantry company.

Anderson's company became part of the 1st Florida Infantry, and on April 5, 1861, a week before the firing at Fort Sumter, he was named the regiment's colonel, initially serving at Pensacola under the command of General Bragg. Anderson was a strict disciplinarian like his superior, and the two formed a bond of loyalty. When Anderson's brigadier, Richard H. Anderson, left for the Army of Northern Virginia in January 1862, Bragg requested Patton Anderson's promotion to brigadier general, and he received his general's star on February 10. In the next month, Bragg transferred Anderson to Corinth and put him in command of a brigade in Ruggles's Division.

After Shiloh, Anderson would be trusted with a brigade or a division in most of the battles in the West, and would vindicate Bragg's faith.

In 1864, while leading a fruitless attack at Jonesboro, before the fall of Atlanta, Anderson was wounded by a minie ball that carried away part of his jaw, much of his tongue, and some teeth. He was able to rejoin the army in North Carolina just prior to its surrender at Greensboro. After the war, he returned to Memphis, but had difficulty working as a result of his war wound. He died from the effects of his wound in 1872, in poverty.

1st Division, 2nd (Anderson's) Brigade at Shiloh

Anderson's Brigade numbered 1,628 men in three regiments and two battalions of infantry: the 17th and 20th Louisiana, 9th Texas, 1st Florida Battalion, and Confederate Guards Response Battalion.

The brigade was a polyglot unit, thrown together at Corinth in the days before the attack on Pittsburg Landing. The 1st Florida Battalion consisted of four companies from Patton Anderson's own Pensacola regiment who had recently re-enlisted. The 17th Louisiana and the German-Irish 20th Louisiana were two of the seven regiments in "Ruggles's Brigade," sent north by railroad from New Orleans. The Confederate Guards Response Battalion followed, sent by Louisiana's Governor Moore after Beauregard's plea to the Southern governors. The 9th Texas was sick, poorly drilled, without reliable weapons, and down to 226 effectives. The brigade's infantry were supported by the dapper, upper-crust 5th Company, Washington Artillery of New Orleans. None had seen combat.

On Sunday morning, Anderson's brigade occupied the center of Ruggles's division. His regiments were lined up, from left to right: 20th Louisiana, 9th Texas, 1st Florida Battalion, Confederate Guard's Response Battalion, and 17th Louisiana, with the Washington Artillery in the rear. In the advance on Sunday morning the brigade followed Cleburne's brigade in Hardee's line. Later on the first day, Anderson's brigade formed the reserve for Ruggles's division.

Anderson's brigade came up with Cleburne's at 8:30 a.m. to the crossing of Shiloh Branch, connecting with Pond's brigade's right. Anderson's men joined with Cleburne's and Russell's brigades in a charge on Sherman's division northwest of Rhea Field, but all were initially repulsed by the fire of Waterhouse's Battery and its infantry support. The 17th Louisiana made three separate charges. Hildebrand's Union brigade was finally put to flight after being bludgeoned by a series of attacks which included Anderson's men. During the struggle the Washington Artillery, together with artillery of the other brigades, occupied the high ground in the rear and added their firepower.

The 20th Louisiana and 9th Texas, on Anderson's left, were twice repulsed, but with reinforcements carried the position held by Buckland's brigade and joined the righthand regiments in an advance upon McClernand's division's second position at the crossroads of the Corinth Road and the Hamburg-Purdy Road, where Anderson's brigade was reorganized.

About noon Anderson joined Trabue in his engagement with McDowell's brigade.

At 3:00 p.m. Anderson's brigade moved directly east to Duncan Field. The Washington Artillery battery was placed in Ruggles's artillery line and the infantry moved to the right, where it joined other troops in an attack on the Hornets' Nest.

In the fighting at the Hornets' Nest, Anderson was more cautious than Cleburne, who had gone in earlier and been thrown back. Anderson halted his infantry and called for artillery support. After many of his 1st Florida men fled to the rear, Anderson dashed along the line in an attempt to regain order in his old regiment.

Despite his efforts, Anderson's attack on the Hornets' Nest was repulsed, and the 20th Louisiana fled from the field. The other regiments returned to the attack and followed the retiring Union troops to the place of surrender. The brigade then moved forward to a ravine at the head of Dill Branch, where it remained 15 minutes under artillery fire, and then, at sunset, retired.

General Anderson bivouacked with the 9th Texas and 1st Florida in the center of the battlefield. The other regiments were scattered, but were all with the brigade on Monday when it was engaged. The Washington Artillery was engaged on Monday on the right, near the Davis Wheat Field, where it lost three guns. The guns were recaptured, but three caissons, a battery wagon, and a forge were left on the field.

At Shiloh, Anderson's brigade lost 69 killed, 313 wounded, and 52 missing, for a total of 434 out of 1,628 engaged—27% casualties.

3rd Brigade
Colonel Preston Pond, Jr.

Preston Pond, 38, was a poor choice for the leader of a brigade, a perfect example of an administrator out of his depth. In the 1850s he was a lawyer practicing in East Feliciana Parish, near Baton Rouge. Entering politics as an anti-immigrant Know-Nothing, he was elected to the Louisiana House of Representatives in 1851, but was defeated in his run for U. S. Congressman from his district in 1855.

Pond also served in the Louisiana Militia as colonel of the East Feliciana regiment. When Louisiana seceded he was given more responsibility, with an appointment to Inspector General of the 3rd Division of the state militia. When the 16th Louisiana—a regiment with recruits from all parts of the state—was thrown together on September 29, 1861, Pond was well enough politically connected to be named its colonel.

Pond was a painstaking drillmaster, drilling his men five hours a day through the fall and early winter. His reputation as a combat leader, however, would not survive the blunders of his first battle: he was not re-elected colonel of the 16th Louisiana regiment after Shiloh, and resigned from the army on May 2. He returned to involvement in Louisiana politics before dying in June 1864 at age 40.

1st Division, 3rd (Pond's) Brigade at Shiloh

Pond's Brigade numbered 2,644 men in four regiments and one battalion of infantry: the 16th and 18th Louisiana, the Crescent Regiment, the Orleans Guard Battalion, and the 38th Tennessee. They were supported by Ketchum's Alabama artillery battery.

The 16th and 18th Louisiana were recently part of "Ruggles' Brigade," on loan from the state of Louisiana. The 16th Louisiana in particular had gained a high reputation for parade drill. With its colonel, Pond, commanding the brigade, the 16th was led at Shiloh by its major.

The 18th Louisiana had the most recent combat experience of any regiment in the army. Assigned to picket duty at Pittsburg Landing when they arrived at Corinth, on March 1 they repulsed a landing party from the Union gunboats Tyler and Conestoga and drove away the gunboats, losing 21 men. The regiment fought under Col. Alfred Mouton, the son of a Louisiana governor and a West Point graduate, class of 1850.

The Crescent Regiment was a militia unit composed of men from elite New Orleans families and who reported for duty in elegant carriages. The regiment was colorful and well-drilled, viewed war as a glorious enterprise, and carried their servants to camp with them. They had enlisted in the Confederate army for only 90 days.

The Orleans Guard Battalion was, like the Crescent Regiment, a New Orleans militia unit of four companies enlisted for 90 days.

The 38th Tennessee had recently been posted at Eastport, Alabama, to guard the Memphis & Charleston Railroad bridge. This small force, with two smoothbore 24-pound guns, had defeated the Federal gunboats in every attempt to pass.

On Sunday morning, Pond's brigade formed the left of Bragg's line of battle, near Owl Creek, in the order from left to right: 38th Tennessee, Crescent Regiment, 18th Louisiana, Orleans Guard, and 16th Louisiana, with Ketchum's Alabama battery in the rear.

At 8:00 a.m. Sunday morning, the 38th Tennessee, the Crescent Regiment, and one section of the battery were detached and sent 1½ miles to the left to the bridge on the Hamburg-Purdy Road over Owl Creek, where they remained on guard until 2:00 p.m.

The other regiments and two sections of the battery, connecting with the left of Anderson's brigade, advanced to Shiloh Branch, where they became engaged with the skirmishers of McDowell's brigade of Sherman's division. McDowell was ordered to withdraw and Pond gained the first line of camps without a fight. Pond's pursuit then stalled as the troops wasted over 30 minutes rifling through the abandoned tents. Pond's stall proved disastrous to the Confederate fortunes on the left. He decided to await the arrival of Ketchum's Battery before resuming his advance, and nearly two hours elapsed before Pond received a curt order from Beauregard to move his brigade forward.

At noon Pond, with his three regiments, joined the left of Trabue's Kentucky Brigade in Crescent Field. He then moved forward to the valley of Tilghman Branch, where at 4:30 p.m. he was ordered by General Hardee to charge the Union lines. He formed his regiments en échelon, the 18th Louisiana in front on the left, followed by the Orleans Guard in the middle, followed by the 16th Louisiana on the right, and moved directly upon the Union line. He was repulsed with heavy loss and retired to high ground on the west side of Tilghman Branch, where he bivouacked Sunday night with his left at Owl Creek.

At 2:00 p.m. on Sunday, the detached 38th Tennessee, the Crescent Regiment, and the section of Ketchum's Battery guarding the Owl Creek bridge were ordered to the center. They moved east along the Hamburg-Purdy Road to its crossroads with the Corinth Road, where Beauregard ordered them to continue northeast along the Corinth Road. At Duncan Field the section of Ketchum's Battery was placed on the left of Ruggles's artillery line and the two regiments were directed to the left, where they engaged the right flank of troops at the Hornets' Nest. There, the 38th Tennessee assisted in the capture of the 12th Iowa, and the Crescent Regiment also made captures. The 38th Tennessee then rejoined the rest of the brigade at Owl Creek on the army's left on Sunday evening. The Crescent Regiment bivouacked in a nearby camp.

Pond did not receive Beauregard's order on Sunday evening to retire, and did not realize the rest of the army had withdrawn a mile during the night, leaving his brigade dangerously exposed. The next morning he found his command to the left of—and far in front of—the rest of the army. Pond's brigade opened Monday's battle with an artillery duel between Ketchum's guns and those of Lew Wallace's division. After extricating his brigade, Pond received too many orders and his brigade went from one destination to another in the confusion.

The brigade was driven back gradually to the Hamburg-Purdy Road, from where it was sent to join Trabue's right. It soon returned to the left and then fell back to Shiloh Church disorganized. Colonel Looney, with his own 38th Tennessee regiment and parts of five other regiments, made the last charge of the day, his command forming at the church under the personal direction of General Beauregard and charging forward directly over the site of Sherman's headquarters.

Ketchum's Battery was engaged with the brigade all day and lost two guns.

On Monday morning, the Crescent Regiment was sent to the right, where it joined the 19th Louisiana and 1st Missouri in support of the Washington Artillery and then, in conjunction with Col. Joe Wheeler, covered the retreat from that part of the field.

At Shiloh, Pond's Brigade lost 89 killed, 336 wounded, and 169 missing, for a total of 594 out of 2,644 present for duty—22% casualties.

2nd Division

Brigadier General
Jones M. Withers

Jones Withers was a magnetic civilian leader and a dependable wartime commander, but did not escape disapproval from his hypercritical superior, Braxton Bragg. Withers was 48 years old, born in Huntsville, Alabama, son of a former Virginia planter. He was West Point, Class of 1835, but graduated 44th out of 56 cadets, and afterward was assigned to the Regular Army dragoons. Rather than live the life of an army trooper he resigned, returned to Alabama, and practiced law. By 1838, at the age of 25, he was married (he would have 10 children), employed as Secretary of the Alabama State Senate, and ranked captain in the Alabama Militia. During the Mexican War, he rose to colonel of the 9th U.S. Infantry.

After the Mexican War, Withers returned again to Alabama and became a cotton broker before entering local politics. He was elected to the state legislature, and afterward was elected U.S. Congressman in 1855, and then mayor of Mobile in 1858.

Withers remained mayor of the city until the outbreak of the Civil War, when he entered the Confederate service as colonel of the 3rd Alabama Infantry on April 28, 1861, and was posted in Norfolk, Virginia. He rose immediately to the head of the Department of Norfolk in May and was promoted to brigadier general on July 10.

In September, Withers was given command of the District of Alabama, with the responsibility of watching the Gulf seacoast. It was soon after Withers's accession to command that Major General Braxton Bragg visited from Pensacola. Typically, Bragg was scathing. After reviewing Withers' troops, Bragg reported to Secretary of War Benjamin, "General Withers' command need to be put in an efficient condition." "The men," he wrote, "are raw and inefficiently organized, armed and equipped…and…destitute of military instructors." Withers he found "very competent" but "sadly addicted to drinking," and "therefore unsafe for those exposed conditions." He suggested replacing Withers with an officer transferred from Pensacola.

Withers, of course, was quietly outraged by Bragg's insult, and had his own assessment of Bragg: "Bragg is a good officer, a man of fair capacity, of good administrative ability," he wrote to a friend, "but not a man of genius.... I may be as self-willed, arrogant and dictatorial as he...yet he has the advantage in that he has the superior rank." Withers did resolve to stay and serve with Bragg. "Oil and water will mix," he promised, "as soon as we can affiliate."

On January 27, 1862, Bragg's Pensacola, Florida command was enlarged to include the Alabama coast, and Withers's 10,000-man army came under his direct control, re-designated the Army of Mobile. Transferred to Corinth with most of his Mobile army on March 4, Withers was named commander of the 2nd Division of Bragg's Second Corps in the Army of the Mississippi on March 29.

Withers had academic military training, experience in the Mexican War, and seven months' experience commanding the Army of Mobile; however, none of this prepared him adequately for combat at Shiloh. He was not alone in this regard, as the scale of the battle was at the time unprecedented on the continent.

Withers proved to be a dependable division commander, and was promoted to major general in August 1862. He served well in the Perryville and Tullahoma campaigns before poor health forced him to leave the army before Chickamauga. He spent the rest of the war in administrative posts, and died in Mobile in 1890, after once more serving a term as the city's mayor.

Second Corps, 2nd (Withers's) Division at Shiloh

Withers's division numbered 7,873 troops from Bragg's Army of Pensacola and Army of Mobile. They were touted by Bragg as the best-trained men in the Army of the Mississippi.

The division consisted of three brigades under men hand-picked by Bragg. The first was commanded by Brig. Gen. Adley H. Gladden, who had served under Bragg first at Pensacola, then Mobile. The second was under James R. Chalmers, and the third was led by Brig. Gen. John K. Jackson.

The lack of combat experience in the division, however, was almost total. These were men who had been manning coastal defenses for a full year. The only action had been a small affair at Santa Rosa Island in October 1861, and a few skirmishes in the weeks leading up to the battle of Shiloh.

Withers's division was on the right of Bragg's corps and formed in line Sunday morning on the Bark Road a quarter mile east of its fork with the Corinth Road.

Gladden's brigade was detached from Withers's division's line and sent forward to form the right of Hardee's corps' first line. Jackson's brigade formed 300 yards directly in rear of Gladden, on the right of the Bark Road, and Chalmers's brigade was on Jackson's right, extending Withers's line to a tributary of Lick Creek.

In the advance on Sunday morning, Chalmers soon came up to Gladden's right and joined it in an attack upon Prentiss's 6th Division camp.

After the capture of Prentiss's camp, Withers was ordered to take Chalmers's and Jackson's brigades down the Bark Road to Lick Creek to attack on the Confederate right. Withers found Stuart's Union brigade there. He succeeded in driving Stuart back and followed him, pressing back the Union left. Withers's men reached the rear of Prentiss and Wallace in the Union center, and received the surrender of part of these troops.

Withers then moved to the right along the ridge south of Dill Branch, formed in line, and then advanced into the valley of Dill Branch, where he made the last attack late Sunday afternoon. He then withdrew, and his division became disorganized. Chalmers's brigade and one regiment of Jackson's brigade bivouacked in Stuart's abandoned camp; Withers himself spent the night in Prentiss's camp.

On Monday Withers's division had retired a mile from the field when it was recalled and engaged on the right until 2:00 p.m., when it retired.

At Shiloh, the men of Withers's command were those he had brought with him from the Army of Mobile, where he had been their commander. They knew and respected him. Yet the two brigades—Chalmers's and Jackson's—under Withers's control took hours to drive away the three Union regiments of Stuart's brigade. Withers kept his two brigades well in hand, but moved slowly. And even though he moved slowly, his missing were 16% of his casualties, a high figure.

At Shiloh, Withers's 2nd Division lost 298 killed, 1,304 wounded, and 316 missing, totaling 1,918 out of 7,873 present for duty—24% casualties, a slightly higher rate than Ruggles's 1st Division, the other division of the Second Corps.

1st Brigade
Brigadier General Adley H. Gladden

Gladden won the admiration of Braxton Bragg, a tough judge of soldiers, but was mortally wounded at the outset of Shiloh, his first major battle in the Civil War.

Born in South Carolina in 1810, Gladden became a cotton broker in Columbia. He led a militia unit in the Seminole War in the 1830s and was rewarded

with the job of postmaster in Columbia. When the war with Mexico began in 1846, Gladden was appointed major of the celebrated "Palmetto" regiment from South Carolina. In the assault on Churubusco, the regiment's colonel and lieutenant colonel were killed, leaving Gladden as the ranking officer. In the battle for Mexico City he was wounded, and after coming home, took up residence in New Orleans.

When Louisiana seceded at the end of January 1861, Gladden was appointed colonel of the 1st Louisiana Regulars. The regiment was sent to the nearest flashpoint as the war neared, which was Pensacola, Florida. In September, Gladden was promoted to brigadier general and replaced Daniel Ruggles in command of a brigade after Ruggles's unlamented departure. During the bombardment of the Confederate forts in Pensacola Harbor in November 1861, Bragg praised Gladden's defense.

When Bragg's command was enlarged to include Alabama in January 1862, Bragg visited the defenses of Mobile and found its second-in-command, former Secretary of War L. Pope Walker, living a life of too much ease and especially too much drink. To replace him, Bragg called Gladden from Pensacola, and Gladden's new command at Mobile was quickly put in military order. As a pet project, Bragg considered putting Gladden at the head of a model brigade that would be an exemplar of discipline for other brigades to follow.

Events intervened, however. In February, Bragg went to Corinth, Mississippi, to help the ailing General Beauregard assemble an army there, and in March transferred most of his troops from Mobile and Pensacola to Corinth. Gladden was given a brigade, mostly of Alabamians.

Bragg admired Gladden as his best brigadier in camp. It was impossible to know how much ability Gladden would show in the acid test of Civil War combat, however, as he would only have a few minutes to demonstrate it. He was mortally wounded by a cannon shot just after ordering his first attack at Shiloh. His last words to his men were, "Go on, my brave boys, they have hit old dad."

2nd Division, 1st (Gladden's) Brigade at Shiloh

Gladden's Brigade numbered 2,156 men in five regiments, the 21st, 22nd, 25th, and 26th Alabama Infantry, and the 1st Louisiana Infantry, supported by Felix H. Robertson's Florida Battery.

The smartly drilled 1st Louisiana was much admired by General Bragg, and was one of three regiments he had wanted to combine into a model brigade. All except the 26th Alabama were well-drilled regiments, having been trained under Bragg's stern eye in the Army of Mobile. The 26th was the exception, a brand-new regiment formed from fresh recruits on April 3 as the Confederate army moved out of Corinth to attack Grant at Shiloh.

Most of the brigade would be fighting under their accustomed leaders, but the 21st and 26th Alabama regiments would be fighting under new commanders, both lieutenant colonels.

Gladden's brigade was attached temporarily to Hardee's corps and took position Saturday night in the first line of battle at the right of Hardee's line on the Bark Road, in the following order, from left to right: 26th Alabama, 25th Alabama, 22nd Alabama, 21st Alabama, and 1st Louisiana, with Robertson's Battery in the rear.

The brigade advanced at 6:30 a.m. Sunday until, at 8:30 a.m., it became engaged in front of Prentiss's camps. The 22nd Alabama formed across the Eastern Corinth Road. The 26th Alabama, crowded out of position on the left by Shaver's brigade, took position on the right. As they advanced along Lick Creek, difficult terrain ruined Gladden's alignment with Hardee's attack.

Prentiss's defenders greeted Gladden's line with volleys that caused them to fall back and regroup. The two sides continued their fight with long-range firing for the next hour. Unexpectedly, Prentiss ordered a fallback, and seeing the Union army give ground, Gladden ordered a charge.

While his soldiers formed for their assault, Gladden rode forward to get a better view of the Union line. Union cannon fired, and Gladden toppled to the ground, mortally wounded—his arm was amputated on the field, and he died a few days later. Senior colonel Daniel W. Adams, of the 1st Louisiana, assumed command, and at 9:00 a.m. the brigade advanced and took possession of Prentiss's camps. Adams formed the brigade in a square at Prentiss's headquarters, where it remained inactive until about 2:00 p.m.

At 2:30 p.m., Adams's brigade was one of the units sent against the Hornet's Nest. While riding down the battle line, a minié ball struck Adams above the right eye and tore through his head to exit behind his right ear. The gravely wounded officer was put into a wagon headed back to Corinth, Miss., but along the way the driver believed he had died and dumped him on the side of the road. Fortunately, some passing Mississippi soldiers noticed Adams was still alive and rescued him. He eventually recovered, and though blind in his right eye, went on to play leading roles in battles from Perryville to Chickamauga to Selma.

After Adams was wounded, Col. Zach Deas of the 22nd Alabama took command. Soon afterward, Deas led the brigade—minus the 26th Alabama—to the right, where he reported to General Breckinridge and became engaged in the last attack upon Prentiss at the Hornets' Nest. Here the 21st and 25th Alabama became separated from the brigade.

Colonel Deas formed the 1st Louisiana and 22nd Alabama (together only 224 men) on the left of Jackson's brigade and took part in the 6:00 attack on the last Union line. They were then ordered back to camp for the night.

In the meantime, the 26th Alabama made a charge across the west side of the Peach Orchard, supported in the woods on the left by Forrest's cavalry.

On Monday 150 men of the 26th Alabama joined Chalmers in two engagements, and then left the field. On that day the 25th Alabama joined the 1st Missouri, Bowen's brigade, and the 21st Alabama fell under Col. Moore's command.

On Monday the 1st Louisiana and the 22nd Alabama, under Col. Deas, were with Ruggles on the left of the line, where they were engaged until reduced to 60 men.

Robertson's Battery of 12-pounder Napoleons was first engaged on the Eastern Corinth Road in front of Prentiss's camp. After that, it engaged the Union batteries in the Peach Orchard and then reported to Ruggles, east of Review Field. On Monday the battery was with the Confederate right.

At Shiloh, Gladden's Brigade lost 129 killed, 597 wounded, and 103 missing, for a total of 829 out of 2,156 engaged—38% casualties.

2nd Brigade
Brigadier General James R. Chalmers

Chalmers was one of the brigadiers—with Gladden and Jackson—who had impressed Bragg mightily at Pensacola, despite having no military experience.

Thirty-one years old, Chalmers was Virginia-born, but had moved to Holly Springs, Mississippi in his youth, graduated from South Carolina College, and by 1858 he was district attorney in Holly Springs. He was a delegate to Mississippi's secession convention in early January 1861. The following April, when the Civil War began, Chalmers raised an infantry company and was elected colonel of the

9th Mississippi Infantry, which was remarkable in view of his ignorance of all things military. After his regiment was moved to Pensacola, he led it in the raid on the Union garrison at Santa Rosa Island on October 8, 1861, and earned General Bragg's admiration.

Bragg, the commander of the Army of Pensacola, especially esteemed Chalmers's 9th Mississippi regiment's discipline, and Bragg promoted Chalmers to brigadier general on February 13, 1862. Chalmers was given a brigade and ordered with it to Corinth. In the days before the army's final concentration, Chalmers's brigade was stationed at Iuka, on the Confederate army's right flank, guarding the Memphis & Charleston Railroad.

After Shiloh, Chalmers would continue to lead his brigade until he was wounded at Stones River, in a desperate charge against the Round Forest, Thomas's last bastion in the Union center. Afterward he led cavalry in Mississippi, and felt nearly overslaughed when Bedford Forrest arrived in the theater after Chickamauga, whereupon Chalmers became his subordinate. Nevertheless it was as a division commander under Forrest that Chalmers earned his greatest fame. After participating in a series of victories, including the infamous Fort Pillow, Chalmers's cavalry division nearly alone tried to hold the Rebel left at Nashville in December 1864, against Federal cavalry that outnumbered him six to one. After that last main battle of the Army of Tennessee, Chalmers tried but failed to reach Forrest in time to avert the fall of Selma in April 1865, and he finally surrendered with the rest of Taylor's western department the following month.

After the war Chalmers returned to practicing law, and, once Reconstruction had ebbed, was elected to Congress in 1876, serving amid contentious Mississippi politics until 1884. He then resumed his law practice, moving to Memphis, and died there in 1898, at age 67.

2nd Division, 2nd (Chalmers's) Brigade at Shiloh

Chalmers's brigade, called "The Mississippi Brigade," was organized March 6, 1862, by order of General Bragg. It numbered 2,039 men in five infantry regiments—the 5th, 7th, 9th, and 10th Mississippi, and the 52nd Tennessee regiments—supported by Gage's Alabama Battery. Bragg's organizing principle seems to have been the creation of a brigade of Mississippians under his best Mississippi general, with the 52nd Tennessee thrown in at the last minute.

None of the regiments had experience in combat, and none were distinguished in drill except for the 9th Mississipi, which was especially admired by General Bragg. It was one of three regiments he wanted to combine into a model brigade.

Leadership was mixed: The 5th and 10th Mississippi were under long-term colonels, but the 7th and 9th Mississippi were led by lieutenant colonels. The 52nd Tennessee's colonel was woefully inexperienced, and would leave the army soon after Shiloh.

Bragg gave this brigade the informal title of "The High Pressure Brigade." (It may have been the most nicknamed brigade in the army—it was also known as the "Pensacola Brigade.")

Chalmers's brigade formed the right of Bragg's line, the second line in the army's order of attack. Its right rested on the swamps of Lick Creek. It was deployed in the order from left to right: 52nd Tennessee, 5th Mississippi, 9th Mississippi, 7th Mississippi, 10th Mississippi, with Gage's Battery in the rear. It advanced at 6:30 a.m. Sunday, soon joined Gladden's right and made a gradual left wheel until it struck the left of Prentiss's camp. At 9:00 a.m. the 18th Wisconsin was driven from its camp by a charge of the 10th Mississippi, followed by the 7th and 9th Mississippi. The three Mississippi regiments pursued the fleeing Federals until they came under fire from Hurlbut's division in the Peach Orchard, when General Johnston ordered them back to the 18th Wisconsin's captured camp.

From the Federal camp the brigade was conducted to the Confederate far right along the Bark Road until its right rested on Lick Creek. There it re-formed its battle line facing north and advanced across Locust Grove Branch against Stuart's brigade's camps. When this advance began, Union skirmishers fired into the 52nd Tennessee, stampeding the regiment so that only two companies could be rallied. These two companies were attached to the 5th Mississippi. As the infantry advanced, Gage's battery, stationed on high ground south of the ravine, shelled Stuart's camp, compelling Stuart to move to his left rear and form behind the Peach Orchard. Chalmers moved upon this position and drove Stuart back

300 yards to a ridge, where Stuart maintained himself until about 2:00 p.m. Stuart then retreated, closely followed by Chalmers, who was supported on his right by Clanton's cavalry, moving down the bank of the Tennessee. Swinging to the left against the exposed Union left, Chalmers's left reached the Hamburg-Savannah Road, where the brigade assisted in the capture of the troops of Prentiss and Wallace, who were attempting to make their way to the rear.

The brigade then moved directly east until its right was near the river, and then advanced into the valley of Dill Branch. Skirmishers of the 9th Mississippi crossed the ravine and ascended to the brow of the bluff, where they came under fire from Union artillery. The brigade struggled to ascend a steep hill, making repeated unsuccessful charges, but continued to fight until nightfall. Gage's Battery was put in position in rear of the brigade, but was soon disabled and compelled to retire, leaving one gun in the ravine in front of its position. It was not again engaged.

The brigade retired to Stuart's Union brigade's camps, where it bivouacked Sunday night.

On Monday Chalmers was joined by several detached regiments and was engaged on the Confederate right south of the Peach Orchard until 2:00 p.m., when it received orders to retire.

In his official report of the battle, General Bragg said of the brigade, "Brigadier General James R. Chalmers, at the head of his gallant Mississippians, filled—he could not have exceeded—the measure of my expectations. Never were troops and commander more worthy of each other and of their State."

This was uncharacteristic generosity by Bragg. At the battle of Shiloh, the first charge by Chalmers's brigade was piecemeal, since only one regiment heard his order to go forward. Withers, likewise, called him "gallant and impetuous" in his report, but in fact, Chalmers's pugnacity was only sporadic at Shiloh. His regiments were satisfied with skirmishing when they outnumbered Stuart's Union regiments three-to-one on the Confederate right, and Bragg had to order Chalmers forward later in the day when Chalmers stopped to rest his men. Chalmers's control was good, however: despite all-day assaults, his missing were only 4.2% of his casualties.

At Shiloh, Chalmers's brigade lost 83 killed, 343 wounded, and 19 missing, for a total of 445 out of 2,039 present for duty—22% casualties.

3rd Brigade
Brigadier General John K. Jackson

John Jackson was one of the very few officers in the Pensacola and Mobile armies—along with Adley Gladden and James Chalmers—who impressed their hard-to-please commander, Braxton Bragg.

Jackson, 34, was a Georgia lawyer when the war began. Elected colonel of the 5th Georgia, he made it the best regiment in Bragg's Pensacola army. In fact, one captain reported, officers "who have seen most of the troops in the Confederate Army say this Georgia regiment is the finest in the service."

Jackson was a lifetime resident of Augusta, Georgia. He received his education first at Augusta's Richmond Academy, a military school, and later attended South Carolina College in Columbia, where he graduated cum laude in 1846. He then began to study law, passing the bar in 1848 and practicing in Augusta until 1861. He was also active as an officer in the Georgia State Militia, working his way up to lieutenant colonel in command of Augusta's infantry battalion by the time the Civil War began.

In May 1861, Jackson and his 5th Georgia Infantry were ordered to Pensacola, Florida, where he was in command of one of the three battalions that took part in the action at Santa Rosa Island on October 8, 1861. On January 14, 1862, he was promoted to brigadier general and assigned command of a brigade in Bragg's Army of Pensacola.

In February Bragg summoned Jackson to Grand Junction, Tennessee, where he organized into brigades the Confederate soldiers sent there on their way to Corinth. On March 29, Jackson was given a brigade in Bragg's corps of the Army of the Mississippi in its final organization before the battle of Shiloh.

At Shiloh, General Jackson thus had some experience in action at Santa Rosa Island, but was only a few days in brigade command.

Jackson would remain in brigade command to the end of the war, but was never promoted. After Joe Johnston's surrender, he returned to practicing law in Augusta, but was stricken by pneumonia and died at age 38 in 1866.

2nd Division, 3rd (Jackson's) Brigade at Shiloh

Jackson's Brigade numbered 2,208 men in four infantry regiments: the 17th, 18th, and 19th Alabama, and Col. Moore's 2nd Texas, supported by Girardey's Georgia Battery from Augusta. Jackson's regiments were only recently brigaded in Corinth before the march to attack Grant at Pittsburg Landing.

The quality of leadership of the brigade's regiments was of two extremes. The colonels of the 19th Alabama and the 2nd Texas were two of the best in the Army of the Mississippi. The 17th Alabama, on the other hand, was saddled with a hemorrhoid-addled lieutenant colonel new to command, and the 18th Alabama's colonel had no military experience. Both would retire within a week of the battle.

The 2nd Texas arrived on April 1 after a grueling three-week march from Houston, with many of its men nearly barefoot. They received almost no rest before they were again put in road column for their march to battle at Shiloh. They made a unique appearance: just prior to the battle, they received new uniforms of undyed cotton, which gave them a ghostly look and made them easy to spot.

On Sunday morning, Jackson's Brigade formed on the right of the Bark Road in Bragg's second line, to the left of Chalmers's brigade and 300 yards in the rear of Gladden's, in the order from left to right: 17th Alabama, 18th Alabama, 19th Alabama, and 2nd Texas, with Girardey's Battery in the rear of the infantry. The brigade advanced at 6:30 a.m. and came up with Gladden's brigade at Prentiss's headquarters, where General Johnston personally ordered the brigade to the left in conjunction with movements of Wood and Shaver, both of which were brigades of Hardee's first line.

Before long, the order was changed, and Jackson was ordered to follow Chalmers to the right. There, the brigade formed on the south side of the deep Locust Grove Branch ravine. Girardey's battery engaged the enemy in the Peach Orchard from Prentiss's camp, then followed the regiments of Jackson's brigade and took position at Shake-a-rag Church (a black Pentecostal church near Prentiss's headquarters). The brigade crossed Locust Branch and advanced directly against the camps of Stuart's Union brigade, to the left of Chalmers. The right of Jackson's brigade engaged the 71st Ohio of Stuart's brigade at the same time the left of the brigade engaged McArthur's brigade in a ravine east of the Peach Orchard.

At about 1:30 p.m. Bowen's brigade joined Jackson's left, and together they advanced, driving back the Union line and making a left wheel with Chalmers.

Once in possession of Stuart's camps, Jackson's hungry men rummaged through the tents, gorging themselves on beef and drinking coffee.

Jackson's brigade, with Chalmers's, reached Prentiss's rear, and was present when Prentiss surrendered about 5:00 p.m. The 18th Alabama was detached to escort the prisoners to the rear. The other three regiments followed Chalmers to the right and took position in the valley of Dill Branch. Chalmers's skirmishers went forward to the top of the bluff, where they came in range of enemy artillery. Finding an advance unwise, the Confederates withdrew.

In the darkness the brigade became separated. The 17th Alabama returned to its camp of Saturday night, and was out of the fight on Monday. The 19th Alabama and 2nd Texas bivouacked with Chalmers.

On Monday, with the 21st Alabama from Gladden's brigade, these regiments were organized as a temporary brigade, and fought on Chalmers's left. In an advance across an open field this force received an unexpected fire, which broke its line and disorganized the command. The 19th Alabama, under Col. Joseph Wheeler, remained alone on the field until a general retreat was ordered, when it formed a rear guard.

General Jackson, with Girardey's battery, bivouacked Sunday night at Shiloh Church. The battery was engaged with Cleburne on Monday. It lost one gun and had its other guns disabled so that the cannoneers were detailed to help man another battery. General Jackson, unable to find his brigade on Monday, was not employed during the day, and he reported at Corinth at 11:30 p.m. that night.

At Shiloh, Jackson's brigade lost 86 killed, 364 wounded, and 194 missing, for a total of 644 out of 2,208 present for duty—29% casualties.

Third Corps

Major General William J. Hardee

Hardee, a tall, wiry, straight-backed Georgian, 46 years old, was already nationally known as a thinking man's soldier when the Civil War began. He was the author of *Rifle and Light Infantry Tactics*, better known as *Hardee's Tactics*, a drill manual used as the standard reference by both armies. Hardee was fastidious in his dress and grooming and formal in his manner, but even so had the affection of his men, who not only respected his ability but sensed kindness behind his prim persona.

General Albert Sidney Johnston's son, William Preston Johnston, wrote his impression of Hardee's character: "[My] estimate of General Hardee, based upon both social and official intercourse, is very high. His personal appearance was striking. In form he was tall and sinewy, and his bearing was eminently military. His features were somewhat harsh in repose, but his frank and genial smile lit them with a most winning expression. He was good-tempered, friendly, and intelligent in conversation with men, and very charming with women. His deference and gallantry were of the old school. His social success belonged to his perfect poise, in which were mingled frankness, amiability, and tact—qualities which, a classmate says, already characterized him while a cadet at West Point."

Hardee knew no life besides that of a soldier. He graduated 28th out of 45 cadets in the West Point Class of 1838. He fought against the Seminoles in Florida and then traveled abroad to study at the Cavalry School at Saumur, France, for two years. Returning to America, he served in frontier duty until the Mexican War, where he won brevets for Gallant and Meritorious Conduct in two battles. After that war, he again returned to the life of a career soldier, now adding academic credentials to his assignments on the frontier: after publishing his drill manual in 1856, he was named Commandant of Cadets at West Point and taught infantry, cavalry, and artillery tactics until 1860. He resigned from the U.S. Army in January 1861, a few days after his home state of Georgia seceded from the Union.

After entering Confederate service as a colonel in March 1861, Hardee was given command of Fort Moran, in Mobile Bay. In June, he was promoted to brigadier general and assigned an independent brigade in northern Arkansas. At the end of August, he was commissioned by the Confederate government to transfer Arkansas troops—13 infantry regiments and three artillery batteries—to Confederate service. In mid-October, Hardee was ordered east to Bowling Green, Kentucky with his Arkansas army.

At Bowling Green, he was made major general and given command of a division in General Johnston's Central Army of Kentucky. His promotion meant elevation of three of his Arkansas regimental commanders—Patrick R. Cleburne, Thomas C. Hindman, and Robert G. Shaver—to brigade commands. In December, General Johnston, who had known Hardee when they were both officers in the 2nd Cavalry in the Old Army, passed command of the entire Central Army of Kentucky to Hardee. His period in command lasted until February 23, when the army was retreated from Bowling Green and combined with Crittenden's eastern Tennessee army in Murfreesboro, Tennessee, prior to the long march to Decatur, Alabama, and the train ride to Corinth. Once in Corinth, General Beauregard redesignated the Central Army of Kentucky the Third Corps of the Army of the Mississippi and retained Hardee in command.

It was because Johnston was so used to relying on Hardee, perhaps, that he put Hardee's corps in the first line of attack on Grant's army at the battle of Shiloh. Hardee would redeem Johnston's trust with a solid performance during the battle, where he would acquire the nickname "Old Reliable." When Bragg took command of the western Confederate army in the summer of 1862, he reported that Hardee was the only suitable major general with the army.

After Shiloh Hardee commanded a corps in the Army of Tennessee until a falling out with Bragg during the Tullahoma campaign compelled him to request a transfer. He returned to the army after Chickamauga and commanded what had formerly been Polk's corps under Joe Johnston in Georgia until Johnston's replacement by John Bell Hood. Hardee's inability to stomach Hood's rash attacks and heavy casualties prompted him to switch to departmental command in the Carolinas. He lost his only child, a 16-year-old cavalryman, in the war's last major battle, at Bentonville. After the surrender Hardee became a businessman and died in 1873 while on a summer vacation in West Virginia.

Third (Hardee's) Corps at Shiloh

The Central Army of Kentucky was reorganized from its original three divisions into two so-called corps of three brigades each: the Third (Hardee's) Corps and the Reserve (Breckinridge's) Corps—the terminology was adopted, perhaps, to make the Army of the Mississippi sound larger than it actually was.

The Third Corps under Hardee had fought little together but marched much, both during their winter in Kentucky and on the trek from Bowling Green across Tennessee to Decatur, Alabama, on the approach to Corinth. Hardee's brigades flaunted a blue flag bordered in white, bearing a white "silver moon."

Hardee's Third Corps at Shiloh—more properly considered a division—consisted of 6,758 troops in three brigades, containing eight Arkansas regiments, supplemented by one Mississippi and two Tennessee regiments. The brigades were supported by six artillery batteries and a company of cavalry.

The nucleus of this corps had been with General Hardee in northern Arkansas until early October 1861. The Arkansans were mostly backwoodsmen and hardscrabble farmers, a rough-and-tumble, motley bunch, with huge Bowie knives (they called them "toothpicks") and assorted revolvers stuck into their belts. Bragg raised an eyebrow when he reviewed them, and deprecated them as "undisciplined volunteers."

Although Hardee's men were veterans of months' service in central Kentucky, they had hardly any experience in combat. The curious decision to make them first-line troops in the initial assault was probably due to the fact that General Johnston was most familiar with them, having been with them since his arrival at Bowling Green the previous October. Hardee himself also inspired confidence.

On Sunday morning, Hardee's corps formed the first line of battle just behind Wood's Field, with brigades in a line from left to right: Cleburne, Wood, Shaver, Gladden. (The three brigades of Hardee's corps did not make the length of the line desired, so Gladden's brigade from Bragg's corps was brought forward, added to the right, and placed under Hardee's command.) Hardee's corps in line of battle had its center on, and was perpendicular to, the Corinth Road, with its left near Owl Creek and its right across the Bark Road.

Just before the battle, Hardee improvised a shuffling of command, breaking up his corps into two temporary divisions. He himself exercised direct tactical control over only Cleburne's and Gladden's brigades. Brigadier General Hindman was given charge of his own brigade, now led by Col. Robert G. Shaver, and that of Brig. Gen. S. A. M. Wood. However, Hindman seems not to have given any orders to Wood. Hindman was disabled about 11:00 a.m. on Sunday morning near the northeast corner of the Review Field, further crippling the coordination of this *ad hoc* division.

On Sunday morning the pickets of Hardee's corps, under Major Hardcastle, stationed at the corner of Fraley's and Wood's fields, were attacked at 4:55 a.m. by a reconnoitering party sent out by General Prentiss. This affair between pickets lasted over an hour, and Hardee's corps in the meantime formed its battle line. It then advanced, drove back the Union party, and followed it to the first line of camps, where the battle became general. General Hardee himself moved with the right of his line, where General Johnston was directing the battle, until the first camps were passed. Hardee, after consulting with Johnston, then went to the left and took general direction of the left flank of the Army of the Mississippi.

Hardee's corps did not remain intact after about 9:00 a.m. on Sunday morning, when his troops intermingled with oncoming friendly troops. With the possible exception of two or three regiments of Cleburne's brigade, none of Hardee's men were under his command on Sunday after he moved to the left.

On Monday Hardee was in command on the extreme right of the line. None of his brigades were under his command. Under General Beauregard's orders, Hardee commenced the withdrawal of his troops in the early afternoon.

At Shiloh, Hardee's Third Corps lost 404 killed, 1,936 wounded, and 141 missing, for a total of 2,481 out of 6,758 present for duty—37% casualties, by far the highest rate of the four Confederate corps.

Hardee's losses to enemy fire were 35% of the total, also a far higher rate than any other corps in the Army of the Mississippi.

1st Brigade
Brigadier General Thomas C. Hindman

There was a violent passion in Thomas Hindman's commitment to the independence of the Confederacy. However, he was a failure as a general. "Poor Hindman, he was a pleasant general and kind, a nice ladies' man," wrote one of his subordinates, "but utterly unfit to command a division of fighting men." This became more and more evident as the war progressed. After the battle of Chickamauga, Brig. Gen. A. P. Stewart, speaking of Hindman, said curtly, "The right man was not there in command." Arthur Manigault, a brigade commander under Hindman at Chickamauga, concurred: "He was not up to the work, it being far beyond his capacity as a general. Had there been a proper man to manage for us, I have little doubt but that a most brilliant success would have been achieved."

Hindman, 34, was an eminent citizen-soldier, a son of the whole South. Born in Tennessee and raised in Alabama and Mississippi, he acquired his military experience by raising a hometown Ripley, Mississippi, company and commanding it in the Mexican War before he was 20, despite the fact that, as a result of an earlier accident that had broken a bone, one of Hindman's legs was shorter than the other, and he wore boots with different sized heels.

After returning home to Ripley, Hindman studied law, was admitted to the bar in 1851, and started a legal practice. In the early 1850s, the Ripley lawyer evolved into a Mississippi politician. He became active in the temperance movement, and in 1853 campaigned successfully for a seat in the Mississippi state legislature.

Soon, however, he sensed greater opportunity directly across the Mississippi River in Arkansas, and moved his law practice to Helena, where he battled the anti-immigrant, anti-Catholic Know-Nothing Party. It was during this time that he became friends with Irish immigrant Patrick Cleburne, when both of them were wounded in a street fight with Know-Nothing thugs. (Cleburne would be best man at his wedding.) In taking on the Know-Nothings, he established himself as a voice in the Arkansas Democratic party, and by 1857, when he became the editor of the Helena Democratic newspaper, he was the clear leader of the Democrats in eastern Arkansas. He easily won the U.S. Congressional seat from the district in 1858, and by 1860 Hindman headed the faction that ruled Arkansas politics.

In the secession debate, Hindman was one of Arkansas's most visible Fire-Eaters, and rather than taking his newly won seat in Congress in 1861, Hindman stayed in Helena and raised "Hindman's Legion," more properly the 2nd Arkansas Infantry regiment, for the Confederate army. He was commissioned brigadier general on September 28, 1861, and on October 28, after General Johnston moved Hardee's Arkansas contingent to Bowling Green, Hindman was given command of a brigade.

In Kentucky, however, Hindman demonstrated his lack of tactical skill at the battle of Rowlett's Station, where on December 17, 1861, a regiment of the Army of the Ohio, which had just advanced to the south side of the Green River in

Central Kentucky, repulsed his 1,350-man force. The victorious Union force was less than half the size of Hindman's.

After the war, retaining his Fire-Eater stance, Hindman fled to Mexico rather than surrender, but returned to Arkansas two years later, despite President Andrew Johnson refusing to issue him a pardon. Hindman soon resumed his habit of political agitation until September 1868, when he was killed by unknown assailants who fired through the window of his home.

Hindman at Shiloh

Despite the fact that General Hardee had put Hindman in charge of an improvised division of two brigades, Hindman remained with his own brigade and seems to have given not a single order to Wood's brigade (the other brigade under Hindman's improvised command). There was no doubt about Hindman's personal bravery, and, except for perhaps one prominent instance later in the war, aggressiveness would be the constant feature of Hindman's style. According to Hardee, Hindman's leadership "upon the field was marked by a courage which animated his soldiers and a skill which won their confidence." Hindman was riding at breakneck speed in front of his lines, cheering his men on, when his horse was killed by a cannon shot. The general was "disabled by the concussion of the ball and the fall of his horse."

1st Brigade
Colonel Robert G. Shaver

"Fighting Bob" Shaver, 30 years old at Shiloh, was born in northeast Tennessee and was educated at Emory and Henry College, just a few miles away across the state line, in Virginia. When he was 20, he came to Batesville, in north central Arkansas, to make a living as a merchant and lawyer.

Although he had not had any military training, when the war broke out he was put in charge of recruiting volunteers over a 10-county area, and Shaver raised enough men for 32 companies. He kept 10 companies, which became the 7th Arkansas Infantry on June 16, 1861. It would be known as "Shaver's Regiment" throughout the war. Shaver and his men were first stationed in Columbus, Kentucky, with General Polk, and were then moved to Bowling Green with their fellow Arkansans under Hardee.

On the second day of Shiloh, Col. Shaver was grievously injured in the head and left side by a shell burst that left him unconscious for hours. He would suffer from the wounds for the rest of his life. Able to still volunteer for duty, he was later transferred to the Trans-Mississippi Department. After the war Shaver remained active in veterans associations until his death in Arkansas in 1915.

Shaver's (Hindman's) Brigade at Shiloh

The brigade Shaver led at Shiloh numbered 2,360 men spread across four infantry regiments—the 2nd, 6th, and Shaver's own 7th Arkansas, and the 3rd Confederate—supported by Swett's Mississippi and Miller's Tennessee batteries.

According to the 6th Arkansas's Henry Morton Stanley, a man who would one day be a world-renowned journalist and African adventurer, his regiment was one-fifth educated gentlemen, and the rest rough, untutored, knife-toting backwoodsmen. The companies came from all over the state. These were true frontiersmen—one company could count only one married man. This motley quality was shared by all the Arkansas regiments.

During its early months, Shaver's 7th Regiment was called the "Ragged Seventh" due to the men's ragged civilian clothing and rough appearance.

The brigade was inexperienced in combat, and Shiloh would be its first time under fire. It was also poorly armed—it shared about a thousand modern Enfield rifles with Cleburne's brigade, but most of its men were armed with old flintlock muskets.

Corps commander Hardee improvised a two-division structure to the Third Corps, and Shaver's—until now, Hindman's—brigade was included with Wood's brigade in an ad hoc division under Hindman.

Shaver's brigade formed line of battle late Saturday evening on Wood's brigade's right and Gladden's brigade's left, its line extending from the Corinth Road on its left to the Bark Road in the order, from left to right: 7th Arkansas, 2nd Arkansas, 6th Arkansas, and 3rd Confederate, with Swett's Battery in the rear.

The brigade moved forward at 6:30 a.m. Sunday, meeting little resistance until within a half-mile of the Union camps. Here Swett's and Harper's batteries took position on the right near the Eastern Corinth Road and engaged Hickenlooper's and Munch's Union batteries.

Shaver's brigade soon struck the first hard blow in the battle. The Arkansas troops initially rushed into the camps of Peabody's brigade. The Union troops stood their ground until the Arkansas soldiers were within 30 feet of them. Then the Federals broke and fled for their lives, while Peabody himself was killed. Men in flight crowded the narrow streets in the camps. The Confederates pushed in among them and a fierce hand-to-hand melee followed. Shaver's brigade had rushed forward so fast that General Hardee had to halt them until the line of battle could catch up to them. The 3rd Confederate regiment, however, continuing the pursuit, became detached from the brigade and advanced until it was engaged at the Hornets' Nest soon after 9:00 a.m.

Colonel Shaver reorganized his command and was ordered to change front to the left, in conjunction with Wood's left wheel, to attack the camp of Raith's brigade, part of McClernand's division. Before completing the movement, Shaver was ordered to re-form and move by the left flank one-half mile, after which he attacked Hare's brigade (also in McClernand's division) behind a large field. Here, at 10:30 a.m., Hindman was riding "at full gallop, his long hair streaming behind him…waving his cap over his head and cheering the men on." Hindman's horse was torn to shreds by a cannon shell, and the general was thrown ten feet in the air. He broke his thighbone in the fall, and had to be carried off the field.

Shaver's left regiments passed through the field in front, drove back Hare's brigade, and occupied the ground for 1½ hours. The right of the brigade passed to the right of the Review Field and became engaged with Sweeny's and Tuttle's brigades, where it was exposed to a heavy crossfire from the Union batteries in the rear of Tuttle. Swett's Battery took position on Shaver's right and engaged those batteries.

Brigadier General A. P. Stewart of Polk's corps—who had started the day in the third line, behind Hardee's and Bragg's—took command of Hindman's force, consisting of Shaver's brigade and the 16th Alabama and 55th Tennessee of Wood's brigade, and, placing his (Stewart's) own 4th Tennessee on the left of Shaver, moved directly east from the northwest corner of Review Field to attack the troops behind Duncan Field, at the right of the enemy's Hornets' Nest line. Stewart was quickly repulsed, and Shaver's brigade retired about a mile to replenish ammunition.

Swett's Battery, after its first participation in the attack on the Hornets' Nest, was placed by General Ruggles in his line of batteries on the east side of Review Field, where it was supported by the 154th (Senior) Tennessee.

Between 2:00 and 3:00 p.m. Shaver's brigade made another attack at the Hornets' Nest and was again repulsed. The brigade then fell back and was not again engaged on Sunday. It went to the rear and bivouacked for the night.

On Monday the brigade formed on the Bark Road. After some time, the 2nd and 6th Arkansas advanced to the left with General Cheatham, where they made an attack about noon and captured some guns. Union troops, however, soon retook the guns and drove Shaver's men back in disorder. In attempting to rally his force, Col. Shaver was knocked senseless by the explosion of a shell, and his command became disorganized.

The 7th Arkansas supported a battery on Monday and later in the day became engaged on the right. On Monday the 3rd Confederate was detached to the right.

At Shiloh, Shaver's (Hindman's) Brigade lost 109 killed, 546 wounded, and 38 missing, for a total of 693 out of 2,360 present for duty—29% casualties.

2nd Brigade
Brigadier General Patrick R. Cleburne

Patrick Ronayne Cleburne, 34, seems always to have been animated by a sensitivity to the fortunes of the downtrodden. He was born in County Cork, Ireland, and absorbed the travail of his people, who in the mid-19th century were not only long-suffering under British rule, but also starving from the effects of the Potato Famine. Cleburne was the son of a doctor, so was not himself destitute, but when he failed his entrance exams to Trinity College, in Dublin, he chose to avoid the shame by enlisting in the British infantry. There, subject to the notoriously brutal British military system, he learned the compensating pleasures of active service and camaraderie with his fellow soldiers, as well as the value of discipline.

In 1848, at the age of 24, Cleburne purchased his discharge from the British Army and sailed for New Orleans. He finally settled upriver, in the frontier town of Helena, Arkansas. There, after partnering in a drug store, he became a lawyer. Although he was opposed to secession, when the Civil War broke out, he joined the Confederate army as a private.

Shy and withdrawing by nature, Cleburne in uniform was assertive and confident. Once back in the military, his rise was meteoric. Though enlisted as a private, he immediately raised a Helena company called the Yell Rifles, who respected his experience and elected him their captain. When his unit went to Little Rock to form a regiment with other early Arkansas companies, his ability and leadership were obvious to the men of every company, and Captain Cleburne was unanimously elected to the head of the new 1st Arkansas regiment, and on May 14, one month after the firing on Fort Sumter, he was promoted to colonel.

Cleburne took his regiment and a battery of artillery and began to construct a fort on a high bluff on the Tennessee side of the Mississippi River, 38 miles north of Memphis, which his men dubbed "Fort Cleburne," and which later became Fort Pillow.

Jefferson Davis appointed Brig. Gen. William Hardee as the head of a brigade of Arkansas regiments in mid-July 1861, and Cleburne and Hardee, recognizing each other's ability, formed an immediate friendship. The drilling of the Arkansas troops continued through August, aided by the unsurpassed expertise of their leaders, but occasionally interrupted by ill-advised raids into Missouri.

When Tennessee's General Polk invaded Kentucky and established his post at Columbus in early September 1861, the 350-mile-long line across the length of the Kentucky border suddenly needed defending. The weak point was in the middle, around Bowling Green, where only 4,500 troops under Brig. Gen. Simon Buckner were stationed, so later that fall General Albert Sidney Johnston, the new Western Department commander, dispatched Hardee's Brigade, including Cleburne's regiment, to double the size of Buckner's force. Once arrived, General Hardee, raised to the command of a division in Johnston's Central Army of Kentucky, named Cleburne to the head of one of his three brigades.

Cleburne's brigade was stationed in an advanced position about five miles north of Bowling Green during the fall of 1861, and responded to all reports of enemy movement nearby. The Union Army of the Ohio in Kentucky, however, was inert through 1861, encroaching only as far as Green River, about 30 miles to the north.

The next movement that included Cleburne was after Grant's capture of Forts Henry and Donelson, in mid-February 1862. In response, the Central Army of Kentucky retreated to Nashville, then Murfreesboro, then to Decatur, Alabama, then to Corinth, Mississippi. There, in preparation for the attack on Grant's camp at Pittsburg Landing, Cleburne was given his promotion to brigadier general. He had gone from private to general in one year.

His storied career in battle for the Confederate cause was about to begin. Cleburne was too aggressive in his first battle. On Sunday morning, he threw his men forward in a murderous frontal attack. Later in the war, however, his good sense became part of what led to his reputation as the "Stonewall of the West," a major general universally respected for his fighting and strategic abilities. From Perryville to the Atlanta Campaign, Cleburne was a stalwart of the Army of Tennessee. At Chattanooga alone he practically saved the army. Cleburne led from the front, which ultimately resulted in his death before Union breastworks at the battle of Franklin in 1864.

Cleburne's Brigade at Shiloh

Cleburne's Brigade numbered 2,789 men in six regiments—the 15th Arkansas, 6th Mississippi, and the 2nd (Bate's), 5th (Hill's), 23rd, and 24th Tennessee—supported by three artillery batteries in Shoup's Battalion—Trigg's, Calvert's, and Hubbard's batteries from Arkansas.

Cleburne's men were green—none had been in combat, although Bate's regiment had been present at First Manassas and had spent the previous autumn in Virginia. Like others in the Confederate army, the regiments had no practice at maneuvering as a brigade.

Besides lack of fighting experience, Cleburne's most pressing problem was his lack of experienced officers: three of his six regiments were without their colonels. Of the colonels present, only one, William Bate, had any military experience, in Mexico. The artillerymen, too, were inexperienced. They would provide no support for the brigade's disastrous attack on Sunday morning.

On April 6, Cleburne's brigade formed the left of Hardee's line, the first line of attack for the Army of the Mississippi. Cleburne's regiments were in the order from left to right: (Bate's) 2nd Tennessee, 24th Tennessee, (Hill's) 5th Tennessee, 6th Mississippi, and 23rd Tennessee, with the 15th Arkansas in advance as pickets and skirmishers. The advance was begun at 6:30 a.m. Sunday, and at about 8:00 a.m. the brigade became engaged along Shiloh Branch, its three batteries on high ground in the rear.

Cleburne's progress was slowed by the marshy ground and briers of the Shiloh Branch, and the units diverged. Three of his regiments remained west of the stream while Cleburne and his rightmost regiments, the 6th Mississippi and 23rd Tennessee, crossed the stream and entered Rhea Field. They charged through the exposed camp of the 53rd Ohio, but were repulsed by the fire of Waterhouse's Battery and the infantry of Raith's and Hildebrand's brigades. The 23rd Tennessee was rallied only with difficulty, but the 6th Mississippi renewed the attack with vigor, and charged again and again, until it had lost 300 men out of 425 engaged.

The left of the brigade met a similar defeat in attempting to charge the position of Buckland's brigade and Barrett's Battery, and was unable to advance until reinforced by Anderson's brigade from Bragg's second-line corps, and by Russell's and Johnson's brigades from Polk's third line. At 9:30 a.m. the

Confederates were finally able to coordinate their attack. Anderson, Russell, and Cleburne's left regiments attacked simultaneously. The remnants of Hildebrand's brigade and Waterhouse's battery retreated toward Shiloh Church.

Colonel William Bate of the 2nd Tennessee was wounded in front of Buckland's brigade, and his 2nd Tennessee regiment was disorganized and out of the fight for the rest of the day Sunday.

On his brigade's right, Cleburne rallied 60 men of the 6th Mississippi and about half of the 23rd Tennessee, and in conjunction with troops from other brigades, advanced along the Corinth Road. There, Cleburne was joined by the 8th Arkansas of Wood's brigade to his right. With the fragments of these three regiments, Cleburne joined Brig. Gen. A. P. Stewart at noon in an attack upon the enemy position at Duncan Field. At 12:30 p.m., the 6th Mississippi retired from the field, and Cleburne ordered the 23rd Tennessee to the rear to reorganize.

Cleburne then went in search of what had started the day as the three leftmost regiments of his brigade and, at 3:00 p.m., found them—the 5th and 24th Tennessee and 15th Arkansas—resting under the brow of a hill. These three regiments had advanced through Buckland's camp at about 10 a.m., and had joined Pond and Trabue. With them, Cleburne's regiments had been engaged from noon to 2:30 p.m. in front of Marsh's brigade's camp, and had passed through those tents.

Soon after Cleburne found his left wing, they were joined by the remnants of his 23rd Tennessee. With these he advanced to the east side of Tilghman Branch, where he was engaged at 4:30 p.m. in the attack upon McClernand's remainder. He then moved forward until he came under the fire of artillery and gunboats, where he halted. At dark, Cleburne was ordered to the rear, and he retired to a camp near where his men started the day, at the Bark Road.

Trigg's and Hubbard's batteries formed a part of Ruggles's massed artillery on the Hornet's Nest at about 4:00 p.m.

On Monday, soon after daylight, Cleburne advanced along the Bark Road with four regiments—the 5th, 23rd, and 24th Tennessee, and the 15th Arkansas—together reduced to 800 men, and became engaged in the thick underbrush to the left of Brig. Gen. Breckinridge and the right of Brig. Gen. Wood, where his brigade was repulsed and completely routed. The 15th Arkansas was the only regiment that rallied. The 15th continued in the fight until reduced to 58 men. These were then ordered to the rear to replenish ammunition.

On Monday, Bate's 2nd Tennessee was engaged on the right under A. P. Stewart. There is no mention of Cleburne's batteries in reports of the fighting on Monday.

At Shiloh, Cleburne's brigade lost 188 killed, 790 wounded, and 65 missing, totaling 1,043 out of 2,789 engaged—37% casualties.

3rd Brigade
Brigadier General
Sterling A. M. Wood

Sterling Alexander Martin Wood—or more commonly, S. A. M. Wood—was a 39-year-old lawyer, newspaper editor, and legislator from Florence, Alabama. He had no previous military experience.

Born in Florence, he attended St. Joseph College in Kentucky, and then started a law practice in Tennessee. At the age of 28 he returned to Florence, where he served in the state legislature and edited *The Gazette*, a Democratic newspaper. He was elected captain of his hometown militia company just before Fort Sumter erupted, then was elected colonel of the 7th Alabama regiment the next month. Wood and the 7th Alabama were sent to Pensacola, the nearest potential flashpoint.

In October Wood was given command of a brigade in General Johnston's Central Army of Kentucky at Bowling Green, and was promoted to brigadier general on January 7, 1862. On February 23, when General Johnston created a division in his army for General Pillow, Wood served as the de facto division commander while Pillow was absent, politicking in Memphis. When, on March 16, Jefferson Davis sacked Pillow, Wood reverted to command of his brigade, directly under General Hardee.

Before Shiloh, Wood had never seen combat in his life. His talent as a leader in battle was shown in the fact that, on Sunday morning, his regiments swept forward until he was disabled at about 11:00 a.m. With Wood out of action, they became disorganized and declined to advance. When Wood returned at 2:30 p.m., he managed to collect four regiments and go forward again. However, once its regiments separated, Wood's Brigade never fought again as a unit at Shiloh.

Wood was an able brigadier, as indicated by the fact that he remained in command of his brigade through the battles of Perryville, Stones River, and Chickamauga. Division commander Cleburne's report after Chickamauga included no praise for Wood, however, and Wood resigned within the month. After the war he returned to law and politics. He died in 1891 in Tuscaloosa.

Wood's Brigade at Shiloh

Wood's Brigade numbered 2,508 men in five understrength regiments—the 16th Alabama, 8th Arkansas, and 27th, 44th, and 55th Tennessee—and two battalions, the 9th Arkansas and 3rd Mississippi Battalions, supported by Harper's Mississippi Battery and the Georgia Dragoons. The two Arkansas units had been with Hardee's original Arkansas brigade.

Wood's Brigade accompanied the Central Army of Kentucky in its retreat to Nashville and Murfreesboro, where it was reported in Pillow's short-lived division in the organization of February 23. It was in this organization that the 16th Alabama and the 27th and 55th Tennessee were first reported belonging to the brigade. Pillow's division was dissolved on March 16, 1862, when President Davis relieved Pillow of command, and in the three weeks before the battle of Shiloh, Wood's brigade was organized as the 3rd Brigade of Hardee's Third Corps.

Prior to April 1862, only one regiment, the 16th Alabama, had seen combat, at Mill Springs.

On Sunday morning at Shiloh, Wood's brigade occupied the center of Hardee's line of battle, the first line of the attacking Army of the Mississippi, with Cleburne's brigade on its left and Hindman's (Shaver's) brigade on its right. It was lined up in the order from left to right: 27th Tennessee, 16th Alabama, 44th Tennessee, 9th Arkansas Battalion, 8th Arkansas and 55th Tennessee. The 3rd Mississippi Battalion was forward on picket duty, and Harper's Battery was in the rear of the infantry. Wood's brigade's right was on the Corinth Road.

Major Hardcastle with the 3rd Mississippi, on picket a quarter-mile in advance of the main line, was attacked at 4:55 Sunday morning by a reconnoitering party sent out by General Prentiss. Hardcastle fought Prentiss's party until 6:30 a.m., when the rest of the brigade advanced to his support and, pursuing the retreating reconnoitering party, moved directly forward to attack the Union camps, which were reached at 9:00 a.m. In this movement Wood's brigade was the guide for Hardee's entire first line. The left of Wood's brigade struck the front of the 53rd Ohio camp, in Sherman's division. Its right extended into the camps of Peabody's brigade of Prentiss's division. On the brigade's left, the 27th Tennessee, by a movement to the right, avoided the approach to the 53rd Ohio camp, which was being swept by the fire of Waterhouse's Union battery, while the brigade's right passed directly through a part of Peabody's camp, pressing the Union forces back.

Soon, Wood's left had passed Waterhouse's Battery and become exposed to a left flank and rear fire, and the right had reached a field in the rear of Peabody's camp. Here the brigade wheeled to the left and attacked McClernand's 3rd (Raith's) Brigade's camps to the rear of Waterhouse's guns. After wheeling and adjusting his line by bringing the 9th Arkansas Battalion and 8th Arkansas to the left flank, Wood moved directly forward, bending back the left of Raith's brigade and attacking Marsh's brigade on the Corinth Road. There, Wood's men captured Burrows's Battery.

In this attack, at about 11:00 a.m., General Wood was thrown from his horse and disabled, forcing him to leave the field until 2:30 p.m. The brigade became disorganized and its regiments did not fight together again for the rest of the day.

The 27th Tennessee rested from about 11:00 until 3:00 p.m., then joined Wood when he resumed command. The 16th Alabama and the 55th Tennessee joined Shaver's brigade in its movement to the right under Brig. Gen. A. P. Stewart and then, with the 3rd Mississippi Battalion, went to the rear with a collection of Union prisoners, returning to the field Monday morning.

The 44th Tennessee became separated from the brigade during the morning fighting and drifted to the right of Shaver's brigade at the Hornets' Nest. It joined Wood again at 3:00 p.m.

The 8th Arkansas and 9th Arkansas Battalion rested an hour, then after 12:00 noon joined Cleburne's and Shaver's forces in an attack at Duncan Field, and at 3:00 p.m. rejoined General Wood.

The 3rd Mississippi Battalion was not engaged. It joined the 16th Alabama and 55th Tennessee as guard for the Union prisoners, and returned to the field on Monday.

Harper's Battery became detached Sunday morning and was engaged in the morning with Shaver's brigade and in the afternoon with General Cheatham at the Peach Orchard. Avery's Georgia Dragoons went to the right as a guard at Greer's Ford over Lick Creek.

At 2:30 p.m. on Sunday, General Wood resumed command and brought together four of his units, the 27th and 44th Tennessee and the 8th Arkansas and 9th Arkansas Battalion, reporting to General Ruggles west of Duncan Field. At 4:00 p.m. he was sent with General Anderson to the right, to attack the Union force at the Hornets' Nest. Wood did not become engaged but followed the retiring troops of Tuttle's Union brigade until their surrender. At sunset he retired to McClernand's Union camps for the night.

On Monday morning Wood formed the remnant of his four regiments, not over 650 men, and went into action on the south end of Jones Field. At 11:00 a.m.

he fell back to Shiloh Church, where the 3rd Mississippi Battalion rejoined him, and soon afterward moved to the right and made a charge at the Water Oaks Pond, where he engaged McCook's division and units from Sherman's division. He then retired to the high ground south of Shiloh Branch. On Monday, Harper's Battery was on the right.

At Shiloh, Wood's brigade lost 107 killed, 600 wounded, and 38 missing, for a total of 745 out of 2,508 engaged—30% casualties.

Reserve Corps

Brigadier General John C. Breckinridge

"A perfect gentleman" was how many described John C. Breckinridge. Born in 1821 in Lexington, Kentucky, to a venerable Bluegrass family, Breckinridge's antecedents included an attorney general in Thomas Jefferson's cabinet and a president of Princeton University. With his self-image shaped by these forebears and possessing good looks, a powerful voice, and a magnetic personality, Breckinridge dedicated himself to a life of public service and scholarship.

He attended three colleges: Center College in nearby Danville, the College of New Jersey (now Princeton), and Transylvania College in Lexington, the first college west of the Allegheny Mountains. He made the law his profession and showed no fondness for the military. However, after a stirring eulogy for Mexican War dead made him a celebrity, he was made major in the 3rd Kentucky Volunteers and marched with them to Mexico City. He saw no action in Mexico, however.

Returning to Kentucky, Breckinridge won a state legislature seat as a Democrat in 1849 and a seat in the U.S. Congress in 1851. The Kentucky Democrats hitched their wagon to his rising star, and in 1856, as the darling of a slave state, he was courted as the running-mate of the three leading Democratic presidential candidates. One Arkansas delegate admired "his manner, his severely simple style of delivery with scarcely an ornament [or] gesture and deriving its force and eloquence solely from the remarkably choice, ready flow of words, the rich voice and intonation. …Every member," this observer went on, "seemed riveted to his seat and each face seemed by magnetic influence to be directed to him." When Breckinridge's choice for a running mate—James Buchanan, a Pennsylvanian—was elected, Breckinridge became the youngest vice president in the nation's history, and served from 1857 to 1861.

Although he was not a secessionist, he accepted his party's nomination for president as a States Rights Democrat in the 1860 presidential election, losing to Abraham Lincoln but coming in second out of four candidates. When his term as vice president came to an end in March of 1861, he took a Senate seat and argued for compromise. However, in September 1861, when Kentucky's initial neutrality was ended in favor of the North, Breckinridge, known as a political hero in the South, was ordered arrested by Union authorities.

Breckinridge fled south and joined the Confederate Army. On November 2, he was made brigadier general and given command of the "Kentucky Brigade" in General Simon Bolivar Buckner's army that had established itself at Bowling Green.

On March 29, 1862, one week before Shiloh, after General Crittenden was relieved of command of the recently created Reserve Corps for drunkenness, Breckinridge was promoted to command of the corps.

At Shiloh, Breckinridge was only a few days in command, and with no military training or battle experience. However, on the second day of the battle, he was the only corps commander to maintain control of his intact command, a testament to his attention to organization.

Bragg was complimentary of Breckinridge's performance at Shiloh. At the battle of Murfreesboro eight months later, however, Breckinridge showed a healthy caution when Bragg ordered a suicidal charge. The two soon developed an intense dislike for each other. Breckinridge temporarily went west to serve under Joe Johnston during the Vicksburg campaign, but returned to Bragg's army for the battles of Chickamauga and Chattanooga in the fall of 1863. At the latter battle Bragg once again criticized Breckinridge, suspecting him of drunkenness, but it was Bragg who would be relieved of command.

In 1864 Breckinridge was brought east to command in the Shenendoah Valley, and won a remarkable victory at New Market that May. Thereafter he reinforced Lee at Cold Harbor, and was dispatched back to the Valley, under Jubal Early, for further operations. After the Rebels finally lost the Shenendoah, in February 1865 Breckinridge was named Confederate Secretary of War by President Davis, and participated in the surrender conference between Sherman and Joe Johnston in North Carolina.

Refusing to surrender personally, he fled first to Cuba, then to Britain and Canada, before finally returning to the United States in early 1869. Although his prior connections allowed him to resume a career in law and business, his health rapidly declined, and he died in Lexington at age 54, in 1875.

Reserve (Breckinridge's) Corps at Shiloh

The 7,211 men of the Reserve Corps under Breckinridge—more properly considered a division—were in battle for the first time, except for the veterans of the battle of Mill Springs. The Reserve Corps consisted of three brigades, commanded by Brig. Gen. John S. Bowen and Colonels Robert Trabue and Walter Statham. Bowen was the best of these. Trabue and Statham were able but not particularly distinguished.

Trabue's 1st Brigade was "The Orphan Brigade," pro-Confederate Kentucky regiments "orphaned" when Kentucky's government aligned itself with the Union.

Bowen's 2nd Brigade consisted mainly of regiments subtracted from Polk's garrison at Columbus, Kentucky, the previous fall. These two brigades had been combined for months in Bowling Green as part of the Central Army of Kentucky.

Statham's 3rd Brigade was largely the Mississippi and eastern Tennessee troops that had been Zollicoffer's brigade, veterans of the battle of Mill Springs.

The three brigades were brought together during their brief stay in Murfreesboro, Tennessee, in February 1862, after the Central Army of Kentucky's retreat from Bowling Green by way of Nashville, and Zollicoffer's brigade's retreat from the battle of Mill Springs by way of Carthage, Tennessee. From Murfreesboro, they moved together, southwest to their concentration with the Army of the Mississippi in Corinth. In mid-March these three brigades were designated the Reserve Corps.

On Sunday morning at Shiloh, Breckinridge's corps was the last in the four successive lines of attack organized by General Beauregard. It bivouacked Saturday night along the Bark Road, in column of brigades, the 1st (Trabue's) Brigade in advance, 2nd (Bowen's) Brigade behind it, and the 3rd (Statham's) Brigade in the rear.

At the intersection of the Bark and Corinth roads, Trabue's brigade was detached and sent north on the Corinth Road directly to Shiloh Church. General Breckinridge led Bowen's and Statham's brigades east along the Bark Road, then north along the Eastern Corinth Road.

General Johnston personally positioned Bowen's and Statham's brigades for attack south of the Peach Orchard, where they were first engaged about 1:00 p.m. Breckinridge was physically courageous—he went forward with his men and shared their danger. However, on this day the former presidential candidate's magnetism was lacking. In the afternoon, Breckinridge needed Johnston's help to

urge one balky regiment forward. After Johnston's death a short time later, Bragg found Breckinridge holding back, undecided what to do.

General Breckinridge served personally all day with Bowen's and Statham's brigades, reuniting them with Trabue's brigade where Prentiss surrendered between 5:00 and 6:00 p.m. He then conducted the entire command to the east, along the ridge south of Dill Branch to near the Tennessee River, where it came under fire from gunboats and field batteries. At dark Breckinridge withdrew to the enemy camps east of Shiloh Church.

On Monday Breckinridge's Reserve Corps engaged the enemy with his three brigades intact behind Duncan Field facing northeast—the only Confederate corps to have all its brigades together on the second day. His right joined Hardee around the Peach Orchard and fought Crittenden's Union division for most of the day; his left joined Anderson's brigade and faced Rousseau's Union brigade of McCook's division. This portion of the battlefield—between the deep ravines of Tilghman Branch on the left and Dill Branch on the right—was the only level part of the field, and Beauregard chose it, and Breckinridge's intact command, for his most sustained attack of the second day.

When the army retired, Breckinridge formed the rear guard.

At Shiloh, Breckinridge's Reserve Corps lost 386 killed, 1,682 wounded, and 165 missing and captured, for a total of 2,233 out of 7,211 engaged—31% casualties, the second highest (after Hardee's corps) loss rate of the four Confederate corps.

Breckinridge's losses to enemy fire (the killed and wounded) were 29% of the total, also the second highest rate in the Confederate army.

1st Brigade
Colonel Robert P. Trabue

Colonel Trabue, "Old Trib" to his men (though he was only 38) came from one of the oldest families in the prosperous Kentucky Bluegrass. He entered the Mexican War as a private with a regiment of Kentucky volunteers and returned the captain of a company. In the 1850s he lived and practiced law in Mississippi, but in early 1861, when war appeared certain, he returned to Kentucky to raise a regiment.

His main organizational problem was an excess of officer candidates. In this, Trabue was a master of tact, moving quietly among the hopefuls, speaking soothingly and reminding them that there would be opportunities for advancement as the war progressed. His diplomatic spirit of compromise soon

suffused his officer corps. This was his first victory with his regiment. Trabue would demonstrate the same coolness in the midst of battle. He was not showy, but aristocratic, cool, and self-possessed.

Trabue assumed command of the Kentucky brigade only days before Shiloh, when Breckinridge, the previous brigade commander, was promoted to the command of the Reserve Corps.

After the battle, Breckinridge would recommend Trabue for promotion to brigadier general "for gallant and meritorious conduct at Shiloh." However, Trabue was back in regimental command at the battle of Murfreesboro at the end of 1862, and died of disease before he could receive his commission.

Trabue's "Kentucky Brigade" numbered 2,678 men in five infantry regiments—the 3rd, 4th, 5th, and 6th Kentucky, and the six-company 31st (Hale's) Alabama; two infantry battalions—Clifton's 4th Alabama Battalion and Crews's Tennessee Battalion; two batteries—Cobb's Battery and Byrne's Battery; and John Hunt Morgan's cavalry squadron. Trabue's brigade was nicknamed "The Orphan Brigade" because it was composed mostly of regiments from Kentucky that were unable to return home after their state fell into Union hands.

The story of the brigade started at Camp Boone, a recruitment camp near Clarksville, Tennessee, near the southern Kentucky border, where secessionist Kentuckians swarmed in the first months of the war to sign up for Confederate service. There, the first two Confederate Kentucky regiments, the 2nd and 3rd Kentucky Infantry, were organized in July 1861. At Camp Burnett two miles away, the 4th Kentucky was organized on September 13. On September 18, an invasion column—consisting of the 2nd Kentucky and the armed portions of the 3rd and 4th Kentucky under Brig, Gen. Simon B. Buckner—entered Kentucky and dug in around Bowling Green. Soon, the 5th and 6th Kentucky were being organized on home soil.

These regiments were brigaded under Buckner on October 28, 1861, the same day Albert Sidney Johnston came to Bowling Green and assumed command of the Central Army of Kentucky.

The 3rd and 4th Kentucky regiments, having completed their organization and acquiring uniforms, drill, and the routine of camp life before the arrival of the 5th and 6th, called the new regiments "dandies." The 5th and 6th Kentucky, in turn, called the 3rd and 4th "roughs" and "plug uglies." Shiloh would be the battle that brought the two groups together. Soon, they would become known as one of the most dependable brigades in the Confederate Army of Tennessee.

In November, the Kentucky Brigade was put under the command of the former U.S. vice president from Kentucky, Brig. Gen. John C. Breckinridge.

During the next three months, the brigade divided its time between training in Bowling Green and occupying Russellville, 25 miles to the west, and parts in between.

At the surrender of Fort Donelson on February 17, 1861, the 2nd Kentucky and General Buckner were captured and subtracted from the brigade.

On February 23, 1862, in Murfreesboro, Tennessee, Clifton's Alabama Battalion, Crews's Tennessee Battalion and Morgan's Cavalry Squadron were assigned to the brigade.

On March 21, 1862, in Corinth, Mississippi, the 31st Alabama regiment (Hale's) was assigned to the brigade.

On March 29, 1862, Col. Robert P. Trabue of the 4th Kentucky took command of the brigade when Breckinridge was promoted to the head of the Reserve Corps, only one week before the battle of Shiloh.

Trabue's Brigade at Shiloh

Aside from lack of combat experience, arming the Kentucky troops was still a problem, even as they filed into their lines at Shiloh on Sunday morning. When Breckinridge assumed command, there weren't enough muskets and rifles to supply each man with one, and the lack of uniformity was a drag on efficiency. The 2nd, 3rd, and 4th Regiments had been partially supplied with Belgian rifles, but many, even in those regiments, were armed with old muskets with their barrels newly rifled, and some of them had flintlocks. Many could be fired only by a match or a firebrand. There were weapons of almost every kind: squirrel rifles of every age, style, and bore; shotguns, double- and single-barreled, old and new; flintlocks, carbines, pistols, and knives. As late as January 2, 1862, complaint was made that the 5th Kentucky had no arms of any kind for half its men, and reports showed that there were but 246 really serviceable guns, besides 70 old flintlocks.

On Sunday morning, Trabue's brigade formed the advance of Breckinridge's Reserve Corps and reached the fork of the Bark Road and Corinth Road about 8:00 a.m. General Breckinridge sent it forward on the Corinth Road to support Polk's line, and soon afterward the brigade deployed to the left of the road in the order from left to right: 4th Kentucky, 6th Kentucky, 31st Alabama, 5th Kentucky, Clifton's 4th Alabama Battalion, Crews's Tennessee Battalion, and the 3rd Kentucky, with Cobb's Battery and Byrne's Battery in the rear. The Kentucky Brigade passed Shiloh Church in line of battle about 11:30 a.m., advancing due north from the church to Crescent Field.

Here, the 3rd Kentucky, the 4th Alabama Battalion, Crews's Tennessee Battalion and Byrne's Battery were detached by General Beauregard and ordered to support General Patton Anderson on the right. The 3rd and 4th Kentucky remained detached all day.

Cobb's Battery was put in position in front of the 5th Kentucky in the avenue in front of Marsh's brigade's camp. Colonel Trabue sheltered his command in a slight ravine on the edge of Crescent Field and rode forward to make observations. He saw camps to his left and his front, Union troops still in occupation. He moved his command by the left flank into Crescent Field and confronted the enemy. Here he was joined on the left by parts of Russell's, Stewart's, and Cleburne's brigades, and on his right by part of Anderson's brigade.

The Union troops in Trabue's front were the 46th Ohio and 6th Iowa (both from McDowell's brigade, Sherman's division) and the 13th Missouri (from McArthur's brigade, W. H. L. Wallace's division). After an engagement of about an hour, at about noon, Trabue brought up the 31st Alabama, which was in reserve, and ordered a charge. The Alabamians moved forward on the double-quick and drove the enemy through Marsh's camps and into the woods in the rear. Soon afterward, Trabue and his brigade reached the field where Prentiss surrendered. There he met troops from the Confederate right, completing the encircling of the unlucky Hornets' Nest survivors who had not escaped the jaws of the trap. Crews's Battalion was detached to take the prisoners to the rear.

In the meantime Cobb's Battery, occupying its first position in Marsh's camp, was taken by the enemy, then retaken. It had lost all of its horses and was abandoned. Four of its guns were removed with mules on Sunday night, but the battery was not again in action. Byrne's Battery was engaged in Ruggles's grand artillery line.

After the surrender of Prentiss, Trabue, with the 4th, 5th, and 6th Kentucky, and 31st Alabama, rejoined Breckinridge and moved east along the ridge south of Dill Branch. Trabue and his men occupied a position on the crest of the hill overlooking the Tennessee River, where they came under fire from the Union gunboats, which they endured until nearly dark. They then withdrew, traversing the battlefield to the crossroads of the Corinth Road and Hamburg-Purdy Road, where they were joined by the 3rd Kentucky, Clifton's 4th Alabama Battalion, and Byrne's Battery. Trabue's reunited regiments then further withdrew to the Union camps nearest Owl Creek, on the Confederate far left, where they passed Sunday night. Trabue says he rode until 11:00 p.m., trying to find a general officer to whom he could report for orders, and then sent an aide with an escort, who likewise rode all night without finding any of Trabue's superiors.

The Sunday battle had demanded that Trabue lead the brigade in a day of almost constant attack, and the brigade had performed well under his command. But Trabue's 3rd and 4th Kentucky were detached all day, and his lack of control was indicated by the fact that the missing were 11.5% of the casualties in his brigade, a rate much higher than the average for brigade-sized Rebel units at Shiloh.

On Monday morning the Kentucky Brigade formed on the Hamburg-Purdy Road. In a short time it was moved by the right flank to a point three-quarters of a mile east of Shiloh Church, and formed in line facing northeast, with Byrne's Battery at the edge of Duncan Field. Anderson's brigade was on the brigade's left and Bowen's brigade on its right. They held this position for four hours, and then the brigade, except the 4th Kentucky and Clifton's 4th Alabama Battalion, moved to the right of Duncan Field and was engaged for an hour more, after which it fell back to the right of Shiloh Church.

The 4th Kentucky and Clifton's 4th Alabama Battalion were engaged in a severe firefight north of Duncan Field, where they lost very heavily.

At Shiloh Church the contest was continued for two hours, when the brigade fell back to the fork of the Bark Road and Corinth Road, where it remained as a rear guard on Monday night. On Tuesday the brigade retired to Mickey's, where it remained three days.

At Shiloh, Trabue's Kentucky brigade lost 151 killed, 557 wounded, and 92 missing, for a total of 800 out of 2,691 engaged—30% casualties.

2nd Brigade
Brigadier General John S. Bowen

John S. Bowen, at 31 years old, was rather young for a brigade commander. He was born in Bowen's Creek, Georgia, to a prosperous merchant father who did business in nearby Savannah. A good student, he received an excellent formal education. He entered West Point in 1848, but in 1851 was suspended for a year for failing to report the absence of a fellow cadet. He graduated 13th of 52 cadets in the class of 1853, and was assigned to the Mounted Rifles.

In the U.S. Army, he served at the Carlisle cavalry school and on the frontier. He then resigned his commission in 1856 and became an architect in Savannah, Georgia, where he put his military training to use as lieutenant colonel of Georgia militia. He moved to St. Louis in 1857 because he recognized it as a flashpoint in the growing sectional crisis. There, he continued as an architect and by 1861 was captain of a pro-secessionist Missouri militia company. In the early months of

1861, he was sent with militiamen to southwest Missouri to guard the state against incursions by Freesoil Kansas Jayhawkers.

At the beginning of the Civil War in April, Bowen and his fellow St. Louis-area secessionists were captured at Camp Jackson by Union troops under Captain Nathaniel Lyon. As he waited to be exchanged, he went to Memphis, where he opened a recruiting depot for secessionist Missourians and enlisted more than 1,000 men in 10 companies. He was commissioned a colonel in the Confederate States Army and assumed command of his regiment, designated the 1st Missouri Infantry, on June 11, 1861. The 1st Missouri was soon shipped upriver to General Polk's army at Columbus, Kentucky.

Detached by Polk in early October to command a garrison at Camp Beauregard, a strongpoint in western Kentucky halfway between Columbus and Fort Henry, Bowen on October 24 was made commander of a two-brigade force, designated the 4th Division of the Western Department.

Bowen's division was transferred to Bowling Green in late December and he took charge of a brigade in Johnston's Central Army of Kentucky. When in mid-March of 1862 Generals Johnston and Beauregard combined their armies for the attack upon Grant at Pittsburg Landing, Bowen belatedly received his commission as brigadier general, and his brigade was assigned to the Reserve Corps. When the corps commander, General Crittenden, was dismissed from the army for drunkenness a week before the battle of Shiloh, Bowen was considered as his replacement, but he gave way to former U.S. Vice President John Breckinridge, who had less military background but more prestige.

Bowen, though without prior battlefield experience, distinguished himself at Shiloh, aggressively pushing his brigade forward until he was wounded as a result of his habit of commanding from the front. He nevertheless supervised his regiments closely; his missing were only 4.5% of casualties.

In 1863, he was recommended for promotion to major general for his aggressive defensive effort against Grant's superior forces at the battle of Port Gibson, the prelude action east of the Mississippi River on the way to the siege of

Vicksburg. Bowen received his promotion and brilliantly led his division at Champion Hill and Vicksburg, where he was General Pemberton's most trusted officer. That was his last command, however, for Bowen died of dysentery on July 13 shortly after the Vicksburg siege ended.

Bowen's Brigade at Shiloh

Bowen's brigade numbered 1,744 men in four infantry regiments—the 9th and 10th Arkansas, 2nd Confederate, and 1st Missouri—supported by two batteries, Hudson's and Watson's (Belzhoover's).

Elements of the brigade had been together since the fall of 1861. That October the force detached with Bowen from Polk's garrison at Columbus to occupy Camp Beauregard included Bowen's own 1st Missouri regiment, the 2nd Confederate (then known as the 1st Mississippi Valley regiment), the 9th and 10th Arkansas, and Hudson's Mississippi Battery. By November 30, Watson's Louisiana Battery (now known as Belzhoover's Battery), which had seen combat at the battle of Belmont, had been added to the garrison.

In mid-December 1861, when elements of the Union Army of the Ohio advanced along the Louisville & Nashville Railroad to Munfordville on the Green River, General Johnston in Bowling Green ordered Polk to reinforce Bowen. The report of the Army of Central Kentucky for January 31, 1862, shows Bowen's Brigade at Bowling Green.

Johnston's army return of February 23, after its retreat to Murfreesboro, Tennessee, shows Bowen's Brigade still attached. By this time, the 2nd Confederate regiment had been added to the brigade.

General Bowen was fortunate in the quality and experience of his regimental commanders. All were colonels, and only Merrick of the 10th Arkansas was unpopular with his men—alone among Bowen's colonels, he would not be reelected in the reorganization of the Army of the Mississippi in May 1862.

On Sunday morning, April 6, Bowen's brigade marched north from its Saturday night bivouac on the Corinth Road, turned east on the Bark Road, and then followed the Eastern Corinth Road north to a position between the Peach Orchard and Locust Grove Branch, where it formed a line of battle at noon under the personal direction of General Johnston. It deployed in the order from left to right: 9th Arkansas, 10th Arkansas, 2nd Confederate, and 1st Missouri, with Hudson's and Watson's batteries in the rear. Bowen's brigade's right was 800 yards to the rear of the left of Jackson's brigade.

General Johnston himself readied Bowen's troops, brandishing a tin cup he had picked up that morning from a Union campsite and calling it "My share of the spoils." He addressed the regiment, saying, "Men of Mississippi and Arkansas, the enemy is stubborn. I want you to show General Beauregard and General Bragg what you can do with your bayonets and toothpicks [Bowie knives]!" Sometime around 12:30 p.m., Bowen's men went forward with a cheer, passed Johnston at a run and disappeared into the thicket in front. In 20 minutes, hundreds of Bowen's men had gone down, but McArthur's Union brigade east of the Peach Orchard was driven back.

Here General Johnston, following close on the rear of Bowen's brigade, received his mortal wound: a spent minie ball tore an artery just below his knee, and he bled to death soon afterward.

Bowen was next engaged for two hours at Wicker Field, where he was wounded. His brigade fell back a half-mile to the fork of the Hamburg-Savannah and Hamburg-Purdy roads, where Col. John D. Martin took command. The brigade moved forward again in time to join Breckinridge in his advance toward the river after the surrender of Prentiss. Martin halted within 300 or 400 yards of the river when the batteries near Pittsburg Landing and the Tyler and Lexington gunboats opened on him. In the failing light, Martin fell back and bivouacked for the night in Peabody's Union camps.

On Monday the brigade was engaged under Breckinridge on the Confederate right astride the Eastern Corinth road, and fell back with him to the Bark Road, where he bivouacked Monday as rear guard.

At Shiloh, Bowen's brigade lost 98 killed, 498 wounded, and 28 missing, for a total of 624 out of 1,744 engaged—36% casualties.

3rd Brigade
Colonel Walter S. Statham

Walter Scott Statham, known as "Scott" to his friends, was an attorney, a youthful 30 years old at Shiloh, born in Georgia and reared in Grenada, Mississippi. His well-to-do family sent him to Dartmouth College, from which he graduated in 1855. When at the beginning of the Civil War his hometown organized the Grenada Rifles infantry company, Statham was elected its captain. He was then elected colonel of the 15th Mississippi Infantry on June 6, 1861, although his command credentials were based not on his military accomplishments but entirely on his high social standing in Grenada.

On August 13, 1861, Statham moved with his regiment to Knoxville, Tennessee, where it took its place with other regiments in Felix Zollicoffer's brigade. Statham was accidentally shot in the shoulder by a careless Confederate cavalryman in September 1861, which caused him to miss the brigade's first combat at the battle of Mill Springs. At Shiloh, he was still bothered by the wound.

A month after Shiloh, Statham was re-elected colonel of the 15th Mississippi regiment, and soon afterward he was re-appointed brigade commander. It was said that "All the men loved Colonel Statham." He continued to lead the brigade until July 27, 1862, when, just days before he was to receive a promotion to brigadier general, he died of what official reports described as "a hot fever."

Statham's Brigade at Shiloh

Statham's brigade was a large one, numbering 3,079 men in six infantry regiments—the 15th and 22nd Mississippi, and the 19th, 20th, 28th, and 45th Tennessee, supported by Rutledge's Battery and Nathan B. Forrest's Tennessee cavalry.

Statham's was one of the only battle-experienced brigades in the Army of the Mississippi, due to the fact that the 15th Mississippi and 19th, 20th, and 28th Tennessee regiments, as well as Rutledge's Battery had been in Zollicoffer's brigade and had fought at Mill Springs in eastern Kentucky on January 19, 1862.

The brigade, defeated at Mill Springs and mourning the death of General Zollicoffer there, retreated south across the Cumberland River, licking its wounds in Carthage, Tennessee, for a month after the battle. Command of Zollicoffer's brigade fell to its senior colonel, Walter Statham.

Retreating further to Murfreesboro in February, Statham's four veteran regiments rendezvoused with General Johnston's Central Army of Kentucky, which had also retreated to Murfreesboro. There, in the February 23 reorganization of the army, Statham's brigade was placed in Crittenden's division (what would be the Reserve Corps at Shiloh), and its battle-tested regiments were augmented by the 22nd Mississippi and 45th Tennessee. The two new regiments had not seen combat, and the 45th Tennessee had not even made a march.

From Murfreesboro, the brigade slogged with Johnston's army through mud and rain to Decatur, Alabama, and then went by rail to Corinth, Mississippi. After reaching Corinth, Forrest's Tennessee Cavalry regiment, which had escaped from the debacle at Fort Donelson, was added to Statham's Brigade.

Statham was unfortunate in the leadership of his infantry regiments at Shiloh. One of his regiments was led by a lieutenant colonel, and one by a major. Of the four regiments led by full colonels, only one, Col. Battle of the 20th Tennessee, was esteemed. Two others would not be reelected by their men in the army reorganization the following month, and, in the case of the 22nd Mississippi, the incompetent, malingering Col. Schaller's departure due to a foot wound was unlamented.

On Sunday morning, Statham's brigade was at the rear of the army. It followed Bowen's brigade, and at noon was put in line near the army's right, south of the Peach Orchard, with its right 800 yards in rear of Bowen's brigade's left. It moved forward into the orchard, and at about 2:20 p.m. was put in position by Tennessee's governor Isham Harris and ordered to attack the Union forces at Bloody Pond. After being personally ordered to charge across Sarah Bell Field by General Breckinridge and then General Johnston, Statham's men made a spirited bayonet charge across the field and into the Peach Orchard in cooperation with three regiments of Stephens's brigade, now under Col. George Maney. As one Iowa soldier recorded it, "a shout arose, and [Statham's] brigade moved on magnificently." The brigade fought here for about two hours. The attack forced Stuart's and McArthur's Union brigades, along with elements of Hurlbut's division, to fall back, exposing Prentiss's left flank at the Hornets' Nest. The Confederates then wheeled to the left and helped to surround Prentiss.

After Prentiss's surrender Statham's brigade joined Breckinridge in the day's last movement, to the east on the ridge south of Dill Branch. Stymied here by a stout Federal last-ditch line in front of Pittsburg Landing, and enfiladed from the right by the two gunboats on the Tennessee River, Statham then retired with the rest of the Reserve Corps.

It is not recorded where Statham's men bivouacked Sunday night.

On Monday Statham's brigade was engaged with Breckinridge, staging an attack in the Hornets' Nest area from the south side of Duncan Field, with Statham's Brigade to the left and Bowen's Brigade, now under Col. John D. Martin, to the right. In the back-and-forth fighting at mid-day, Statham's men counter-attacked the same ground at the Hornets' Nest that the Confederate army had attacked the day before.

The 20th Tennessee must have been engaged Monday with Breckinridge—its colonel, Joel A. Battle, was captured in the vicinity of Lost Field late in the day.

At Shiloh, Statham's Brigade lost 137 killed, 627 wounded, and 45 missing, for a total of 809 out of 3,079 men engaged involved—26% casualties.

Colonel Nathan Bedford Forrest

Born in 1821 to an illiterate blacksmith in Bedford County in south central Tennessee, the 17-year-old Forrest became head of a family of seven children upon his father's death. By the time the Civil War opened, his canny speculations in land, cotton, and slaves had made him, at the age of 40, a Memphis millionaire, owner of two plantations, and one of the wealthiest men in Tennessee. He had no military experience and entered Confederate service as a private, but rose to the rank of lieutenant general—the only man on either side to rise so far. He revolutionized mobile warfare, using his troopers as mounted infantry. In the course of the war, he was wounded four times, had 30 horses shot out from under him, and killed 31 men in hand-to-hand combat. Union general William T. Sherman called him "the most remarkable man our Civil War produced on either side." Civil War author Shelby Foote voiced his opinion that the Civil War produced two geniuses: Abraham Lincoln and Nathan Bedford Forrest. For his exploits, Forrest acquired the sobriquet "The Wizard of the Saddle."

On July 24, 1861, authorized by Tennessee's Governor Isham Harris to raise a cavalry battalion of 500 troopers, Nathan Bedford Forrest started his recruitment with an advertisement in the *Memphis Appeal.* He immediately went to Kentucky to procure weapons for his command, and recruited his first company there. He returned to Memphis in August. In October 1861, Forrest's Tennessee Cavalry battalion—650 troopers from five Confederate states, mostly armed with double-barreled shotguns—was organized. It reported to Col. Adolphus Heiman, who was constructing Forts Henry and Donelson on the Tennessee and Cumberland rivers. Proceeding to Hopkinsville, Kentucky, the battalion was reinforced by two Alabama companies, bringing Forrest's command to 800 men.

Forrest's command's first skirmish was at Sacramento, Kentucky, on December 28, 1861, in the no-man's-land of western central Kentucky, where he routed a Federal cavalry force nearly twice the size of his own. There, he demonstrated tactics for which he would later become famous: dividing his force into groups, using deception and encirclement, and leading the cavalry charge personally. His superior at the time, Brig. Gen. Charles Clark, noted his "skill, energy and courage." Soon afterward, in February of 1862 at the battle for Fort Donelson, Forrest was astonished and angered when his fellow Confederate commanders, in a nighttime council of war, decided to surrender. Forrest shouted, "I did not come here for the purpose of surrendering my command," stormed out of the meeting, gathered 700 troopers, and escaped in the dark, leading his men on a snowy two-day, 75-mile trek to join General A.S. Johnston's army in Nashville.

Forrest immediately supervised the removal of huge amounts of army supplies from Nashville and rejoined the Confederate army under Johnston at Murfreesboro. Johnston ordered Forrest's command to Huntsville, Alabama, then to the vicinity of Corinth in mid-March. There Forrest and his men were attached to Statham's brigade in the final organization of the Army of the Mississippi before the battle of Shiloh.

After the battle Forrest embarked on his storied career as an independent raider, wreaking havoc with Union supply lines, while sometimes joining main battles as at Chickamauga and Franklin. His last action was attempting to hold Selma in April 1865, and he subsequently surrendered with the rest of Richard Taylor's department the following month.

After the war, Forrest became president of the Selma, Marion, & Memphis Railroad, but under his direction the company went bankrupt in the 1870s. His last years were spent in declining health. Forrest spent his final days living in a log cabin he and his wife had salvaged from his plantation and running a prison work farm. Forrest, who in his prime was a physically imposing man of 6'2" and 200 pounds, died in 1877 at the age of 56, weighing little more than a hundred pounds, from what may have been diabetes. His death certificate gave the cause of death as chronic diarrhea.

Forrest's 3rd Tennessee Cavalry at Shiloh

Prior to the battle, Forrest led a small scouting mission in the vicinity of Hamburg Landing. On the evening of April 5, Forrest was ordered to deploy his entire regiment to guard a crossing at Lick Creek, a short distance south of Pittsburg Landing, on the far right of the Confederate army. They camped there for the night, and remained there during the opening hours of the battle of Shiloh the next morning.

However, around 11:00 a.m., as the battle raged and no enemy approached the Lick Creek crossing, Forrest and the infantry commander on the flank watch,

Col. George Maney, saw that it was folly to remain idle. Forrest called to his men, and in a few minutes his cavalry was galloping toward the sound of the guns. As the troopers approached Prentiss's position at the Hornets' Nest, shells from a Union artillery barrage started falling among the cavalry. Forrest asked General Cheatham, whose division was retiring from the front, for permission to attack. Cheatham refused. A little while later, Forrest asked again, and Cheatham refused again, saying, "If you want to charge, you must do it on your own authority."

Forrest, who was always quick to seize the moment, gave the order, and the cavalry's charge carried it to within fifty yards of the Union line when the horses struck soft, marshy ground. The cavalry pulled back, but Cheatham, observing that the approach of the thundering cavalry had caused unsteadiness in the enemy line, ordered his tattered division forward once more. In the chaos of the renewed fighting among the infantry, the Union men started filtering toward the rear. Forrest directed his cavalry around the marsh and fell on the rear of the retreating Federals, scattering them and hurrying them toward the shelter of Pittsburg Landing.

The fighting on Sunday was over for the cavalry. That night, Forrest pleaded with Brig. Gen. Chalmers, then General Breckinridge, then General Hardee to make an immediate attack, having heard from his scouts that Buell's army was arriving. None were willing to authorize an attack, and Beauregard was not to be found.

On Monday, after falling back from his advance picket line at the start of Buell's advance, Forrest's men were mainly assigned to provost duty, stiffening up stragglers behind the Confederate lines. As the withdrawal began, Beauregard employed the cavalry as a mobile reserve, dispatching it to different parts of the front that seemed threatened.

On Tuesday, April 8, Forrest initiated the last major clash of the battle. That morning General Sherman ventured out in pursuit, with two of his re-gathered brigades plus a regiment of Union cavalry. About four miles out they came in sight of a large Rebel field hospital, guarded by cavalry. It was about 150 men under Forrest, buttressed by Texas Rangers from the 8th Texas, and contingents from Wirt Adams's Mississippi cavalry and Kentuckians led by John Hunt Morgan.

Upon seeing Sherman's skirmish line flounder in soft ground in a stretch of fallen timber, Forrest ordered a hellbent charge, and the Rebel horsemen, some 350 strong, came thundering down from their ridgeline. They overran the lead Federal regiment, and dispersed the Illinois cavalry. Sherman readied his following brigades for the impact, but it was only Forrest himself who kept charging. Nearly surrounded, shot in the side, and with his horse mortally wounded, Forrest somehow managed to escape—though without the tall tale of him pulling a Union soldier up behind him on his horse as a shield.

Afterward Sherman walked the field, which he thought should have been easily defended against cavalry, and counted 15 of his dead and 40 wounded. Some 70 other men had been hauled off by the Rebels as prisoners. In his report of the action, written that day, Sherman curiously said he had been attacked by "General Forrest in person." Forrest was still a colonel at Shiloh, but it was as if Sherman had gained a premonition of the nemesis he would have to vie with for the rest of the war.

At Shiloh, Forrest's Cavalry numbered about 679 men present for duty. Its casualties were not reported.

Afterword

The strategic consequences of Shiloh were profound. The defeat of the Confederate concentration at Shiloh opened the way to capturing the rail hub of Corinth, Mississippi, just a handful of weeks later. With its lifeline to the east thus severed, the Memphis, Tennessee—the capital of the South's Cotton Empire, and, with New Orleans, the most important Southern city on the Mississippi River—fell quickly on June 6, 1862. This was the climax of the struggle for only the Mississippi Valley, and one that had been predictable since the appearance of Union ironclad gunboats six months earlier. When the war in the Western Theater shifted away from the rivers dominated by the "turtles" and moved to the highlands along Louisville- Nashville-Chattanooga-Atlanta axis, the pace of the Union war was slowed by two years of hard fighting, this time with Rebel cavalry as the spearheads instead of Federal gunboats.

Shiloh introduced to history many of the future chieftains—the major generals, lieutenant generals and full generals—who would guide the war in the West for the next three years. The one prominent name that would not be among them was Albert S. Johnston. The South had high hopes that his leadership would help guide the Confederacy to independence. His shocking death during the early hours of the battle left a command vacuum and volatility in the upper echelon of leadership that would not solidify until Braxton Bragg assumed the reins of army command. Of those who survived, P. G. T. Beauregard, Braxton Bragg, Ben Cheatham, Patrick Cleburne, Nathan Bedford Forrest, William Hardee, Thomas

Hindman, Bushrod Johnson, Leonidas Polk, Alex P. Stewart, and Jones Withers would lead the way.

Future Union leaders of the war effort included Ulysses Grant, William Sherman, Don Carlos Buell, Ralph Buckland, Charles Cruft, William Hazen, Jacob Lauman, John McArthur, and James Veatch. George Thomas, alone among the Union armies' division commanders, arrived too late for this first great battle, which may explain why it took him so long to attain his rightful place in the top flight of Union generals.

Shiloh was without question one of the Civil War's major turning points. The large scale combat signaled in bloody fashion that the end of the mostly quiescent early stage of the conflict was over, and another—more terrible, much darker, and more destructive—beginning. The Confederate attack was thrown back in tactical defeat, but that strong thrust reversed the Union momentum of early 1862. After being surprised at Shiloh, Grant was discredited. The plodding, methodical Henry Halleck took command of the Union army and applied a tremendous brake on Union progress in the Western Theater. Halleck's caution squandered the advantages won by Grant's impetuosity. Within six months General Bragg and his Army of Mississippi had reversed the Federal tide, invaded Kentucky, and threatened the Ohio River line.

The horrific casualty totals printed in the nation's newspapers produced both the most immediate and perhaps the longest-lasting result of the battle: it shocked the nation's psyche. More than 24,000 men had been killed or wounded (including 20 of the 66 leaders presented on these pages), a number that shocked and dismayed American North and South. These were unimaginable losses—higher in one battle than the Revolutionary War, War of 1812, and Mexican War combined.

In the Eastern Theater, news of the Shiloh holocaust further convinced Maj. Gen. George McClellan, stalled on the Virginia peninsula around Yorktown, that his campaign must be won by strategy and maneuver; the hard head-to-head fighting that had produced such hideous gore at Shiloh must be avoided. McClellan's siege of Yorktown was followed by a slow and careful march up the neck of land to the outskirts of Richmond. In late June, Robert E. Lee demonstrated that he had no such compunction about pitched action and drove him away in defeat during the Seven Days's Battles. As Bragg was invading Kentucky in the West the next fall, Lee was similarly turning the tables in the East, scoring one victory after another until his momentum carried him beyond the Potomac River.

What followed was a war that took on the horrific dimensions first glimpsed after the Shiloh bloodletting. Hundreds of thousands more casualties and three more years of blood and misery were required to bring the war to an end. "Shiloh was the severest battle fought at the West during the war," wrote Grant in his memoirs, "and but few in the East equaled it for hard, determined fighting." If McClellan and perhaps others learned one lesson from Shiloh, U. S. Grant learned something altogether different. It was only after Shiloh, he continued, that "indeed, I gave up all idea of saving the Union except by complete conquest." After capturing Vicksburg and breaking the siege of Chattanooga in late 1863, President Lincoln promoted Grant to lieutenant general and Commanding General of the Army, brought him to Washington, and set him loose. General Grant brought with him the blunt-force, attritional style of warfare he had used so successfully in the West.

Critical Bibliography

Civil War-era senator Charles Sumner wrote the famous epigram, "Nobody sees a battle." This was never more true than in the thickets and the ravines, amid the smoke and deafening roar, of Shiloh. That battle, acknowledged Ulysses S. Grant, was "perhaps less understood or persistently misunderstood" than any other Civil War engagement.

The first place to begin any serious research is a close reading of the reports, letters, and telegrams found within the pages of *The Official Records of the War of the Rebellion,* an indispensable reference source for an understanding of the experiences of the officers as they remembered them a few days or weeks later. Shaping a full narrative of a battle as fluid and confused as Shiloh, however, required the passage of four decades.

It was not until after the turn of the century that the first attempt to craft a full-length account of the battle appeared. David W. Reed's *The Battle of Shiloh and the Organizations Engaged* was published by the Government Printing Office in 1902. Reed's book is still an invaluable source for anybody researching this most chaotic of combats. Reed was a veteran of the 12th Iowa regiment (Tuttle's brigade, W. H. L. Wallace's division), and had been wounded in the thigh at the Hornets' Nest. He was also the first historian of the Shiloh National Military Park (established by Congress in 1894), and had thus spent decades after the war walking the ground, meticulously tracing the movements and firefights of the armies on Sunday and Monday, April 6 and 7, 1862. Reed recorded those movements and firefights at the brigade level. Since I examined leadership of the brigadiers that guided those brigades at Shiloh, Reed's book was essential in informing my account of those men and their commands in the mayhem of those two days.

It took many more decades before the first modern study of the battle appeared. Wiley Sword's *Shiloh: Bloody April* (Morrow, 1974) was the first book on the battle I devoured, many years ago. I recommend it for its well-researched vignettes and its lively writing. Its detailed small actions and quotes by participants make this a book rich with color. My only cavil with Sword's work is that concentrating on those small actions comes somewhat at the expense of the larger picture.

Another fine study on the battle was written years before Sword's book in 1966 at Louisiana State University under the eye of the great historian T. Harry Williams. Although highly regarded and heavily used by rangers and historians at the park, O. Edward Cunningham's dissertation was not published for another 41 years until historian Gary Joiner and Shiloh park ranger Timothy Smith brought it to the attention of Theodore P. Savas, the managing director of Savas Beatie. Cunningham's *Shiloh and the Western Campaign of 1862* (Savas Beatie, 2007), a thoroughly researched account decades ahead of other scholarship on several major issues, had finally reached the audience it so richly deserved. It includes an account of the run-up to the battle, starting with the strategic picture in the first months of 1862 and sketching Grant's capture of Forts Henry and Donelson, an approach I particularly like because until one understands the reasons for a battle, it is not possible to understand the battle itself.

In 1977, three years after Sword's book appeared, came another Shiloh narrative. James Lee McDonough's *Shiloh—In Hell Before Night* (University of Tennessee Press, 1977) agreed with David Reed's thesis that the Hornets' Nest was at the crux of the battle. Cunningham's research, together with contemporary analysis, including a study of casualties in this book, has brought the primacy of the Hornets' Nest into question.

In 1997, Larry J. Daniel's *Shiloh: The Battle That Changed the Civil War* (Touchstone Books) appeared. Like Cunningham, Daniel devoted much space to the lead-up to the battle before describing the battle proper. I like his frequent switches of setting, from the capitals of the two warring nations, to the far-flung headquarters of the three armies in the weeks before the eventual clash at Shiloh, to the converging stations of the combat units as they made their way unsurely toward the battle that only became a virtual certainty the night before the first shots were fired. It was then that Confederate General Albert Sidney Johnston had determined to plunge headlong into the camps of the more numerous Union army, declaring "I would fight them if they were a million."

Timothy Smith's *Shiloh: Conquer or Perish* (University Press of Kansas, 2014) is the most recent of the Shiloh volumes and, together with Cunningham's, the best of them all. It reveals Smith as the greatest of the battle's contemporary historians, who as a park ranger has walked every yard of that sprawling battlefield. Smith also penned *This Great Battlefield of Shiloh* (2006) and *The Untold Story of Shiloh* (2006). His *Conquer or Perish* also offers the best telling of the battle's second day, which until now has been given short shrift by historians, and demonstrates the importance of the terrain on the battle.

Finally, I am grateful for Joseph Allan Frank and George A. Reaves's *"Seeing the Elephant": Raw Recruits at the Battle of Shiloh* (University of Illinois Press, 2003), a vivid record that draws on the letters and diaries of the men in the more than 160 regiments that saw combat for the first time at Shiloh.

Beside the important studies on the battle itself, other books treating the events and characters leading up to the battle are indispensable in understanding how Shiloh came about, and how it was the culmination of the first year of the War in the West.

Of the books I kept handy during the writing of this book, the earliest to appear in print was Arthur L. Conger's *The Rise of U. S. Grant* (New York, NY: Century Co., 1931). For some reason, I have not one but two well-worn copies of Bruce Catton's towering *Grant Moves South* (Boston, MA: Little Brown and Company, 1960), which, even after half a century, serves as a model for Civil War writing. I also learned much from T. K. Kionka's *Key Command: Ulysses Grant's District of Cairo* (Columbia, MO: University of Missouri Press, 2006), a recent reference that more closely examines the importance of Grant's earliest district command from which he set the critical Western events of 1862 in motion.

The books on the Western battles in the months previous to Shiloh are also illuminating. The early war combat at Belmont is treated by Nathaniel Cheairs Hughes, Jr.'s *The Battle of Belmont: Grant Strikes South* (University of North Carolina Press, 1991); the capture of the river forts, examined in Benjamin Franklin Cooling's *Forts Henry and Donelson: The Key to the Confederate Heartland* (University of Tennessee Press, 1987), Kendall D. Gott's *Where the South Lost the War: An Analysis of the Fort Henry—Fort Donelson Campaign, February 1862* (Mechanicsburg, PA: Stackpole Books, 2003), and Timothy B. Smith's *Grant invades Tennessee: The 1862 Battles for Forts Henry and Donelson* (University Press of Kansas, 2016).

Studies about the gathering armies that converged on Shiloh offer revealing insights about the leaders, recruits, habits of mind, and the state of the military art in early 1862. Many were constantly close at hand as I wrote this book. Stanley F. Horn's *The Army of Tennessee* (University of Oklahoma Press, 1941) is the forerunner here. Other useful works on this Western Confederate army include Thomas Lawrence Connelly's *Army of the Heartland: The Army of Tennessee, 1861-1862* (Louisiana State University Press, 1967), and Larry J. Daniel's *Soldiering in the Army of Tennessee: A Portrait of Life in a Confederate Army* (University of North Carolina Press, 1991).

The books on the Union armies also offer invaluable reading. Grant's army is the subject of Steven F. Woodworth's 760-page *Nothing but Victory: The Army of the Tennessee* (Alfred Knopf, 2005). Buell and his army are treated in the insightful *All for the Regiment: The Army of the Ohio, 1861-1862* (University of North Carolina Press, 2001) by Gerald J. Prokopowicz, and Larry J. Daniel's *Days of Glory: The Army of the Cumberland, 1861-1865* (Louisiana State University Press, 2004). Particularly interesting to me, and emphasized in all these books, are not only the primary importance of the character of the leaders, but the extent to which logistics—the movement of supplies—determines where, when, and often how battles are fought.

Biographies of the principals, of course, proved indispensable. Some of the Confederate studies I consulted include (in no particular order of importance): William Preston Johnston's *The Life of General Albert Sidney Johnston* (D. Appleton, 1878), Charles P. Roland's *Albert Sidney Johnson, Soldier of Three Republics* (University Press of Kentucky, 2013), Earl Hess' *Braxton Bragg: The Most Hated Man in the Confederacy* (University of North Carolina Press, 2016), Grady McWhiney's *Braxton Bragg and Confederate Defeat*, Vol. 1 (University of Alabama Press, 1969), Sam Davis Elliott's *Soldier of Tennessee: General Alexander P. Stewart and the Civil War in the West* (Louisiana State University Press, 1999), Christopher Losson, *Tennessee's Forgotten Warriors: Frank Cheatham and His Confederate Division* (University of Tennessee Press, 1990), Dianne Neal and Thomas Kremm's *The Lion of the South: General Thomas C. Hindman* (Mercer University Press, 1997) and John Allan Wyeth's *That Devil Forrest: Life of General Nathan Bedford Forrest* (Louisiana State University Press, 1959), Nathaniel Cheairs Hughes' *General William J. Hardee: Old Reliable* (Louisiana State University Press, 1987), and T. Harry Williams' *P. G. T. Beauregard: Napoleon in Gray* (Louisiana State University Press, 1955).

On the Union side, in addition to Conger's and Catton's books on Grant noted above, I consulted, among others (and once more in no order of importance or significance), U. S. Grant, *Personal Memoirs of U. S. Grant* (Charles L. Webster & Co., 1885), Christopher C. Meyers, *Union General John A. McClernand and the Politics of Command* (McFarland & Co., 2010), Isabel Wallace, *Life and Letters of General W.*

H. L. Wallace (R. R. Donnelley, 1909), Jeffrey N. Lash, *A Politician Turned General: The Civil War Career of Stephen Augustus Hurlbut* (Kent State University Press, 2003), William T. Sherman, *Memoirs*, 2 vols. (Appleton, 1875), Dan Lee, *Kentuckian in Blue: A Biography of Major General Lovell Harrison Rousseau* (McFarland & Co., 2010), and William Babcock Hazen's *A Narrative of Military Service* (Ticknor and Co., 1885).

My understanding was improved, too, by reading the regional biographers, which included Victor Hicken, *Illinois in the Civil War* (University of Illinois Press, 1991), Addison A. Stuart, *Iowa Colonels and Regiments: Being a History of Iowa Regiments in the War of the Rebellion* (Mills & Co., 1865), James Grant Wilson, *Biographical Sketches of Illinois Officers Engaged in the War Against the Rebellion of 1861* (J. Barnet, 1862), Thomas J. Lindsey, *Ohio at Shiloh: Report of the Commission* (C. J. Krehbiel & Company, 1903), and Whitelaw Reid, *Ohio in the War: Her Statesmen, Her Generals, and Soldiers* (Robert Clarke Company, 1895).

Unit histories at the brigade level that I consulted in writing this book include Stuart Salling, *Louisianans in the Western Confederacy: The Adams-Gibson Brigade in the Civil War* (McFarland & Company, 2010), William C. Davis, *The Orphan Brigade: The Kentucky Confederates Who Couldn't Go Home* (NY: Knopf Doubleday, 2012), Edwin Porter Thompson, *History of the First Kentucky Brigade* (Caxton Publishing House, 1868), and Mark W. Johnson, *That Brave Body of Men: The U.S. Regular Infantry and the Civil War in the West* (Da Capo Press, 2003).

Jack D. Welsh, M.D., penned *Medical Histories of Confederate Generals* and *Medical Histories of Union Generals* (Kent State University Press, 1995, 1997). They are invaluable for information on medical backgrounds, wounds, injuries, and general health issues related to the men in question. Vincent J. Esposito's *The West Point Atlas of American Wars*, Vol. 1 (Henry Holt and Co., 1995), offers outstanding cartography of the Shiloh area of operations.

Acknowledgments

The assistance of many persons was indispensable in the writing of this book, starting with my excellent publisher, Theodore P. (Ted) Savas, to whom I am indebted for the use of his library, his knowledge of the subject, his conversations over beer, and his good sense in guiding the book through its many stages to completion. I am also extremely grateful to my editor, Steven Smith, for glimpsing the essence of the book inside the much larger original manuscript. It was under his guidance that I chipped away at the marble slab until I uncovered the statue within. To both, I am indebted for their gentle urgings, without which I would have gone to considerably less trouble.

I also owe many thanks to cartographer Tim Kissel, who took my laundry list of landmarks in the campaign theater and the battlefield and produced two magnificent maps that illuminate the context and the progress of this most chaotic of battles.

I am also in debt to Timothy B. Smith, the foremost author on the subject of Shiloh, for his willingness to answer my many questions about the battle, particularly regarding Confederate artillery, overlooked references, and regimental histories. Tim also helped with obtaining some of the photographs of my subjects, and recommended Ashley Berry, supervisory park ranger of Shiloh National Military Park, who was also very helpful. It was she who pointed me to David Raith, who was kind enough to mail me the photograph of his courageous forebear, Julius Raith.

Finally, I would like to thank my wife, Lori Jablonski, for her unfailing support and constant yumminess.

About the Author

Born in Lincoln, Illinois, Larry Tagg graduated from the University of Texas at Austin. He recently retired after teaching high school drama, English, and Asian and Middle Eastern literature in the prestigious Humanities and International Studies program in Sacramento, California.

A bass player/singer of world renown, Larry co-founded and enjoyed substantial commercial success with the group Bourgeois Tagg in the mid-1980s. He went on to play bass for Todd Rundgren, Hall and Oates, and other acts; was a staff songwriter for Warner/Chappell Music; and released two solo albums, "With a Skeleton Crew" and "Rover." He is also historian and designer for the computer game company "Scourge of War."

Larry is the author of the bestselling *The Generals of Gettysburg: The Leaders of America's Greatest Battle* (1998, 2003), and *The Unpopular Mr. Lincoln: The Story of America's Most Reviled President* (2009; published in trade paperback as *The Battles that Made Abraham Lincoln: How Lincoln Mastered his Enemies to Win the Civil War, Free the Slaves, and Preserve the Union*, 2013).